CANNIBALS AND KINGS

CANNIBALS AND KINGS

The Origins of Cultures

Marvin Harris

VINTAGE BOOKS
A DIVISION OF RANDOM HOUSE, INC.
NEW YORK

VINTAGE BOOKS EDITION, JUNE 1991

 Published in the United States by Random House, Inc., New York, and simultaneously in Canada by Random House of Canada Limited, Toronto. Originally published by Random House, Inc., in October 1977.

Library of Congress Cataloging in Publication Data
Harris, Marvin, 1927-
Cannibals and kings.
Bibliography: p.
1. Social evolution. 2. Culture—Origin.
3. Man—Influence of environment. 4. Food supply.
I. Title.
[GN358.H37 1978] 301.2 90-55701
ISBN 0-679-72849-X

Manufactured in the United States of America
10 9 8 7 6 5

Contents

Introduction

For centuries the Western world has been comforted by the belief that material progress will never end. We take our cars, telephones, and central heating as proof that living is far easier for us today than it was for our grandparents. And although we recognize that progress may be slow and uneven, with temporary setbacks, we feel that living will, on balance, be a lot easier in the future than it is now.

Scientific theories, for the most part formulated a hundred years ago, nourish this belief. From the vantage point of Victorian scientists, the evolution of culture seemed to be a pilgrimage up a steep mountain from the top of which civilized peoples could look down at various levels of savagery and barbarism yet to be passed by "lower" cultures. The Victorians exaggerated the material poverty of the so-called savages and at the same time inflated the benefits of industrial "civilization." They pictured the old stone age as a time of great fear and insecurity, when people spent their days ceaselessly searching for food and their nights huddled about fires in comfortless caves besieged by saber-toothed tigers. Only when the secret of how to plant crops was discovered did our "savage" ancestors have enough leisure time to settle down in villages and build comfortable dwellings. And only then could they store surplus food and have time to think and experiment with new ideas. This in turn supposedly led to the invention of writing, to cities, to organized governments and the flowering of art and science. Then came the steam engine, ushering in a new and more rapid phase of progress, the industrial revolution, with its miraculous cornucopia of mass-produced labor-saving machines and life-enhancing technology.

It isn't easy to overcome this kind of indoctrination. Nevertheless, growing numbers of people can't help feeling that industrial society has a hollow core and that despite media images of fun-filled leisure hours our progeny will have to work harder and harder to hold on to the few luxuries we now enjoy. The great industrial cornucopia has not only been polluting the earth with wastes and poisons; it has also been spewing forth increasingly shoddy, costly, and defective goods and services.

My purpose in this book is to replace the old onwards-and-upwards Victorian view of progress with a more realistic account of cultural evolution. What is happening to today's standard of living has happened in the past. Our culture is not the first that technology has failed. Nor is it the first to reach its limits of growth. The technologies of earlier cultures failed again and again, only to be replaced by new technologies. And limits of growth have been reached and transcended only to be reached and transcended again. Much of what we think of as contemporary progress is actually a regaining of standards that were widely enjoyed during prehistoric times.

Stone age populations lived healthier lives than did most of the people who came immediately after them: during Roman times there was more sickness in the world than ever before, and even in early nineteenth-century England the life expectancy for children was probably not very different from what it was 20,000 years earlier. Moreover, stone age hunters worked fewer hours for their sustenance than do typical Chinese and Egyptian peasants—or, despite their unions, modern-day factory workers. As for amenities such as good food, entertainment, and aesthetic pleasures, early hunters and plant collectors enjoyed luxuries that only the richest of today's Americans can afford. For two days' worth of trees, lakes, and clear air, the modern-day executive works five. Nowadays, whole families toil and save for thirty years to gain the privilege of seeing a few square feet of grass outside their windows. And they are the privileged few. Americans say, "Meat makes the meal," and their diet is rich (some say too rich) in animal proteins, but two-thirds of the people alive today are involuntary vegetarians. In the stone age, everyone maintained a high-protein, low-starch diet. And the meat wasn't frozen or pumped full of antibiotics and artificial color.

But I haven't written this book to talk down modern American and European standards of living. No one can deny that we are better off today than were our great-grandparents in the last century. And no one can deny that science and technology have helped to improve the diet, health, longevity, and creature comforts of hundreds of millions of people. In matters such as contraception, security against natural calamities, and ease of transportation and communication, we have obviously surpassed even the most affluent of earlier societies. The question uppermost in my mind is not whether the gains of the last 150 years are real, but whether they are permanent. Can the recent industrial cornucopia be looked upon as the tip of a single continuously rising curve of material and spiritual uplift or is it the latest bubble-like protuberance on a curve that slopes down as often as it slopes up? I think the second view is more in accord with the evidence and explanatory principles of modern anthropology.

My aim is to show the relationship between material and spiritual well-being and the cost/benefits of various systems for increasing production and controlling population growth. In the past, irresistible reproductive pressures arising from the lack of safe and effective means of contraception led recurrently to the intensification of production. Such intensification has always led to environmental depletion, which in general results in new systems of production—each with a characteristic form of institutionalized violence, drudgery, exploitation, or cruelty. Thus reproductive pressure, intensification, and environmental depletion would appear to provide the key for understanding the evolution of family organization, property relations, political economy, and religious beliefs, including dietary preferences and food taboos. Modern contraceptive and abortion techniques enter this picture as potentially decisive new elements, since they remove the excruciating penalties associated with all preexisting techniques for coping directly with reproductive pressures through fertility control. But the new technology of contraception and abortion may have come too late. Contemporary state societies are committed to the intensification of the industrial mode of production. We have only begun to pay the penalties for the environmental depletions associated with this new round of intensification, and no one can predict what new constraints will be needed to transcend the limits of growth of the industrial order.

I am aware that my theories of historical determinism are likely to provoke an unfavorable reaction. Some readers will be offended by the casual links I point to among cannibalism, religions of love and mercy, vegetarianism, infanticide, and the cost/benefits of production. As a result, I may be accused of seeking to imprison the human spirit within a closed system of mechanical relationships. But my intention is exactly the opposite. That a blind form of determinism has ruled the past does not mean that it must rule the future.

Before going any further, I should clarify the meaning of the word "determinism." In the context of twentieth-century science, one no longer speaks of cause and effect in the sense of a mechanical one-to-one relationship between dependent and independent variables. In subatomic physics Heisenberg's "indeterminacy principle," substituting cause-and-effect probabilities about micro-particles for cause-and-effect certainties, has long held sway. Since the paradigm "one exception falsifies the rule" has lost its reign in physics, I, for one, have no intention of imposing it on cultural phenomena. By a deterministic relationship among cultural phenomena, I mean merely that similar variables under similar conditions tend to give rise to similar consequences.

Since I believe that the relationship between material processes and moral preferences is one of probabilities and similarities rather than certainties and identities, I have no difficulty in believing both that history is determined and that human beings have the capacity to exercise moral choice and free will. In fact, I insist on the possibility that improbable historical events involving the unpredictable reversal of normal cause-and-effect relationships between material processes and values can occur and that therefore we are all responsible for our contribution to history. But to argue that we human beings have the capacity to make culture and history conform to standards of our own free choice is not to say that history is actually the expression of that capacity. Far from it. As I shall show, cultures on the whole have evolved along parallel and convergent paths which are highly predictable from a knowledge of the processes of production, reproduction, intensification, and depletion. And I include here both abhorred and cherished rituals and beliefs throughout the world.

In my opinion, free will and moral choice have had virtually no significant effect upon the directions taken thus far by evolving systems of social life. If I am correct, it behooves those who are concerned about protecting human dignity from the threat of mechanical determinism to join me in pondering the question: why has social life up to now consisted overwhelmingly of predictable rather than unpredictable arrangements? I am convinced that one of the greatest existing obstacles to the exercise of free choice on behalf of achieving the improbable goals of peace, equality, and affluence is the failure to recognize the material evolutionary processes that account for the prevalence of wars, inequality, and poverty. As a result of the studied neglect of the science of culture, the world is full of moralists insisting that they have freely willed what they were unwittingly forced to want, while by not understanding the odds against free choice, millions who would be free have delivered themselves into new forms of bondage. To change social life for the better, one must begin with the knowledge of why it usually changes for the worse. That is why I consider ignorance of the causal factors in cultural evolution and disregard of the odds against a desired outcome to be forms of moral duplicity.

CANNIBALS AND KINGS

1
Culture and Nature

The explorers sent out during Europe's great age of discovery were slow to grasp the global pattern of customs and institutions. In some regions—Australia, the Arctic, the southern tips of South America and Africa—they found groups still living much like Europe's own long-forgotten stone age ancestors: bands of twenty or thirty people, sprinkled across vast territories, constantly on the move, living entirely by hunting animals and collecting wild plants. These hunter-collectors appeared to be members of a rare and endangered species. In other regions—the forests of eastern North America, the jungles of South America, and East Asia—they found denser populations, inhabiting more or less permanent villages, based on farming and consisting of perhaps one or two large communal structures, but here too the weapons and tools were relics of prehistory.

Along the banks of the Amazon and the Mississippi, and on the islands of the Pacific, the villages were bigger, sometimes containing a thousand or more inhabitants. Some were organized into confederacies verging on statehood. Although the Europeans exaggerated their "savagery," the majority of these village communities collected enemy heads as trophies, roasted their prisoners of war alive, and consumed human flesh in ritual feasts. The fact that the "civilized" Europeans also tortured people—in witchcraft trials, for example—and that they were not against exterminating the populations of whole cities should be kept in mind (even if they were squeamish about eating one another).

Elsewhere, of course, the explorers encountered fully developed states and empires, headed by despots and ruling classes, and defended by standing armies. It was these great empires, with their cities, monuments, palaces, temples, and treasures, that had lured all the Marco Polos and Columbuses across the oceans and deserts in the first place. There was China—the greatest empire in the world, a vast, sophisticated realm whose leaders scorned the "red-faced barbarians," supplicants from puny kingdoms beyond the pale of the civilized world. And there was India—a land where cows were venerated and the unequal burdens of life were apportioned according to what each soul had merited in its previous incarnation. And then there were the native American states and empires, worlds unto themselves, each with its distinctive arts and religions: the Incas, with their great stone fortresses, suspension bridges, ever-normal granaries, and state-controlled economy; the Aztecs, with their bloodthirsty gods fed from human hearts and their incessant search for fresh sacrifices. And there were the Europeans themselves, with their own exotic qualities: waging warfare in the name of a Prince of Peace, compulsively buying and selling to make profits, powerful beyond their numbers because of a cunning mastery of mechanical crafts and engineering.

What did this pattern signify? Why did some peoples abandon hunting and plant collecting as a way of life while others retained it? And among those who adopted farming, why did some rest content with village life while others moved steadily closer to statehood? And among those who organized themselves into states, why did some achieve empires and others not? Why did some worship cows while others fed human hearts to cannibal gods? Is human history told not by one but by ten billion idiots—the play of chance and passion and nothing more? I think not. I think there is an intelligible process that governs the maintenance of common cultural forms, initiates changes, and determines their transformations along parallel or divergent paths.

The heart of this process is the tendency to intensify production. Intensification—the investment of more soil, water, minerals, or energy per unit of time or area—is in turn a recurrent response to threats against living standards. In earliest times such threats arose mainly from changes in climate and migrations of people and animals. In later times competition between states became the major stimulus. Regardless of its immediate cause, intensification is always counterproductive. In the absence of technological change, it leads inevitably to the depletion of the environment and the lowering of the efficiency of production since the increased effort sooner or later must be applied to more remote, less reliable, and less bountiful animals, plants, soils, minerals, and sources of energy. Declining efficiency in turn leads to low living standards—precisely the opposite of the desired result. But this process does not simply end with everybody getting less food, shelter, and other necessities in return for more work. As living standards decline, successful cultures invent new and more efficient means of production which sooner or later again lead to the depletion of the natural environment.

Why do people try to solve their economic problems by intensifying production? Theoretically, the easiest way to achieve a high-quality diet, a vigorous long life free of toil and drudgery, is not to increase production but to reduce population. If for some reason beyond human control—an unfavorable shift of climate, say—the supply of natural resources per capita is cut in half, people need not try to compensate by working twice as hard. Instead, they could cut their population in half. Or, I should say, they could do this were it not for one large problem.

Since heterosexual activity is a genetically mandated relationship upon which the survival of our species depends, it is no easy task to thin out the human "crop." In preindustrial times the effective regulation of population itself involved lowering the standard of living. For example, if population is to be reduced by avoiding heterosexual intercourse, a group's standard of living can scarcely be said to have been maintained or enhanced. Similarly, if the fecundity of the group is to be lowered by midwives jumping on a woman's stomach to kill the fetus and often the mothers as well, the survivors may eat better but their life expectancy will not be improved. Actually, the most widely used method of population control during much of human history was probably some form of female infanticide. Although the psychological costs of killing or starving one's infant daughters can be dulled by culturally defining them as non-persons (just as modern pro-abortionists, of whom I am one, define fetuses as non-infants), the material costs of nine months of pregnancy are not easily written off. It is safe to assume that most people who practice infanticide would rather not see their infants die. But the alternatives—drastically lowering the nutritional, sexual, and health standards of the entire group—have usually been judged to be even more undesirable, at least in pre-state societies.

What I am getting at is that population regulation

was often a costly if not traumatic procedure and a source of individual stress, just as Thomas Malthus suggested it would have to be for all future time (until he was proven wrong by the invention of the rubber condom). It is this stress—or reproductive pressure, as is might more aptly be called—that accounts for the recurrent tendency of pre-state societies to intensify production as a means of protecting or enhancing general living standards. Were it not for the severe costs involved in controlling reproduction, our species might have remained forever organized into small, relatively peaceful, egalitarian bands of hunter-collectors. But the lack of effective and benign methods of population control rendered this mode of life unstable. Reproductive pressures predisposed our stone age ancestors to resort to intensification as a response to declining numbers of big-game animals caused by climatic changes at the end of the last ice age. Intensification of the hunting and collecting mode of production in turn set the stage for the adoption of agriculture, which led in turn to heightened competition among groups, an increase in warfare, and the evolution of the state—but I am getting ahead of the story.

2
Murders in Eden

The accepted explanation for the transition from band life to farming villages used to go like this: Hunter-collectors had to spend all their time getting enough to eat. They could not produce a "surplus above subsistence," and so they lived on the edge of extinction in chronic sickness and hunger. Therefore, it was natural for them to want to settle down and live in permanent villages, but the idea of planting seeds never occurred to them. One day an unknown genius decided to drop some seeds in a hole, and soon planting was being done on a regular basis. People no longer had to move about constantly in search of game, and the new leisure gave them time to think. This led to further and more rapid advances in technology and thus more food—a "surplus above subsistence"—which eventually made it possible for some people to turn away from farming and become artisans, priests, and rulers.

The first flaw in this theory is the assumption that life was exceptionally difficult for our stone age ancestors. Archaeological evidence from the upper paleolithic period—about 30,000 B.C. to 10,000 B.C.—makes it perfectly clear that hunters who lived during those times enjoyed relatively high standards of comfort and security. They were no bumbling amateurs. They had achieved total control over the process of fracturing, chipping, and shaping crystalline rocks, which formed the basis of their technology, and they have aptly been called the "master stoneworkers of all times." Their remarkably thin, finely chipped "laurel leaf" knives, eleven inches long but only four-tenths of an inch thick, cannot be duplicated by modern industrial techniques. With delicate stone awls and incising tools called burins, they created intricately barbed bone and antler harpoon points, well-shaped antler throwing boards for spears, and fine bone needles presumably used to fashion animal-skin clothing. The items made of wood, fibers, and skins have perished, but these too must have been distinguished by high craftsmanship.

Contrary to popular ideas, "cave men" knew how to make artificial shelters, and their use of caves and rock overhangs depended on regional possibilities and seasonal needs. In southern Russia archaeologists have found traces of a hunters' animal-skin dwelling set in a shallow pit forty feet long and twelve feet wide. In Czechoslovakia winter dwellings with round floor plans twenty feet in diameter were already in use more than 20,000 years ago. With rich furs for rugs and beds, as well as plenty of dried animal dung or fat-laden bones for the hearth, such dwellings can provide a quality of shelter superior in many respects to contemporary inner-city apartments.

As for living on the edge of starvation, such a picture is hard to reconcile with the enormous quantities of animal bones accumulated at various paleolithic kill sites. Vast herds of mammoth, horses, deer, reindeer, and bison roamed across Europe and Asia. The bones of over a thousand mammoth, excavated from one site in Czechoslovakia, and the remains of 10,000 wild horses that were stampeded at various intervals over a high cliff near Solutré, France, testify to the ability of paleolithic peoples to exploit these herds systematically and efficiently. Moreover, the skeletal remains of the hunters themselves bear witness to the fact that they were unusually well-nourished.

The notion that paleolithic populations worked round the clock in order to feed themselves now also appears ludicrous. As collectors of food plants they were certainly no less effective than chimpanzees. Field studies have shown that in their natural habitat the great apes spend as much time grooming, playing, and napping as they do foraging and eating. And as hunters our upper paleolithic ancestors must have been at least as proficient as lions—animals which alternate bursts of intense activity with long periods of rest and relaxation. Studies of how present-day hunters and collectors allocate their time have shed more light on this issue. Richard Lee of the University of Toronto kept a record of how much time the modern Bushman hunter-collectors spend in the quest for food. Despite their habitat—the edge of the Kalahari, a desert region whose lushness is hardly comparable to that of France during the upper paleolithic period—less than three hours per day per adult is all that is needed for the Bushmen to obtain a diet rich in proteins and other essential nutrients.

The Machiguenga, simple horticulturalists of the Peruvian Amazon studied by Allen and Orna Johnson, spend a little more than three hours per day per adult in food production and get less animal protein for this effort than do the Bushmen. In the rice-growing regions of eastern Java, modern peasants have been found to spend about forty-four hours per week in productive farm work—something no self-respecting Bushman would ever dream of doing—and Javanese peasants seldom eat animal proteins. American farmers, for whom fifty-and-sixty-hour work weeks are commonplace, eat well by Bushman standards but certainly cannot be said to have as much leisure.

I do not wish to minimize the difficulties inherent in comparisons of this sort. Obviously the work associated with a particular food-production system is not limited to time spent in obtaining the raw product. It also takes time to process the plants and animals into forms suitable for consumption, and it takes still more time to manufacture and maintain such instruments of production as spears, nets, digging sticks, baskets, and plows. According to the Johnsons' estimates, the Machiguenga devote about three additional hours per day to food preparation and the manufacture of essential items such as clothing, tools, and shelter. In his observations of the Bushmen, Lee found that in one day a woman could gather enough food to feed her family for three days and that she spent the rest of her time resting, entertaining visitors, doing embroidery, or visiting other camps. "For each day at home, kitchen routines, such as cooking, nut cracking, collecting firewood, and fetching water, occupy one to three hours of her time."

The evidence I have cited above leads to one conclusion: The development of farming resulted in an increased work load per capita. There is a good reason for this. Agriculture is a system of food production that can absorb much more labor per unit of land than can hunting and collecting. Hunter-collectors are essentially dependent on the natural rate of animal and plant reproduction; they can do very little to raise output per unit of land (although they can easily decrease it). With agriculture, on the other hand, people control the rate of plant reproduction. This means that production can be intensified without immediate adverse consequences, especially if techniques are available for combating soil exhaustion.

The key to how many hours people like the Bushmen put into hunting and collecting is the abundance and accessibility of the animal and plant resources available to them. As long as population density—and thus exploitation of these resources—is kept relatively low, hunter-collectors can enjoy both leisure and high-quality diets. Only if one assumes that people during the stone age were unwilling or unable to limit the density of their populations does the theory of our ancestors' lives as "short, nasty, and brutish" make sense. But that assumption is unwarranted. Hunter-collectors are strongly motivated to limit population, and they have effective means to do so.

Another weakness in the old theory of the transition from hunting and collecting to agriculture is the assumption that human beings naturally want to "settle down." This can scarcely be true given the tenacity with which people like the Bushmen, the aborigines of Australia, and the Eskimo have clung to their old "walkabout" way of life despite the concerted efforts of governments and missionaries to persuade them to live in villages.

Each advantage of permanent village life has a corresponding disadvantage. Do people crave company? Yes, but they also get on each other's nerves. As Thomas Gregor has shown in a study of the Mehinacu Indians of Brazil, the search for personal privacy is a pervasive theme in the daily life of people who live in small villages. The Mehinacu apparently know too much about each other's business for their own good. They can tell from the print of a heel or a buttock where a couple stopped and had sexual relations off the path. Lost arrows give away the owner's prize fishing spot; an ax resting against a tree tells a story of interrupted work. No one leaves or enters the village without being noticed. One must whisper to secure privacy —with walls of thatch there are no closed doors. The village is filled with irritating gossip about men who are impotent or who ejaculate too quickly, and about women's behavior during coitus and the size, color, and odor of their genitalia.

Is there physical security in numbers? Yes, but there is also security in mobility, in being able to get out of the way of aggressors. Is there an advantage in having a larger cooperative labor pool? Yes, but larger concentrations of people lower the game supply and deplete natural resources.

As for the haphazard discovery of the planting process, hunter-collectors are not so dumb as this sequence in the old theory would suggest. The anatomical details in the paintings of animals found on the walls of caves in France and Spain bear witness to a people whose powers of observation were honed to great accuracy. And our admiration for their intellects has been forced to new heights by Alexander Marshak's discovery that the faint scratches on the surface of 20,000-year-old bone and antler artifacts were put there to keep track of the phases of the moon and other astronomical events. It is unreasonable to suppose that the people who made the great murals on the walls of Lascaux, and who were intelligent enough to make calendrical records, could have been ignorant of the biological significance of tubers and seeds.

Studies of hunter-collectors of the present and recent past reveal that the practice of agriculture is often forgone not for lack of knowledge but as a matter of convenience. Simply by gathering acorns, for example, the

Indians of California probably obtained larger and more nutritious harvests than they could have derived from planting maize. And on the Northwest coast the great annual migrations of salmon and candlefish rendered agricultural work a relative waste of time. Hunter-collectors often display all the skills and techniques necessary for practicing agriculture minus the step of deliberate planting. The Shoshoni and Paiute of Nevada and California returned year after year to the same stands of wild grains and tubers, carefully refrained from stripping them bare, and sometimes even weeded and watered them. Many other hunter-collectors use fire to deliberately promote the growth of preferred species and to retard the growth of trees and weeds.

Finally, some of the most important archaeological discoveries of recent years indicate that in the Old World the earliest villages were built 1,000 to 2,000 years before the development of a farming economy, whereas in the New World plants were domesticated long before village life began. Since the early Americans had the idea for thousands of years before they made full use of it, the explanation for the shift away from hunting and collecting must be sought outside their heads. I'll have more to say about these archaeological discoveries later on.

What I've shown so far is that as long as hunter-collectors kept their population low in relation to their prey, they could enjoy an enviable standard of living. But how did they keep their population down? This subject is rapidly emerging as the most important missing link in the attempt to understand the evolution of cultures.

Even in relatively favorable habitats, with abundant herd animals, stone age peoples probably never let their populations rise above one or two persons per square mile. Alfred Kroeber estimated that in the Canadian plains and prairies the bison-hunting Cree and Assiniboin, mounted on horses and equipped with rifles, kept their densities below two persons per square mile. Less favored groups of historic hunters in North America, such as the Labrador Naskapi and the Nunamuit Eskimo, who depended on caribou, maintained densities *below* .3 persons per square mile. In all of France during the late stone age there were probably no more than 20,000 and possibly as few as 1,600 human beings.

"Natural" means of controlling population growth cannot explain the discrepancy between these low densities and the potential fertility of the human female. Healthy populations interested in maximizing their rate of growth average eight pregnancies brought to term per woman. Childbearing rates can easily go higher. Among the Hutterites, a sect of thrifty farmers living in western Canada, the average is 10.7 births per woman. In order to maintain the estimated .001 percent annual rate of growth for the old stone age, each woman must have had on the average less than 2.1 children who survived to reproductive age. According to the conventional theory such a low rate of growth was achieved, despite high fertility, by disease. Yet the view that our stone age ancestors led disease-ridden lives is difficult to sustain.

No doubt there were diseases. But as a mortality factor they must have been considerably less significant during the stone age than they are today. The death of infants and adults from bacterial and viral infections—dysenteries, measels, tuberculosis, whooping cough, colds, scarlet fever—is strongly influenced by diet and general body vigor, so stone age hunter-collectors probably had high recovery rates from these infections. And most of the great lethal epidemic diseases—smallpox, typhoid fever, flu, bubonic plague, cholera—occur only among populations that have high densities. These are the diseases of state-level societies; they flourish amid poverty and crowded, unsanitary urban conditions. Even such scourges as malaria and yellow fever were probably less significant among the hunter-collectors of the old stone age. As hunters they would have preferred dry, open habitats to the wetlands where these diseases flourish. Malaria probably achieved its full impact only after agricultural clearings in humid forests had created better breeding conditions for mosquitoes.

What is actually known about the physical health of paleolithic populations? Skeletal remains provide important clues. Using such indices as average height and the number of teeth missing at time of death, J. Lawrence Angel has developed a profile of changing health standards during the last 30,000 years. Angel found that at the beginning of this period adult males averaged 177 centimeters (5′ 11″) and adult females about 165 centimeters (5′ 6″). Twenty thousand years later the males grew no taller than the females formerly grew—165 centimeters—whereas the females averaged no more than 153 centimeters (5′ 0″). Only in very recent times have populations once again attained statures characteristic of the old stone age peoples. American males, for example, averaged 175 centimeters (5′ 9″) in 1960. Tooth loss shows a similar trend. In 30,000 B.C. adults died with an average of 2.2 teeth missing; in 6500 B.C., with 3.5 missing; during Roman times, with 6.6 missing. Although genetic factors may also enter into these changes, stature and the condition of teeth and gums are known to be strongly influenced by protein intake, which in turn is predictive of general well-being. Angel concludes that there was "a real depression of health" following the "high point" of the upper paleolithic period.

Angel has also attempted to estimate the average age of death for the upper paleolithic, which he places at 28.7 years for females and 33.3 years for males. Since Angel's paleolithic sample consists of skeletons found all over Europe and Africa, his longevity estimates are not necessarily representative of any actual band of hunters. If the vital statistics of contemporary hunter-collector bands can be taken as representative of paleolithic bands, Angel's calculations err on the low side. Studies of 165 !Kung Bushman women by Nancy Howell show that life expectancy at birth is 32.5 years, which compares favorably with the figures for many modern developing nations in Africa and Asia. To put these data in proper perspective, according to the Metropolitan Life Insurance Company the life expectancy at birth for non-white males in the United States in 1900 was also 32.5 years. Thus, as paleodemographer Don Dumond has suggested, there are hints that "mortality was effectively no higher under conditions of hunting than under those of a more sedentary life, including agriculture." The increase in disease accompanying sedentary living "may mean that the mortality rates of hunters were more often significantly lower" than those of agricultural peoples.

Although a life span of 32.5 years may seem very short, the reproductive potential even of women who live only to Angel's 28.7 years of age is quite high. If a stone age woman had her first pregnancy when she was sixteen years old, and a live baby every two and a half years thereafter, she could easily have had over five live births by the time she was twenty-nine. This means that approximately three-fifths of stone age children could not have lived to reproductive age if the estimated rate of less than .001 percent population growth was to be maintained. Using these figures, anthropological demographer Ferki Hassan concludes that even if there was 50 percent infant mortality due to "natural" causes, another 23 to 35 percent of all potential offspring would have to be "removed" to achieve zero growth population.

If anything, these estimates appear to err in exaggerating the number of deaths from "natural" causes. Given the excellent state of health the people studied by Angel seemed to enjoy before they became skeletons, one suspects that many of the deceased died of "unnatural" causes.

Infanticide during the paleolithic period could very well have been as high as 50 percent—a figure that corresponds to estimates made by Joseph Birdsell of the University of California in Los Angeles on the basis of data collected among the aboriginal populations of Australia. And an important factor in the short life span of paleolithic women may very well have been the attempt to induce abortions in order to lengthen the interval between births.

Contemporary hunter-collectors in general lack effective chemical or mechanical means of preventing pregnancy—romantic folklore about herbal contraceptives notwithstanding. They do, however, possess a large repertory of chemical and mechanical means for inducing abortion. Numerous plant and animal poisons that cause generalized physical traumas or that act directly on the uterus are used throughout the world to end unwanted pregnancies. Many mechanical techniques for inducing abortion are also employed, such as tying tight bands around the stomach, vigorous massages, subjection to extremes of cold and heat, blows to the abdomen, and hopping up and down on a plank placed across a woman's belly "until blood spurts out of the vagina." Both the mechanical and chemical approaches effectively terminate pregnancies, but they are also likely to terminate the life of the pregnant woman. I suspect that only a group under severe economic and demographic stress would resort to abortion as its principal method of population regulation.

Hunter-collectors under stress are much more likely to turn to infanticide and geronticide (the killing of old people). Geronticide is effective only for short-run emergency reductions in group size. It cannot lower long-term trends of population growth. In the case of both geronticide and infanticide, outright conscious killing is probably the exception. Among the Eskimo, old people too weak to contribute to their own subsistence may "commit suicide" by remaining behind when the group moves, although children actively contribute to their parents' demise by accepting the cultural expectation that old people ought not to become a burden when food is scarce. In Australia, among the Murngin of Arnhem Land, old people are helped along toward their fate by being treated as if they were already dead when they become sick; the group begins to perform its last rites, and the old person responds by getting sicker. Infanticide runs a complex gamut from outright murder to mere neglect. Infants may be strangled, drowned, bashed against a rock, or exposed to the elements. More commonly, an infant is "killed" by neglect: the mother gives less care than is needed when it gets sick, nurses it less often, refrains from trying to find supplementary foods, or "accidentally" lets it fall from her arms. Hunter-collector women are strongly motivated to space out the age difference between their children since they must expend a considerable amount of effort merely lugging them about during the day.

Richard Lee has calculated that over a four-year period of dependency a Bushman mother will carry her child a total of 4,900 miles on collecting expeditions and campsite moves. No Bushman woman wants to be burdened with two or three infants at a time as she travels that distance.

The best method of population control available to stone age hunter-collectors was to prolong the span of years during which a mother nursed her infant. Recent studies of menstrual cycles carried out by Rose Frisch and Janet McArthur have shed light on the physiological mechanism responsible for lowering the fertility of lactating women. After giving birth, a fertile woman will not resume ovulation until the percentage of her body weight that consists of fat has passed a critical threshold. This threshold (about 20–25 percent) represents the point at which a woman's body has stored enough reserve energy in the form of fat to accommodate the demands of a growing fetus. The average energy cost of a normal pregnancy is 27,000 calories—just about the amount of energy that must be stored before a woman can conceive. A nursing infant drains about 1,000 extra calories from its mother per day, making it difficult for her to accumulate the necessary fatty reserve. As long as the infant is dependent on its mother's milk, there is little likelihood that ovulation will resume. Bushman mothers, by prolonging lactation, appear to be able to delay the possibility of pregnancy for more than four years. The same mechanism appears to be responsible for delaying menarche—the onset of menstruation. The higher the ratio of body fat to body weight, the earlier the age of menarche. In well-nourished modern populations menarche has been pushed forward to about twelve years of age, whereas in populations chronically on the edge of caloric deficits it may take eighteen or more years for a girl to build up the necessary fat reserves.

What I find so intriguing about this discovery is that it links low fertility with diets that are high in proteins and low in carbohydrates. On the one hand, if a woman is to nurse a child successfully for three or four years she must have a high protein intake to sustain her health, body vigor, and the flow of milk. On the other hand, if she consumes too many carbohydrates she will begin to put on weight, which will trigger the resumption of ovulation. A demographic study carried out by J. K. Van Ginneken indicates that nursing women in underdeveloped countries, where the diet consists mostly of starchy grains and root crops, cannot expect to extend the interval between births beyond eighteen months. Yet nursing Bushman women, whose diet is rich in animal and plant proteins and who lack starchy staples, as I have said, manage to keep from getting pregnant four or more years after each birth. This relationship suggests that during good times hunter-collectors could rely on prolonged lactation as their principal defense against overpopulation. Conversely, a decline in the quality of the food supply would tend to bring about an increase in population. This in turn would mean either that the rate of abortion and infanticide would have to be accelerated or that still more drastic cuts in the protein ration would be needed.

I am not suggesting that the entire defense against overpopulation among our stone age ancestors rested with the lactation method. Among the Bushmen of Botswana the present rate of population growth is .5 percent per annum. This amounts to a doubling every 139 years. Had this rate been sustained for only the last 10,000 years of the old stone age, by 10,000 B.C. the population of the earth would have reached 604,463,-000,000,000,000,000,000.

Suppose the fertile span were from sixteen years of age to forty-two. Without prolonged nursing, a woman might experience as many as twelve pregnancies. With the lactation method, the number of pregnancies comes down to six. Lowered rates of coitus in older women might further reduce the number to five. Spontaneous abortions and infant mortality caused by disease and accidents might bring the potential reproducers down to four—roughly two more than the number permissible under a system of zero population growth. The "extra" two births could then be controlled through some form of infanticide based on neglect. The optimal method would be to neglect only the girl babies, since the rate of growth in populations that do not practice monogamy is determined almost entirely by the number of females who reach reproductive age.

Our stone age ancestors were thus perfectly capable of maintaining a stationary population, but there was a cost associated with it—the waste of infant lives. This cost lurks in the background of prehistory as an ugly blight in what might otherwise be mistaken for a Garden of Eden.

3
The Origin of Agriculture

The period from 30,000 to 12,000 years ago marked the climax of millions of years of slow technological evolution during which our stone age ancestors gradually perfected the tools and techniques for making a living by hunting large land animals. There are Old World habitation sites dating back hundreds of thousands of years at which archaeologists have found remains of a few pachyderms, giraffes, and buffalo, but these animals probably died natural deaths or were trapped or wounded by nonhuman predators. During this time our ancestors may have scavenged rather than hunted the meat from big game. But by 30,000 years ago the situation had changed, and bands of hunter-collectors in both the Old and New Worlds possessed the means for killing and butchering even the largest animals on a routine basis.

In Europe and Asia vast herds of reindeer, mammoth, horses, bison, and wild cattle grazed on lush grasses fed by glacial melt waters. The pursuit of these creatures came to dominate the food quest. Hunters rounded up their prey by setting fires, drove them over cliffs, and dispatched them with an arsenal of stone and bone projectile points, spears, darts. long knives, and bows and arrows. For thousands of years human predators and animal prey remained in ecological balance.

Then, about 13,000 years ago, a global warming

trend signaled the beginning of the terminal phase of the last ice age. The glaciers that had covered much of the Northern Hemisphere with mile-high sheets of ice began to back away toward Greenland. As the climate became less severe, forests of evergreens and birches invaded the grassy plains which nourished the great herds. The loss of these grazing lands in combination with the toll taken by the human predators produced an ecological catastrophe. The woolly mammoth, woolly rhinoceros, steppe bison, giant elk, European wild ass, and a whole genus of goats suddenly became extinct. While horses and cattle survived, their numbers in Europe sharply decreased. Other species like the saiga antelope and the musk ox survived only in scattered pockets in the far north. Scientists do not agree about the relative impact of the climatological changes and human predation in bringing about the extinction of these animals. Human predation definitely played a role because elephants and rhinos had managed to survive several earlier warming trends caused by previous glacial retreats.

The collapse of the big-game hunting cultures in northern Europe was followed by the mesolithic period (or middle stone age), during which people obtained their proteins from fish, shellfish, and forest deer. In the Middle East (what is now southern Turkey, Iraq, Iran, Syria, Jordan, and Israel), where the age of the big-game hunters had come to an end much earlier than in the north, the pattern of subsistence became even more diversified. Here people turned from hunting giant wild cattle and red deer to preying on smaller species such as sheep, goats, and antelope and paid increasing attention to fish, crabs and other shellfish, birds, snails, acorns, pistachios and other nuts, wild legumes, and wild grains. Kent Flannery of the University of Michigan has called this system "broad spectrum" hunting and collecting. The retreat of the glaciers and the intensification of big-game hunting did not have precisely the same consequences in Europe and the Middle East, but both regions probably suffered similar environmental depletions which raised the costs of obtaining animal proteins. According to Karl Butzer, most of Turkey, northeastern Iraq, and Iran were treeless during the last ice age, and this would have facilitated the hunting of herd animals. True, the reforestation that occurred at the end of the glacial period was not as extensive as in Europe, but this may actually have made the ecological crisis in the Middle East more severe because of a deficit of both open-country and forest species.

Turning to North and South America, one can see the same process at work. The terminal phase of the last ice age represented the peak of specialized big-game hunting in the New World. At sites in Venezuela, Peru, Mexico, Idaho, and Nevada archaeologists have found beautifully crafted leaf-shaped projectile points, blades, and burins dating from 13,000 to 9000 B.C., some of which are associated with extinct species of antelope, horses, camels, mammoth, mastodon, giant ground sloths, and giant rodents. Between 11,000 and 8000 B.C. big-game hunters equipped with fluted and channeled points were active over a wide expanse of North America, but by 7000 B.C. predation and the climatological changes brought about by the receding glaciers had resulted in the total extinction of thirty-two whole genera of large New World animals including horses, giant bison, oxen, elephant, camels, antelope, pigs, ground sloths, and giant rodents.

Paul C. Martin of the University of Arizona has suggested that the ancestors of the American Indians killed off all of these large animals—called collectively the "Pleistocene Megafauna"—in one short burst of intense predation. Martin attributes this rapid extinction to the fact that the animals had never been hunted by human beings prior to the arrival of bands of Siberian migrants who crossed the Bering Straits land bridge 11,000 years ago. We now know, however, that the discovery of America by migrants from Asia took place much earlier —at least 15,000 and possibly even 70,000 years ago. Although Martin's overall theory is thus disproven, his idea of rapid extinction deserves careful consideration. Using a computer program to simulate various kill rates practiced by a small initial human population, Martin has shown that all the big animals from Canada to the Gulf Coast could have been wiped out in three centuries if the hunters had permitted their own population to double each generation—a rate of growth well within the reproductive capacity of paleolithic hunters.

> We introduce 100 Paleoindians at Edmonton. The hunters take an average of 13 animal units per person per year. One person in a family of four does most of the killing, at an average rate of one animal unit per week....
>
> The hunting is easy; the [band] doubles every 20 years until local herds are depleted and fresh territory must be found. In 120 years the Edmonton population grows to 5,409. It is concentrated on a front 59 miles deep at a density of 0.37 persons per square mile. Behind the front, the megafauna is exterminated. By 220 years, the front reaches northern Colorado . . . in 73 years, the front advances the remaining 1,000 miles [to the Gulf of Mexico], attains a depth of 76 miles, and reaches a maximum of just over 100,000 people. The front does not advance more than 20 miles in one year. In 293 years the

hunters destroy the megafauna of 93 million animal units.

Martin's scenario remains useful as an illustration of the vulnerability of large, slow-breeding species to hunter-collectors who decide to increase their kill rates as a result of reproductive pressures and threats to their standard of living. I suspect that the extinction was caused not by any sharp increase in the human population, but simply by an attempt to maintain dietary standards and low abortion and infanticide rates in the face of fewer numbers of prey animals.

After the decline of the New World big-game hunters, cultures appeared in the Americas whose subsistence systems resembled those of the Middle Eastern "broad spectrum" hunters and collectors. Details of the process of intensification and depletion are clearest in the remarkable studies carried out in the Tehuacán Valley under the direction of Richard MacNeish of the Peabody Museum of Archaeology. The Tehuacán Valley, a long, narrow depression located in the southeast part of the Mexican state of Puebla at an altitude of 4,500 feet, is surrounded by high mountains that give it a hot, dry climate. Here, during the Ajuereado period (7000–5000 B.C.), horses and antelope were hunted to extinction. The hunters then intensified the predation of jackrabbits and giant turtle, and these too soon became extinct. MacNeish estimates that at this time meat comprised 89 to 76 percent of the hunters' total caloric intake at maximum and minimum seasons of the year. During the following El Riego (5000–3400 B.C), Coxcatlán (3400–2300 B.C.), and Abejas (2300–1850 B.C.) periods, the maximum-minimum seasonal calorie percentage of meat fell to 69–31, 62–23, and 47–15 percent, respectively. By about 800 B.C., when fully sedentary villages based on agriculture were finally established in the valley, the proportion of calories provided by animal proteins had fallen still farther and the difference in eating habits between hunting and nonhunting seasons had virtually disappeared. Eventually, as we shall see later on, meat in ancient Mexico was to become a luxury whose production and consumption was the occasion for some of the must brutal institutions in human history.

The implacable decline in the proportion of animal protein in the Tehuacán diet was the result of a continuous series of intensifications and depletions, accompanied by improvements in the technology of hunting. As each species was depleted, the hunters attempted to compensate for the declining return in the effort they invested by using more efficient hunting weapons and techniques. Lances, spear-throwers, darts, and finally the bow and arrow were pressed into service, all to no avail.

According to MacNeish's estimates, the labor efficiency (calories obtained per calorie expended) of Ajuereado rabbit drives was 2.5:1. Lance ambushing started with an efficiency of 3.2:1 in the early Ajuereado period but fell to 1:1 in Abejas and then died out. Dart stalking of deer began at 7:1 but dropped to about 4:1 as the animal became less plentiful. Later the bow and arrow provided a new high of about 8:1 or 9:1, but by then game was so scarce that meat could contribute only insignificantly to the diet.

As they fought their long and futile delaying action against the consequences of the depletion of animal species, the people of Tehuacán gradually shifted their primary subsistence effort away from animals toward plants. Intensification of plant production resulted in a slowly increasing proportion of domesticated plants among the "broad spectrum" that was initially obtained entirely by collecting activities. By late El Riego times the hunting bands had succeeded in domesticating squash, amaranth, chili peppers, and avocados. They added maize and beans during the Coxcatlán period, and these crops steadily gained in importance as settlements increased in size and became more sedentary.

MacNeish estimates that the percentage calorie contribution of domesticated and/or cultivated plants was only 1 percent during the El Riego period, 8 percent during Coxcatlán, and 21 percent during Abejas. Even by the time the first permanent settlements appeared, domesticated and/or cultivated plants provided only 42 percent of the total caloric intake.

As in the case of hunting, intensification of farming gave rise to a series of technological advances. Horticulture, or rudimentary gardening, was followed by agriculture, which came to rely more and more on irrigation. The labor efficiencies of these different systems of food production advanced from 10:1 to 30:1 to 50:1. MacNeish does not discuss the possibility that successive declines in labor efficiency prompted the shifts to agriculture and irrigation. And I would not insist that such declines are always necessary to explain the shift to more efficient modes of farming. The decline in the production of animal protein could after all be compensated only by raising the output of plant proteins. The important point is, despite the fact that irrigation agriculture was five times more productive per man-hour than horticulture, the entire 9,000-year sequence of intensifications, depletions, and technological innovations resulted in an overall deterioration in nutritional status.

It seems clear that the extinction of the Pleistocene megafauna triggered the shift to an agricultural mode of production in both the Old and New Worlds. But the two sequences involve crucial differences vital to the understanding of all subsequent human history. Tehuacán Valley villages were not built until several thousand years after the first plants were domesticated. And this was generally the sequence throughout the Americas. (Villages in Peru may have been built by sea-mammal hunters in more remote times, but these did not play a role in the main sequence of cultural evolution.) In the Old World the sequence was reversed. People built villages first and then, 2,000 years later, domesticated the wild plants whose seeds they had been collecting. To understand this difference, let us take a closer look at the two best-known regions: first the Middle East and then Mesoamerica (Central America and Mexico).

The earliest Middle Eastern villages are now known to have been built in conjunction with a mode of subsistence that involved gathering the seeds of wild barley, wheat, and other grasses. These seeds ripen during a three-week period in the late spring. Stands of wild wheat still grow thick enough in Anatolia for an individual using a flint-bladed sickle to harvest over two pounds of grain per hour—or for a family of experienced plant collectors to gather as much grain during a three-week period as they would need for a whole year. The "broad spectrum" hunter-collectors built the first permanent villages to provide a place for storing the grain, grinding it into flour, and converting it into cakes or porridge. Their houses, walls, storage pits, roasting ovens (for cracking the husks), and heavy grinders (for making the flour) were investments that, unlike temporary campsites, could not easily be given up.

At Mount Carmel in Israel, for example, eleventh-millennium B.C. prehistoric hunter-collectors known as

Natufians carved out basin-shaped depressions at the front of their rock shelters, laid courses of stone pavement, and built rings of stone around permanent hearths. In the Jordan River Valley, at the 12,000-year-old site of Mallaha, seed eaters made stone foundations for round houses and plastered storage pits. Flint "sickles," which acquired a telltale sheen from cutting the stalks of wild grains, have also been found at these sites. There is similar evidence, dating back to 10,000–8000 B.C., of preagricultural grain-cutting and grain-roasting or grain-storing village life at Zawi Chemi Shanidar in Iraq along the upper drainage of the Tigris River and at Karim Shahir on the flanks of the Zagros Mountains. At Tell Mureybat, at the headwaters of the Euphrates River in Syria, archaeologists have found 10,000-year-old clay-walled houses, grinding stones, roasting pits, and eighteen separate types of wild seeds including the ancestors of wheat and barley.

The New World sequence was very different. The earliest New World domesticated plants, those found by MacNeish in the Tehuacán Valley, are about 9,000 years old. Primitive forms of maize with a small cob containing only two or three rows of kernels were being grown about 7,000 years ago. Yet it was not until 5,400 years ago that the inhabitants of the Tehuacán Valley built permanent houses. And even then the houses were inhabited only part of the year, since semimigratory collecting continued to furnish 50 percent of the plants used for food.

Incidentally, the long but peculiarly different sequence of steps and the entirely different set of plants involved in the incipient phases of agriculture in the Old and New worlds should lay to rest once and for all the hoary notion that one development was derived from the other. If people from the Middle East somehow managed to get to Tehuacán 9,000 years ago, they came empty-handed and were obviously not very helpful. The American Indians still had to spend several thousand additional years improving and expanding their own inventory of crops. Some die-hard diffusionists—scholars who believe that it was unlikely for something as complex as agriculture to have been developed independently more than once—attempt to get around the absence of wheat, barley, rye, or any other Old World food plants or domesticated animals in Mesoamerica by proposing that the *idea* of crops was transmitted and not the crops themselves. Yet I have already shown that what keeps hunter-collectors from switching over to agriculture is not ideas but cost/benefits. The idea of agriculture is useless when you can get all the meat and vegetables you want from a few hours of hunting and collecting per week.

I think the reason why the two sequences were different is that different kinds of plant and animal communities existed in the Old and New worlds after the big game were destroyed. In the Middle East the combination of animals and plants was such that, by settling down in villages, the "broad spectrum" hunter-collectors could increase their consumption of both meat and food plants. But in Mesoamerica to settle down in permanent seed-collecting villages was to do without meat.

The zones in which Middle Eastern agriculture arose happened to contain not only wheat, barley, peas, and lentils in a wild state but also the precursors of domesticated sheep, goats, pigs, and cattle. When permanent preagricultural settlements were built in the middle of dense fields of grain, herds of wild sheep and goats—whose major source of food was wild grasses, including the ancestors of wheat and barley—were forced into closer contact with the villagers. Aided by dogs, villagers could bring the movement of these herds under control. The sheep and goats were kept on the margins of the grain fields and were allowed to eat the stubble but not the ripening grain. In other words, the hunters no longer had to go to the animals; the animals, attracted by the fields of concentrated foodstuff, came to the hunters.

The ripening grain could have been so irresistible, in fact, that the animals threatened to destroy the crops. This gave the hunters a double incentive as well as a double opportunity to intensify their production of meat, thereby threatening sheep and goats with overkill and extinction. And that is probably what would have happened to these species, like so many before them, were it not for the advent of domestication—the greatest conservation movement of all times.

The actual steps by which the animals were saved from extinction could have been simple. Many modern-day hunter-collectors and village horticulturalists keep animals as pets. Just as it was not lack of knowledge about plants that delayed the development of farming, so was it not lack of knowledge about animals that prevented earlier cultures from raising large numbers of sheep and goats as pets and making use of them for food and other economic benefits. The principal limitation was rather that human populations would soon run out of wild plant foods for themselves if they had to feed captive animal populations. But the cultivation of grains opened new possibilities. Sheep and goats thrive on stubble and other inedible portions of domesticated plants. They could be penned, fed on stubble, and milked and slaughtered selectively. Animals that were too aggressive or too delicate, or that grew too slowly, would have been eaten before they reached reproductive age.

This theory explains why the domestication of plants and animals occurred at the same times and places in the Old World. Both domestications were part of a general region-wide intensification which laid the basis for the emergence of a new production system. At Zawi Chemi Shanidar, one of the earliest villages in Iraq, domesticated sheep were present almost 11,000 years ago. Evidence of domesticated goats dating back 9,500 to 9,000 years, has been found at Ali Kosh in Iran, along with domesticated varieties of wheat, barley, and oats. Archaeologists have identified the same complex —domesticated plants and animals—at Jarmo in Iraq with a date of 8,800 years ago.

Now, back to Mesoamerica. Like their near-contemporaries in the Middle East, the "broad spectrum" hunter-collectors of the Ajuereado period in Tehuacán made good use of grains, two of which—amaranth and maize—were later domesticated. MacNeish notes that seed collection had labor efficiencies comparable to agriculture and that, like agriculture, it provided harvests that could be stored. Why, then, didn't the people of Tehuacán settle down near the wild stands of amaranth or corn? Was it because they lacked geniuses to tell them how to do it? Or was it, as one archaeologist has suggested, because of mysterious "changes in sociopolitical organization which had nothing to do with either climate or population density"? These are poor alternatives given the glaring differences between the remnant animal species in Mexico and those in the Middle East. The domestication of animals in Tehuacán did not keep pace step by step with the domestication of amaranth and corn for the simple reason that all domesticable herd animals had become locally extinct as a result of climatological changes and overkill. If they wanted to eat meat, the people of Tehuacán needed to move about freely in response to the seasonal habits of their prey—mostly woodland deer, rabbits, turtles, and other small animals and birds. Hence their reluctance to invest the kind of effort the Near Eastern seed gatherers put into their houses, roasting pits, and storage facilities. And hence their postponement of full village life until they had depleted even the smaller animals long after they had domesticated many species of plants.

I am not saying that Mesoamerica was entirely devoid of domesticable species. Toward the end of the Tehuacán sequence, dogs and turkeys were being raised for food. But the dietary potential of these animals was insignificant compared to the Old World grass-eating ruminants. Dogs can be significant sources of protein only if they are raised as scavengers, and turkeys compete with human beings for grains. The only New World animals comparable to sheep and goats were llamas and alpacas, which survived exclusively in South America and could play no role in the formative phases of Mesoamerican village life.

South American Indians did, of course, eventually domesticate llamas, alpacas, and guinea pigs (also absent from Mesoamerica). These animals served as an important source of meat for Andean peoples from about 2500 B.C. onwards. Not enough is known about the incipient phases of agriculture in the Andes to explain why preagricultural villages based on seed gathering and semidomesticated llama-alpaca hunting did not occur. One possibility is that the llama and alpaca were very difficult to breed in captivity. Their closest wild relative, the vicuña, whose wool is much sought-after, cannot be domesticated because the animal refuses to go through its elaborate courtship ritual when it is confined. Another posibility is that wild stands of quinoa were not productive enough to serve as an inducement to build a village next to them. But this question cannot be answered without additional research.

The depletion of animal resources in the zones where New World agriculture developed had far-reaching consequences. It set the two hemispheres on divergent trajectories and imparted to each a different pace of development. This explains why it was that Columbus "discovered" America and Powhatan did not "discover" Europe, that Cortés conquered Moctezuma rather than the other way around. In the Old World the domestication of sheep and goats was followed rapidly by that of pigs, cattle, camels, donkeys, and horses. These animals were incorporated into the agricultural system and provided the basis for additional technological advances. In fully sedentary villages, grains could be diverted to feed donkeys and oxen, which could be harnessed to help pull plows and other heavy objects. Loads were hauled first on sleds, then on rollers, and finally on wheels. This led to increasingly efficient transport and, more important, laid the foundation for mechanical engineering and hence for all complex machines. In the New World the wheel was invented by the American Indians, perhaps for making pottery and certainly as a toy, but its further development was halted by the lack of animals suitable for hauling heavy loads. Llamas and alpacas were worthless as a source of traction, and the bison, hard to tame in any case, lived outside the nuclear areas of incipient farming and state formation. Failure to develop the technology of the wheel meant that the New World was left far behind in all lifting, hauling, milling, and manufacturing processes in which pulleys, gears, cogs, and screws play an essential role.

The different faunal endowments of the two hemispheres at the end of the Pleistocene overkill had other consequences as well. Patterns of political economy, religion, and food preferences in both hemispheres cannot be understood without taking into account the role of domestic animals as a source of animal protein. These subjects will be taken up in later chapters.

What I have shown so far is that the emergence of village life was a response to the depletions brought about when the hunting-collecting mode of subsistence was intensified. But in the Middle East, once the investment was made in grain-processing and grain-storage facilities, the improved standards of living and the abundance of both calories and proteins made it extremely difficult not to tolerate or encourage population expansion. Medium-protein, high-calorie diets reduced the effectiveness of prolonged lactation as a means of contraception; women were more sedentary and could take care of a new baby as well as a three- or four-year-old; agricultural tasks sponged up child labor; and villages could expand into virgin lands. Beginning with 100,000 people in 8000 B.C., the population of the Middle East probably reached 3.2 million shortly before 4000 B.C.—a fortyfold increase in 4,000 years. This increase entailed renewed pressures on living standards, starting a new round of intensification and a new cycle of depletions. Forest resources proved particularly vulnerable to the increase in domestic animals. Large areas reverted to scrub, and soils began to erode. Meat once again became scarce, nutritional standards fell, diseases transmitted by domestic animals increased, reproductive pressure soared, and the whole region stood on the threshold of enormous new transformations which would affect every aspect of life. And all this did not take place without another cost which I have yet to discuss: the cost of increased warfare.

4
The Origin of War

Any anthropologist can recite the names of a handful of "primitive" peoples who are reported never to wage war. My favorite list includes the Andaman Islanders, who live off the coast of India, the California-Nevada Shoshoni, The Yahgan of Patagonia, the California Mission Indians, the Semai of Malaysia, and the recently contacted Tasaday of the Philippines. The existence of such groups suggests that organized intergroup homicide may not have been part of the cultures of our stone age ancestors. Perhaps. Yet most of the evidence no longer supports this view. It is true that a few modern band-level peoples have no interest in war and seek to avoid it, but several cultures on my list consist of refugees who have been driven into remote areas by more warlike neighbors. The majority of hunter-collectors known to modern observers carry out some form of intergroup combat in which teams of warriors deliberately try to kill each other. William Divale has identified thirty-seven such groups.

Proponents of the view that warfare originated with village settlements and the growth of the state claim that contemporary hunter-collectors are not really representative of prehistoric peoples. Some experts even hold that all incidents of armed combat between hunter-collectors reflect the debasement of "primitive" ways as a result of direct or indirect contact with state-level societies. Archaeologists have not yet been able to settle this controversy. The problem lies in the fact that the weapons of prehistoric war would have been identical with those used in hunting, and deaths caused by wounds to vital organs cannot easily be detected by examining skeletons. Evidence of mutilated and severed skulls extends back 500,000 years or more. The famous Peking Man skulls had been smashed at the base—probably to provide access to the brains. This is a common practice among modern cannibals, many of whom regard brains as a delicacy. But how can one tell if the individuals to whom the skulls belong died in combat? Much present-day cannibalism is practiced not on enemies but on revered next of kin. As for severed heads, contemporary peoples such as the Manus of New Guinea treasure the skulls of close relatives and use them in rituals. For the first really reliable archaeological evidence of warfare one must wait for the construction of fortified villages and towns. The oldest of these is pre-Biblical Jericho, where by 7500 B.C. an elaborate system of walls, towers, and defensive ditches, or moats had already been constructed, leaving no doubt that warfare was by then an important facet of everyday life.

In my opinion warfare is a very ancient practice, but its characteristics differed in the successive epochs of prehistory and history. During the upper paleolithic period intergroup violence must have been moderated by the absence of sharply defined territorial boundaries and by frequent changes in band membership as a result of intermarriage and a high volume of visiting. Ethnographic studies have shown that the resident core of a typical modern hunter-collector band changes from season to season, and even from day to day, as families shuttle back and forth between the camps of the husband's and wife's relatives. While people identify with the territory in which they were born, they don't have to defend that territory in order to earn their living. Hence acquisition of additional territory through the rout or annihilation of enemy forces is seldom a conscious motive for joining battle. Bands usually initiate combat as the result of an accumulation of personal grievances between influential individuals. If the aggrieved persons can muster a sufficient number of relatives who sympathize with their cause or who have grievances of their own against members of the targeted band, a war party can be organized.

One example of a war between hunter-collector bands took place in the late 1920's between the Tiklaulia-Rangwila and Mandiiumbula bands of Bathhurst and Melville Islands in northern Australia. The Tiklauila-Rangwila men were the instigators. They painted themselves white, formed a war party, and advised the Mandiiumbula of their intentions. A time was set for a meeting. When the two groups had gathered, both sides "exchanged a few insults and agreed to meet formally in an open space where there was plenty of room." As night fell—to continue the account given by Arnold Pilling and C. W. Hart—individuals from the two groups exchanged visits, since the war parties included relatives on both sides and no one regarded every member of the other group as an enemy. At dawn the two groups lined up on opposite sides of the clearing. Hostilities began with some old men shouting out their grievances at one another. Two or three individuals were singled out for special attention.

> Hence when spears began to be thrown, they were thrown by individuals for reasons based on individual disputes.

Since the old men did most of the spear throwing, marksmanship tended to be highly inaccurate.

> Not infrequently the person hit was some innocent noncombattant or one of the screaming old women who weaved through the fighting men, yelling obscenities at everybody, and whose reflexes for dodging spears were not as fast as those of the men. . . . As soon as somebody was wounded, even a seemingly irrelevant crone, fighting stopped immediately until the implications of this new incident could be assessed by both sides.

I do not mean to liken hunter-collector warfare to slapstick comedy. W. Lloyd Warner reported high rates of fatalities for at least one other northern Australian hunter-collector group called the Murngin. According to Warner, 28 percent of adult male Murngin deaths were caused by wounds inflicted on the battlefield. Bear in mind that when a whole band contains only ten adult males, one death per battle every ten years is all it takes to rack up this kind of body count.

Warfare after the development of agriculture probably became more frequent and more deadly. Certainly the scale of combat increased. Permanent houses, food-processing equipment, and crops growing in the fields sharpened the sense of territorial identity. Villages tended to remain enemies across the generations, repeatedly attacking and plundering, seeking to rout each other from their territories. Among the village-dwelling Dani of West Irian, New Guinea, warfare has a regulated "nothing fight" phase, similar to that of the Tiwi, in which there are few casualties. But the Dani also launch all-out sneak attacks that result in the destruction and rout of whole villages and the deaths of several hundred people at a time. Karl Heider estimates that 29 percent of Dani men die as a result of injuries sustained during raids and ambushes. Among the Yanomamo village horticulturalists along the Brazil-Venezuela border, raids and ambushes account for 33 percent of adult male deaths from all causes. Since the Yanomamo are an important test case, I've set aside a whole chapter for them following this one.

The reason some anthropologists deny the reality of high levels of combat among band and village peoples is that the populations involved are so small and spread out as to make even one or two intergroup killings seem utterly irrational and wasteful. The Murngin and the Yanomamo, for example, have population densities of less than one person per square mile. But even groups with such low densities are subject to reproductive pressure. There is considerable evidence indicating that the balance between people and resources does in fact lie behind band and village warfare and that the origin of this scourge stems from the inability of preindustrial peoples to develop a less costly or more benign means of achieving low population densities and low rates of population growth.

Before I discuss this evidence, let me review some alternative explanations and show why I think none of these is adequate to the task. The major alternatives include *war as solidarity, war as play, war as human nature*, and *war as politics*.

War as solidarity. According to this theory, war is the price that is paid for building up group togetherness. Having external enemies creates a sense of group identity and enhances esprit de corps. The group that fights together stays together.

I must admit that aspects of this explanation are compatible with one based on reproductive pressure. If a group is undergoing stress caused by intensification, declining efficiencies, and increased abortions and infanticides, the deflection of aggressive behavior onto neighboring bands or villages would certainly be preferable to letting it fester within the community. I do not doubt that deflecting aggressive behavior onto foreigners can act as a "safety valve." What this approach fails to explain, however, is why the safety valve has to be so deadly. Wouldn't verbal abuse, mock combat, or competitive sports be less costly ways of achieving solidarity? The claim that mutual slaughter is "functional" cannot be based on some vague abstract advantage of togetherness. It must be shown how and why such deadly recourse is necessary to prevent an even more deadly consequence—how, in other words, the benefits of war outweigh its costs. No one ever has shown or will be able to show that the consequences of less solidarity would be worse than deaths in combat.

War as play. Some anthropologists have tried to balance the material costs and benefits of warfare by representing it as a pleasureable, competitive team sport. If people actually enjoy risking their lives in combat, then war can be materially wasteful but psychologically valuable and the puzzle disappears. I agree that people, especially men, are frequently brought up to believe that warfare is a zestful or ennobling activity and that one should enjoy stalking and killing other human beings. Many of the mounted Indians of the Great Plains—the Sioux, the Crow, the Cheyenne—kept a tally of their acts of bravado in war. A man's reputation lay in counting coups. They gave the most points not to the warrior with the highest body count, but to the one who took the most risks. The greatest feat of all was to sneak in and out of an enemy camp without being detected. But indoctrination for military bravado among band and village peoples was not always successful. The Crow and other Indians of the Great Plains took care of their pacifists by letting them put on women's clothing and making them serve as attendants to the warriors. And even the bravest of warriors, as among the Yanomamo, have to be emotionally prepared for the fray by performing rituals and taking drugs. If people can be taught to value war and to enjoy stalking and killing other human beings, one must also grant that they can be taught to hate and fear war and to be revolted by the spectacle of human beings trying to kill each other. Both kinds of teaching and learning actually do take place. So if warlike values cause wars, the crucial problem becomes that of specifying the conditions under which people are taught to value war rather than to abhor it. And this the *war as play* theory cannot do.

War as human nature. A perennially favorite way for anthropologists to avoid the problem of specifying the conditions under which war will be regarded as a valuable or an abhorrent activity is to endow human nature with an urge to kill. War occurs because human beings, especially males, have a "killer instinct." We kill because such behavior has been proved successful from the standpoint of natural selection in the struggle for existence. But *war as human nature* runs into difficulties as soon as one observes that killing is not universally admired and that intensity and frequency of warfare are highly variable. I fail to see how anyone can doubt that these variations are caused by cultural rather than genetic differences, since sharp reversals from extremely warlike to peaceful behavior may occur in one or two generations without any genetic changes whatsoever. The Pueblo Indians in the Southwest of the United States, for example, are known to contemporary observers as peaceful, religious, unaggressive, cooperative peoples. Yet not so long ago they were known to the Spanish governor of New Spain as the Indians who tried to kill every white settler they could get their hands on and who burned every church in New Mexico, together with as many priests as they could lock inside and tie to the altars. One need merely recall the astonishing flip-flop in post-World War II Japanese attitudes toward militarism, or the sudden emergence of the Israeli survivors of Nazi persecution as the leaders of a highly militarized society, to grasp the central weakness of the *war as human nature* argument.

Obviously it is part of human nature to be able to become aggressive and to wage war. But how and when we become aggressive is controlled by our cultures rather than by our genes. To explain the origin of warfare one must be able to explain why aggressive responses take the specific form of organized intergroup combat. As Ashley Montagu has warned us, even in infrahuman species killing is not the goal of aggression. There are no drives or instincts or predispositions in human beings to kill other human beings on the battlefield, although under certain conditions they can easily be taught to do so.

War as politics. Another recurrent explanation of war holds that armed conflict is the logical outcome of an attempt of one group to protect or increase its political, social, and economic welfare at the expense of another group. War occurs because it leads to the expropriation of territory and resources, the capture of slaves or booty, and the collection of tribute and taxes —"To the victor belong the spoils." The negative consequences for the vanquished can simply be written off as a miscalculation—"the fortunes of war."

This explanation makes perfectly good sense in relation to the wars of history, which are primarily conflicts between sovereign states. Such wars clearly involve the attempt on the part of one state to raise its standard of living at the expense of others (although the underlying economic interests may be covered up by religious and political themes). The form of political organization which we call the state came into existence precisely because it was able to carry out wars of territorial conquest and economic plunder.

But band and village warfare lacks this dimension. Band and village societies do not conquer territories or subjugate their enemies. Lacking the bureaucratic, military, and legal apparatus of statehood, victorious bands or villages cannot reap benefits in the form of annual taxes or tribute. And given the absence of large amounts of stored foods or other valuables, the "spoils" of war are not very impressive. Taking prisoners and making slaves of them is impractical for a society that cannot intensify its system of production without depleting its resource base and that lacks the organizational capacity to exploit a hostile, underfed labor force. For all of these reasons, the victors in pre-state wars often returned home carrying a few scalps or heads as trophies or with no spoils at all—except the right to boast about how manly they were in combat. In other words, political expansion cannot explain warfare among band and village societies because most such societies do not engage in political expansion. Their entire mode of existence is dominated by the need not to expand in order to preserve the favorable ratio of people to resources. Hence we must look to the contributions of warfare to the conservation of favorable ecological and demographic relationships in order to understand why it is practiced by band and village societies.

The first such contribution is the dispersal of populations over wider territories. While bands and villages do not conquer each other's lands the way states do, they nonetheless destroy settlements and rout each other from portions of the habitat that they would otherwise jointly exploit. Raids, routs, and the destruction of settlements tend to increase the average distance between settlements and thereby lower the overall regional density of population.

One of the most important benefits of this dispersion—a benefit shared by both victor and vanquished—is the creation of "no man's lands" in areas normally providing game animals, fish, wild fruits, firewood, and other resources. Because the threat of ambush renders them too dangerous for such purposes, these "no man's lands" play an important role in the overall ecosystem as preserves of plant and animal species that might otherwise be permanently depleted by human activity. Recent ecological studies show that in order to protect endangered species—especially large animals that breed slowly—very extensive refuge areas are needed.

The dispersal of populations and the creation of ecologically vital "no man's lands" are very considerable benefits which derive from intergroup hostilities among band and village peoples despite the costs of combat. With one proviso: having dispersed the enemy camps and settlements, the victors cannot allow the population of their camps and settlements to increase to the point where game and other resources are threatened by their own population growth and intensification effort. Warfare under pre-state conditions cannot satisfy this proviso—at least not through the direct effect of combat deaths. The problem is that the combatants are almost always males, which means that most of the battle fatalities are men. Warfare causes only 3 percent of adult female deaths among the Dani and 7 percent among the Yanomamo. Moreover, war-making band and village societies are almost always polygynous, that is, the husband services several wives. Thus there is no possibility that warfare alone can depress the rate at which a band or village—especially if it is victorious—grows and depletes its environment. Male combat deaths, like geronticide, can produce short-run relief from population pressure, but they cannot influence overall trends as long as a few polygynous male survivors continue to service all the noncombatant females. The biological reality is that most males are reproductively superfluous. As Joseph Birdsell has put it, the fertility of a group is determined by the number of its adult women, rather than by its adult men. "Undoubtedly, one able-bodied male could keep ten women continuously pregnant." This is obviously a conservative statement, since at ten pregnancies per woman the male in question would have only a maximum of 100 children while many Arab sheiks and Eastern potentates seem to encounter no great difficulty in siring well over 500 children.

But let us follow Birdsell's logic, which is unassailable even though it is based on the hypothetical example of one man and only ten women:

> This would produce the same number of births as if the group consisted of ten men and ten women. But if we can imagine a local group consisting of ten men and only one woman, the birth rate would necessarily be ten percent of the former example. *The number of women determines the rate of fertility.*

As I will show, warfare does drastically affect the number of women and thus does have a powerful effect on the human crop. But the manner in which it achieves this has hitherto not been understood.

Before I explain how warfare limits the rate at which settlements grow, I want to emphasize one point. The twin demographic effects that warfare produces among band and village societies are not characteristic of state-level military complexes. For the moment, I will address myself only to the origin of pre-state warfare. Among state-level societies warfare may disperse populations, but it seldom depresses their rate of growth. Each of the major wars of this century—World Wars I and II, Korea and Vietnam—has failed to reduce the long-term rate of growth of the combatant populations. While it is true that during World War I the deficit between the projected and actual population for Russia reached 5 million, it took only ten years for this to be overcome. Even short-time population growth may be unaffected. All through the decade of the Vietnam War, the population of Vietnam grew at the phenomenal rate of 3 percent per year. That warfare does not automatically depress the rate of population growth should be obvious from European history. Scarcely a decade went by during the past three centuries without large-scale combat, and yet the European population soared from 103 million in 1650 to 594 million in 1950. One might more readily conclude that European wars—and wars of states in general—have been part of a system for stimulating rapid population growth.

What no one seems to have realized is that, unlike state societies, bands and villages were exceptional in their use of warfare to achieve very low rates of population growth. They achieved this not primarily through male combat deaths—which, as we have just seen, are always easily compensated for by calling upon the remarkable reproductive reserves of the human female—but by another means that was intimately conjoined with and dependent upon the practice of warfare yet was not part of the actual fighting. I refer to female infanticide. Warfare in band and village societies made the practice of infanticide sex-specific. It encouraged the rearing of sons, whose masculinity was glorified in preparation for combat, and the devaluation of daughters, who did not fight. This in turn led to the limitation of female children by neglect, abuse, and outright killing.

Studies recently carried out by William Divale show that among band and village societies practicing warfare when they were first censused the number of males aged fourteen or under greatly exceeded the number of females in the same age bracket. Divale found that the ratio of boys to girls was 128:100, whereas the ratio of adult men to women was 101:100. Since the expected world-wide sex ratio at birth is 105 males to 100 females, the discrepancy between 105 and 128 is a measure of preferential treatment of male children and the drop to 101:100 is probably a measure of the rate of adult male combat deaths. This interpretation was strengthened when Divale compared the sex ratios of groups that had practiced warfare at progressively more remote periods in the past with those that were actively practicing warfare when they were first censused.

For populations that were censused five to twenty-five years after warfare had been stopped, usually by colonial authorities, the average sex ratios were 113 boys and 113 adult men per 100 girls and 100 adult women. (The increase in the adult sex ratio from 101:100 when war was present to 113:100 when war had been stopped is probably the result of the survival of males who previously would have been killed in war.) Among populations that were censused more than twenty-five years after warfare, the sex ratio of persons fifteen years and younger was still lower—106:100, approximating the world norm of 105:100, at birth.

These shifts are even more dramatic when the reported frequency of any kind of infanticide, male or female, and the presence of warfare are taken into consideration. Among populations who were still practicing warfare at the time of census and who according to ethnographers' reports were commonly or occasionally practicing some kind of infanticide, the average sex ratio among the young was 133 boys to 100 girls. Yet among adults it declined to 96 men to 100 women. For populations in which warfare had been stopped twenty-five or more years prior to the census and in which infanticide was reported as not common or not practiced, the sex ratio among the young was 104 boys to 100 girls and 92 men to 100 women.

I am not suggesting that war caused female infanticide or that the practice of female infanticide caused war. Rather, I propose that without reproductive pressure neither warfare nor female infanticide would have become widespread and that the conjunction of the two represents a savage but uniquely effective solution to the Malthusian dilemma.

Regulation of population growth through the preferential treatment of male infants is a remarkable "triumph" of culture over nature. A very powerful cultural force was needed to motivate parents to neglect or kill their own children, and an especially powerful force was needed to get them to kill or neglect more girls than boys. Warfare supplied this force and motivation because it made the survival of the group contingent on the rearing of combat-ready males. Males were chosen to be taught how to fight because armaments consisted of spears, clubs, bows and arrows, and other hand-held weapons. Hence military success depended upon relative numbers of brawny combatants. For this reason males became socially more valuable than females, and both men and women collaborated in "removing" daughters in order to rear a maximum number of sons.

To be sure, preferential female infanticide sometimes occurs in the absence of warfare. Many Eskimo groups maintain high rates of female infanticide even though they have relatively little organized intergroup armed combat. The explanation for this is that in the Arctic environment the superior muscle power of males plays a role in production that is analogous to the role it plays in warfare in other regions. The Eskimo need every extra ounce of brawn to track, trap, and kill their animal prey. Unlike hunters in temperate zones, the Eskimo find it difficult to achieve overkill. Their problem is simply to get enough to eat and to prevent their own population from falling below replacement strength. They cannot rely on the collection of plant foods as their main source of calories. In such a context sons become socially more valuable than daughters, even without frequent warfare, and both men and women collaborate in limiting the number of females, just as if males were needed for combat.

In more favorable habitats, high levels of female infanticide would be difficult to maintain in the absence of warfare. Band and village peoples are perfectly capable of understanding that the number of mouths to be fed is determined by the number of women in the group. But it is difficult for them to limit the number of females in favor of males, because in other regards women are more valuable than men. After all, women can do most of the things that men can do, and they alone can bear and nurse infants. Except for their long-range contribution to the population problem, women are in fact a better cost/benefit bargain than are men. Anthropologists have been misled about women's labor value by the fact that among hunter-collectors women have never been observed to hunt large animals. This does not prove that the observed division of labor naturally follows from the brawn of the male or from the supposed need for women to stick close to the campfire, to cook, and to nurse the children. Men on the average may be heavier, stronger, and faster runners than women, but in favorable habitats there are few production processes in which these physiological features make men decisively more efficient than women. In temperate or tropical zones the rate of production of meat is limited by the rate of reproduction of the prey species rather than by the skills of the hunters. Women hunters could easily substitute for men without reducing the supply of high-quality protein. And several recent studies have shown that among horticulturalists women provide more calories and proteins in the form of food plants and small animals even if they don't hunt big game. Moreover, the need for women to nurse infants does not "naturally" lead to their roles as cooks and "homebodies." Hunting is an intermittent activity, and there is nothing to prevent lactating women from leaving their infants in someone else's care for a few hours once or twice a week. Since bands consist of closely related kinspeople, hunter-collector women are not as isolated as modern working women and have no trouble finding the pre-industrial equivalents of baby-sitters and day-care centers.

The explanation for the near-universal exclusion of women from big-game hunting appears to lie in the practice of warfare, the male supremacist sex roles which arise in conjunction with warfare, and the practice of female infanticide—all of which ultimately derive from the attempt to solve the problem of reproductive pressure. Virtually all band and village societies teach only males how to become proficient in the use of weapons, and frequently women are forbidden even to touch these weapons just as they are generally discouraged or prevented from engaging in front-line combat.

Male military prowess is closely associated with sexually differentiated training for fierce and aggressive behavior. Band and village societies train males for combat through competitive sports such as wrestling, racing, and dueling. Women seldom participate in such sports and never compete with men. Band and village societies also instill masculinity by subjecting boys to intense ordeals involving genital mutilations such as circumcision, exposure to the elements, and drug-induced hallucinatory encounters with supernatural monsters. It is true that some band and village societies also put girls through puberty rituals but these usually involve trials by boredom rather than terror. Girls are kept out of sight in special huts or rooms for a month or more, during which time they are forbidden to touch their own bodies. Even if they develop an itch, they must use an instrument like a back-scratcher. Sometimes they are forbidden to speak throughout the entire period of their seclusion. It is also true that some cultures mutilate the female genitalia by cutting off a portion of the clitoris, but this is a very uncommon practice and occurs far less frequently than does circumcision.

One question that remains is why *all* women are barred from being trained as military co-equals with males. There are women who are brawnier and more powerful than some men. The winner of the 1972 Olympic women's javelin competition set a record of 209′ 7″, which not only surpasses the spear-throwing potential of most males but also betters the performance of several former champion Olympic male javelin throwers (though they used slightly heavier javelins). So if the crucial factor in forming a war party is brawniness, why not include women whose strength matches or exceeds that of the average enemy male? I think the answer is that the occasional military success of well-trained, large, and powerful females against smaller males would conflict with the sex hierarchy upon which preferential female infanticide is predicated. Males who are successful warriors are rewarded with several wives and sexual privileges that depend on women being reared to accept male supremacy. If the whole system is to function smoothly, no woman can be permitted to get the idea that she is as worthy and powerful as any man.

To sum up: War and female infanticide are part of the price our stone age ancestors had to pay for regulating their populations in order to prevent a lowering of living standards to the bare subsistence level. I feel confident that the causal arrow points from reproductive pressure to warfare and to female infanticide rather than the other way around. Without reproductive pressures, it would be senseless not to rear as many girls as boys, even if males were looked upon as more valuable because of their superiority in hand-to-hand combat. The fastest way to expand male combat strength would be to regard every little girl as precious and not to kill or neglect a single one. I doubt very much that any human being has ever failed to grasp the elementary truth that to have many men you must start by having many women. The failure of band and village societies to act in conformity with this truth suggests not that warfare was caused by infanticide, or infanticide by warfare, but that both infanticide and warfare, as well as the sexual hierarchy that went with these scourges, were caused by the need to disperse populations and depress their rates of growth.

5
Proteins and the Fierce People

Warfare and male bravado play such a conspicuous role in Yanomamo life that anthropologist Napoleon Chagnon of Pennsylvania State University calls them the Fierce People. Dramatic monographs and films show the Yanomamo, who live in the forests along the border between Brazil and Venezuela near the headwaters of the Orinoco and the Rio Negro rivers, making virtually perpetual war against one another. I mentioned earlier that 33 percent of Yanomamo male deaths are caused by wounds received in battle. Moreover, the Yanomamo practice an especially brutal form of male supremacy involving polygyny, frequent wife beating, and gang rape of captured enemy women.

The Yanomamo are a crucial case not only because they are one of the best-studied village societies in which warfare is actively being practiced, but because Chagnon—who knows them best—has denied that the high level of homicide within and between villages is caused by reproductive and ecological pressures:

> Enormous tracts of land, most of it cultivable and abounding with game is [*sic*] found between villages. . . . Whatever else might be cited as a "cause" of warfare between the villages, *competition for resources is not a very convincing one* [Chagnon's italics]. The generally intensive warfare patterns found in aboriginal tropical forest cultures do not correlate well with

> resource shortages or competition for land or hunting areas. . . . Recent trends in ethnological theory are tending more and more to crystallize around the notion that warfare . . . must always be explainable in terms of population density, scarcity of strategic resources such as territory or "proteins," or a combination of both. The Yanomamo are an important society, for their warfare cannot be explained in this way.

Despite their cultivation of plantains, bananas, and other crops, the overall density of the Yanomamo is only about .5 persons per square mile—not very different from that of Amazonian hunter-collectors. Their villages are large by hunter-collector standards, but settlements "fission" (that is, split up) well before they reach a total of 200 inhabitants. This makes Yanomamo villages puny by comparison with Indian settlements on the mainstreams of the Amazon and Orinoco rivers, where the first European explorers encountered villages of 500 to 1,000 people and continuous rows of houses lining the banks for five miles at a stretch. If, as Chagnon claims there is an abundance of land and game, why has overall density and village size among the Yanomamo remained so low? The difference cannot be blamed on warfare itself, since mainstream peoples were if anything even more bellicose than those who live in the forests. Donald Lathrap has cogently argued that all groups who live away from the main rivers, like the Yanomamo, are the "wreckage" of more evolved societies "forced off the flood plains into less favorable environments."

The Yanomamo make no attempt to disguise the fact that they practice female infanticide. This results in an extremely unbalanced sex ratio in the age group of fourteen and under. Chagnon has studied twelve Yanomamo villages located in the most intensive war zone, where the average ratio was 148 boys to 100 girls. In one warlike village studied by Jacques Lizot the juvenile sex ratio was 260:100. On the other hand, three villages studied by William Smole in the Parima highlands outside the most intensive war zone had an average juvenile sex ratio of 109:100.

According to Chagnon, the fact that females are at a premium, exacerbated by the practice of polygyny, is a prime source of disunity and strife:

> The shortage of women, indirectly a consequence of an attitude that admires masculinity, ultimately leads to keen competition and thus reinforces the entire *waiteri complex* [male fierceness complex] by resulting in more fighting and aggression. In practical terms, nearly every village fissioning I investigated resulted from chronic internal feuding over women, and in many cases the groups ultimately entered into hostilities after they separated.

The Yanomamo themselves "regard fights over women as the primary causes of their wars."

Yet not all Yanomamo villages are inhabited by fierce, aggressive men. Chagnon emphasizes the difference in ferocity between villages located in what he calls the "central" and "peripheral" areas. Among villages at the "periphery":

> Conflicts with neighbors are less frequent . . . the intensity of warfare is greatly reduced. . . . Villages are smaller. . . . Displays of aggression and violence are greatly reduced in frequency and limited in form.

These, then, are the facts about the Yanomamo that need to be explained: (1) the small villages and low overall population density despite the apparent abundance of resources; (2) the greater intensity of warfare and of the male fierceness complex in "central" Yanomamo land; and (3) the killing of female infants despite the need for more women because of the unbalanced sex ratio and the practice of polygyny—a need strong enough to constitute the motivation for perpetual strife and homicidal violence.

All of these features of Yanomamo social life seem to accord well with the general explanation I have given for the origin of warfare among band and village societies. I believe it is possible to show that the Yanomamo have recently adopted a new technology or intensified a preexisting technology; that this has brought about a veritable population explosion, which in turn has caused environmental depletion; and that depletion has led to an increase in infanticide and warfare as part of a systematic attempt to disperse settlements and to prevent them from growing too big.

Let us first consider the demographic situation. According to Jacques Lizot:

> The indigenous settlements were traditionally established far from navigable rivers and one had to walk several days through dense unexplored forest to find them. . . . It is only recently, following their remarkable expansion into unoccupied areas—an expansion due as much to fissioning, war, and conflict as to an astonishing demographic increase—that some groups established themselves, around 1950, on the Orinoco River and its tributaries.

James Neel and Kenneth Weiss believe that the total number of Yanomamo villages in the area studied by Chagnon has more than doubled in the last 100 years. They estimate that the overall rate of population growth during the same period has been between 0.5 and 1 percent per year. However, the rate of growth among villages where warfare today is most intense appears to have been much greater. Starting from a single village 100 years ago, there are now 2,000 people in twelve villages studied by Chagnon. If the original village split in half when its population reached 200, the rate of growth for these settlements would be over 3 percent per year. But since the average present-day village in the war zone splits up before it reaches 166 people, I suspect that the rate of growth has been still higher in this area.

It may seem confusing that although Yanomamo have exceptionally high rates of infanticide and warfare, they have been undergoing a population explosion. After all, warfare and infanticide are supposed to prevent such an explosion. The problem is that we lack a continuous record of the changing relationship between the growth of Yanomamo villages and the practice of infanticide and warfare. I have not said that peoples who practice warfare will never undergo population increase. Rather, I have said that warfare tends to prevent population from growing to the point where it permanently depletes the environment. Accordingly, the years shortly before and after the breakup of a Yanomamo village should be characterized by a peak intensity of warfare and female infanticide. The peak in warfare results from pressure to maintain living standards by exploiting larger or more productive areas in competition with neighboring villages, while the peak in female infanticide arises from pressure to put a ceiling on the size of the village while maximizing combat efficiency. Consequently the fact that overall the Yanomamo are involved in both warfare and a population explosion does not invalidate the theory that environmental depletions and reproductive pressures lie behind both phenomena. Unfortunately, data needed to test my predictions about the rise and fall of the intensity of warfare in relation to growth and the splitting up of specific villages have not yet been collected. Nevertheless the point can be proved in a more general way by looking again at the variations in sex ratios among the more peaceful and more warlike Yanomamo groups: the juvenile sex ratio of 109:100 in Smole's three Parima highland villages as compared with 148:100 in Chagnon's war zone.

Chagnon's zone is the one that is now undergoing the most rapid population increase and the most rapid dispersion into unoccupied territories. Smole's zone, on the other hand, now has a stable or perhaps a declining population. The peak intensities of warfare and infanticide in Chagnon's zone can be readily interpreted as attempts to disperse the growing population and at the same time to place a limit on the maximum size of villages. As I said earlier, if there were no ecological constraints there would be no incompatibility between practicing warfare *and* rearing as many females as males. True, warfare by itself places a premium on the rearing of males for combat. But the quickest way for the Yanomamo to rear more males is not to kill or neglect 50 percent of their female infants but to rear them all to reproductive age. *Only if population is pressing against resources does it make sense not to rear as many females as males.* I'll discuss which resources are involved in a moment.

Why did the Yanomamo population suddenly start to increase about 100 years ago? Not enough is known about the history of the region to give a definitive answer, but I can suggest a plausible hypothesis. It was about 100 years ago that the Yanomamo began to obtain steel axes and machetes from other Indians who were in contact with white traders and missionaries.

Today their reliance on these instruments is so complete that they have lost all knowledge of how to manufacture the stone axes their ancestors once used. Steel tools made it possible for the Yanomamo to produce more bananas and plantains with less effort. And, like most preindustrial societies, they used the extra calories to feed extra children.

Bananas and plantains may even have represented a new means of production. These are not native American crops, having entered the New World from Asia and Africa in the post-Columbian period. Most Amazonian Indians traditionally relied on manioc for their supply of starchy calories. Evidence for a relatively new emphasis on plantain and banana trees is the fact that it is the Yanomamo men who plant them, take care of them, and own them. Women help out by transporting the heavy cuttings used to start new gardens and by bringing home backbreaking loads of ripe stalks, but gardening is basically men's work among the Yanomamo. As Smole points out. "This is in striking contrast with many other aboriginal South American horticultural peoples," where gardens are "an exclusively female realm."

A factor promoting the shift to or the intensification of banana and plantain production may have been the European pacification and extinction (possibly due to malaria and other European-introduced diseases) of the Arawak and Carib groups who previously dominated all the navigable rivers in this region. In aboriginal times, large gardens with fruiting trees would have constituted an inviting target for these more populous and better-organized groups. An important point to keep in mind is that Yanomamo wars are being fought mainly between villages that have broken off from common parental settlements. The Yanomamo are expanding into territories formerly occupied by more powerful riverine peoples.

I have suggested that in general the adoption of a new means of production—steel tools and bananas and plantain gardens in this case—leads to population growth, which through intensification leads to depletions and renewed pressure against resources at a higher level of population density. The average size of the villages studied by Chagnon has more than doubled—to 166 in the twelve groups reported on. Smole indicates that the typical village in the Parima highland core of Yanomamo territory has between 65 and 85 people and that "populations much over 100 are exceptionally large." Other estimates place the average pre-contact villages in the 40-to-60 range.

What resources have been depleted by permitting villages to grow to 166 people instead of the previous limit of 40 to 85? With the exception of the groups who live along major streams and who depend on narrow flood plains for their garden lands, Amazonian band and village peoples' most vulnerable resources are not forests or soils—of which there are vast reserves—but game animals. Even without much hunting by human beings, tropical forests cannot support an abundance of animal life. As I have said, in pre-Columbian times large Amazonian villages were situated along the banks of the major rivers, which provided fish, aquatic mammals, and turtles. The Yanomamo have only recently occupied sites close to such rivers, and they still lack the technology for exploiting fish and other aquatic resources. But what about Chagnon's statement that the areas between villages are "abounding in game"? In earlier observations, Chagnon gave the opposite impression:

> Game animals are not abundant and an area is rapidly hunted out, so that a group must constantly keep on the move. . . . I have gone on five-day hunting trips with the Yanomamo in areas that had not been hunted for decades, and had we not brought cultivated foods along, we would have been extremely hungry at the end of this time—we did not collect even enough meat to feed ourselves.

Chagnon could easily have gained a false impression of superabundance if his later observation pertains to the "no man's lands" between village territories. Such an impression is exactly what one would expect if these lands are functioning as animal sanctuaries where breeding stocks are preserved.

I do not claim that there is an actual decline in the Yanomamo's per capita protein ration as a result of the depletion of animal resources. By walking longer distances, capturing smaller animals, collecting insects and grubs, substituting plant protein for animal protein, stepping up the rate of female infanticide (slowing the rate of population growth as the village break-up point is neared), people can avoid actual clinical symptoms of protein deficiency. Daniel Gross of Hunter College has pointed out that such symptoms have seldom if ever been reported for Amazonians who maintain their aboriginal way of life. The lack of such symptoms has led some observers to underestimate the causal significance of animal proteins in the evolution of band and village societies. Yet if Yanomamo warfare is part of a population-regulating system, the proper functioning of that system is to prevent populations from reaching densities at which adults become malnourished and sickly. Hence the lack of clinical symptoms cannot be taken as evidence against the existence of acute ecological and reproductive pressures. Gross has estimated that the animal protein intake per capita per day for tropical-forest village groups averages 35 grams. Although this is well above minimal nutritional needs, it is just about half of the 66 grams of animal protein consumed per capita per day in the United States. Americans would reach Gross's average animal protein intake estimate by eating one large (5.5 ounce) hamburger once a day. For skilled hunters living in the midst of the world's greatest jungle, this is not a very impressive comparison. How much meat do the Yanomamo get? William Smole has the only definite statement on the subject. While hunting is indispensable to the Yanomamo life style, and all are very fond of eating fresh meat, Smole reports:

> It is not unusual for days on end to pass during which no men from a *shabono* [village] are hunting or when little or no meat is being eaten.

The fact is that under tropical-forest conditions an enormous amount of land is needed to ensure even the modest animal protein intake of 35 grams per capita per day. Moreover, the proportionate increase in area essential for maintaining this level of consumption is greater than any increase in the size of the village. Large villages cause proportionately greater disturbances than small ones since the daily level of activity in a large village has an adverse effect on the availability of game for miles around. As a village expands, its hunting parties have to travel increasing distances to find game in reasonable abundance. A critical point is soon reached when in order not to return empty-handed the hunters must stay out overnight and this is not something they like to do in a region of intense warfare. As a result, the villagers are forced either to accept cuts in their meat rations or to split up and disperse. They eventually choose the latter.

How do the Yanomamo react to the pressure against protein resources and how do they translate it into the actual breakup of a village? Chagnon emphasizes the fact that village breakups are preceded by a crescendo of fights over women. From the account of Helena Valero, a Brazilian captured by the Yanomamo, we know that wives make a point of taunting their husbands when the supply of game falters—a practice common among many other tropical-forest groups. The men themselves, after returning empty-handed, become touchy about real or imagined insubordination on the part of their wives and younger brothers. At the same time the failure of the men emboldens wives and unmarried junior males to probe the weaknesses of husbands, seniors, and headmen. Adultery and witchcraft increase in fact and fancy. Factions solidify and tensions mount.

The breakup of a Yanomamo village cannot take place peacefully. Those who move away inevitably suffer great penalties since they are forced to transport heavy banana and plantain cuttings to new gardens, seek refuge among allies, and pay for food and protection with gifts of women, while waiting for new trees to mature. Many attacks by one village on another represent the prolongation of intra-village disputes. Raids between unrelated villages also increase as tensions mount within villages. As hunting expeditions range over greater distances in pursuit of dwindling game resources, incursions into buffer zones between villages and even into enemy gardens become more frequent. Tensions over women lead to more frequent raiding for women, as an alternative to adultery and as validation of masculinity and threatened headman statuses.

I will not attempt to describe in detail all the mechanisms that serve to announce and transmit the threat of depletion of animal resources and that mobilize the compensatory behavior of village breakups and dispersion. But I believe I have provided enough evidence to show that the case of the Yanomamo strengthens the theory that band and village warfare is part of a system for dispersing populations and slowing their rate of growth.

6

The Origin of Male Supremacy and of the Oedipus Complex

The practice of warfare is responsible for a wide-spread complex of male supremacist institutions among band and village societies. The existence of this complex is a source of embarrassment and confusion to advocates of women's rights. Many women fear that if male supremacy has been in existence for so long, then perhaps it really is "natural" for men to dominate women. But this fear is groundless. Male supremacist institutions rose as a by-product of warfare, of the male monopoly over weapons, and of the use of sex for the nurturance of aggressive male personalities. And warfare, as I have already shown, is not the expression of human nature, but a response to reproductive and ecological pressures. Therefore, male supremacy is no more natural than warfare.

Unfortunately, feminists have tried to counter the view that male supremacy is natural by denying that it existed among the majority of band and village peoples. Among non-anthropologists this has led to a resurrection of mystical theories about a golden age of matriarchy when women reigned supreme over men. Anthropologists themselves have found nothing that justifies the exhumation of this nineteenth-century corpse. Instead they have tried to show that the extent and intensity of the male supremacist complex has been exaggerated. In more extreme instances feminists have recently insisted that the reported high incidence of male supremacist institutions is an illusion created by the sexist minds of the male observers who were responsible for writing most of the descriptions of band and village life.

Those who believe that male supremacist institutions are no more common than female supremacist or sexually balanced institutional complexes display a lack of understanding of the bias that actually dominates and directs the professional careers of cultural anthropologists, be they male or female. This bias reflects an almost irresistible temptation to claim that one has done field work among a group whose customs are sufficiently removed from the ordinary to justify the effort and expense entailed in learning about them. (I well remember my own chagrin at having chosen to do field work among the Bathonga, a patrilineal group in southern Mozambique, when with a little more foresight I could have convinced the Ford Foundation to let me go to a more exotic and hence professionally more rewarding matrilineal culture slightly to the north.) Far from being inclined to overlook the existence of institutions that moderate male power and authority, most ethnographers can envisage nothing more rewarding than to be able to write journal articles about "uxorilocal postmarital residence" or a nice case of "matrilineal descent with polyandry." With this in mind, I find it impossible to believe that the overwhelming statistical regularities indicative of virtually universal structural biases against women are nothing more than motes in the eyes of male field workers.

There are 1,179 societies listed in George P. Murdock's *Ethnographic Atlas.* In three-fourths of these societies, when women get married they must ideally move to the home of either their husband or their husband's paternal relatives, whereas in only one-tenth must grooms go to live in the home of either their bride or their bride's maternal relatives. The reckoning of the descent of one's children shows a like asymmetry. In the same 1,179 societies children are regarded as members of the father's descent group (lineage or clan) five times more often than they are regarded as members of the mother's descent group; that is, patrilineality is five times more common than matrilineality. And only in about one-third of the cultures where descent is in the maternal line do married children remain with the mother. In another third of such cultures married male children stop living with the mother and take up residence in her brother's household. This pattern, called avunculocality (residence with the *avunculus,* the Latin word for "mother's brother"), implies that it is the mother's brother who controls the kin group's children and property even though descent is in the female line. Remarkably, the opposite pattern is nonexistent, though its absence has not prevented anthropologists from using the word "amitalocality" to identify it. If amitalocality did exist, a married male in a society which had patrilineal descent would be obliged to accompany his wife to the residence of her father's sister. This would imply that despite the reckoning of descent in the male line it was the father's sister who controlled the kin group's children and property.

Marriage types also attest to the dominance of males in domestic affairs. Polygyny (one husband, several wives) occurs over 100 times more often than polyandry (one wife, several husbands) and is the marriage form functionally best-suited for using sex and women as rewards for aggressive "masculine" behavior.

Polyandry, on the other hand, is the form that would be best-suited for a society dominated by women and in which servile husbands were the rewards for fierce, competitive womanhood. Such societies would have little chance of success in warfare against enemies among whom robust, aggressive males were the military specialists. This suggests why so few band and village societies encourage women to collect husbands the way so many of them encourage men to collect wives.

Another common marriage-related institution provides still more evidence of culturally induced male supremacy related to warfare and ultimately to ecological and reproductive pressures. At marriage a transfer of valuables from the groom's family to that of the bride is extremely common. This transfer, known as "bride-price," compensates the bride's family for the loss of her valuable productive and reproductive services. A striking fact is that the logical opposite of bride-price—groom-price—virtually does not exist. (A single case, recently brought to my attention by Jill Nash, is that of the Nagovisi of Bougainville, where economic compensation is given by the bride's sisters and mother to the groom's sisters and mother for the loss of his valuable productive and reproductive services.) The term "groom-price" should not be confused with "dowry," which is still another form of wealth exchange at marriage. Dowry occurs in patrilineal societies and is given by the bride's father and brother to the groom or his father. Yet it is not considered compensation for the loss of the groom's productive and reproductive services. Rather, it is intended to help cover the cost of maintaining an economically burdensome woman or as payment for the establishment of political, economic, caste, or ethnic alliances valuable to the bride's father and brothers.

These male-biased marriage relationships lie behind French anthropologist Claude Lévi-Strauss's theory that marriage is the "gift" of women exchanged between men. "Men exchange women; women never exchange men," insists Lévi-Strauss. Lévi-Strauss, however, has never offered an explanation of why this should be so.

Political institutions in band and village societies also tend to be dominated by males. Patrilineal societies always have village headmen rather than headwomen, and religious leadership in most band and village societies is also male-centered; there are some female shamans—those adept at dealing with supernatural forces—but they are almost always less numerous and less prominent than their male counterparts.

Band and village societies consider women to be ritually unclean during menstruation. They regard menstrual blood as a pollutant. Yet they use semen in rituals aimed at improving the group's health and well-being. Throughout the world, males menace women and children with bullroarers" (noisemakers whirled on a string), masks, and other paraphernalia whose nature is kept a secret from the women. Men's clubhouses, in which these items are stored and from which women are excluded, are also part of the same complex. Women, on the other hand, seldom ritually menace men and I know of no village which has a clubhouse where women gather to protect themselves against pollution given off by their husbands.

Finally, in almost all band and village societies, male dominance is evident in the division of labor. Women do the drudge work, such as weeding, seed grinding and pounding, fetching water and firewood, carrying infants and household possessions, and routine cooking.

My argument is that all of these sexually asymmetric

institutions originated as a by-product of warfare and the male monopoly over military weaponry. Warfare required the organization of communities around a resident core of fathers, brothers, and their sons. This led to the control over resources by paternal-fraternal interest groups and the exchange of sisters and daughters between such groups (patrilineality, patrilocality, and bride-price), to the allotment of women as a reward for male aggressiveness, and hence to polygyny. The assignment of drudge work to women and their ritual subordination and devaluation follows automatically from the need to reward males at the expense of females and to provide supernatural justifications for the whole male supremacist complex.

What has prevented others from seeing the causal connection between warfare and all of these male-biased institutions? The stumbling block has always been that some of the most warlike village societies seem to have either very weak male supremacist complexes or none at all. The Iroquois, for example, are well-known for their incessant warfare and their training of males to be immune to pain. They are also well-known for their merciless treatment of prisoners of war. Captives were forced to run a gauntlet, their fingernails were pulled out and their limbs were hacked off, and they were finally decapitated or roasted alive at the stake—after which their remains were consumed in cannibalistic feasts. Yet the Iroquois were matrilineal, matrilocal, paid no bride-price, were more or less monogamous, and had no elaborate religious complex for intimidating or isolating women. Many societies display a similar pattern of intense militarism combined with matrilineal rather than patrilineal descent and weak rather than strong male supremacist institutions. (Bear in mind, however, that matrilineal societies constitute less than 15 percent of all cases.)

In fact, the association between matrilineal institutions and a ferocious form of militarism is much too regular to result by chance. If one weren't already convinced that warfare was responsible for patrilineal-patrilocal complexes, a logical conclusion would be that it was also somehow responsible for matrilineal-matrilocal complexes. The solution to this quandary, of course, is that there are different types of warfare. Matrilineal village societies tend to practice a brand of warfare different from that practiced by patrilineal village societies such as the Yanomamo. William Divale was the first to show that matrilineal societies typically engage in "external warfare," that is, penetration by large raiding parties deep into the territories of distant enemies who are linguistically and ethnologically distinct from the attackers. Warfare among patrilineal band and village groups like the Yanomamo, on the other hand, is called "internal warfare" because it involves attacks by small groups of raiders on nearby villages in which enemies speak the same language and probably share a fairly recent common ancestry—thus the term "internal warfare."

The logic behind the connection between matrilineality and external warfare is as follows: The married men who move into a matrilocal Iroquois communal house come from different families and villages. Their change of residence prevents them from viewing their interests exclusively in terms of what is good for their fathers, brothers, and sons and at the same time brings them into daily contact with men of nearby villages. This promotes peace between neighboring villages and lays the basis for men to cooperate in forming large war parties capable of attacking enemies hundreds of miles away. (Iroquois armies consisting of over 500 warriors mounted attacks from New York against targets in places as distant as Illinois.) Divale has expanded the number of cases to which this logic applies by suggesting that the patrilineal people who were attacked by matrilineally organized groups would also have to adopt a similar organization in a short time or be destroyed.

But let me enter a caveat here against the conclusion that *all* cases of matrilineal organization are related to the practice of external warfare. The protracted absence of males for any reason may lead to a focus on women as the carriers of titles and the guardians of male interests. Hunting and fishing expeditions and long-distance trading are two male-centered activities which are also associated with matrilineality. The logic is similar to that involved in warfare: Men must join together for hazardous undertakings which will require them to be away from their houses, lands, and other property for weeks or months. Such prolonged absences mean that women must bear the responsibility for the decisions about daily work patterns and the care and training of children, and that they must also shoulder the burden of agricultural production in gardens and fields. Shifts from patrilineal to matrilineal organizations originate as an attempt on the part of absentee males to turn over the care of jointly owned houses, lands, and property to their sisters. Absentee males rely on their sisters rather than their wives because wives are drawn from someone else's paternal interest group and have divided loyalties. Sisters who stay at home, however, have the same property interests as brothers. Absentee brothers therefore discourage marriages which would remove their sisters from the household in which they grew up together.

Sisters are only too happy to comply since patrilocal marriage exposes them to abuses at the hands of male supremacist husbands and unsympathetic fathers-in-law and mothers-in-law.

The actual transition from patrilocality to matrilocality need not involve any sudden traumatic institutional changes. It can take place by the simple expedient of changing bride-price to bride-service. In other words, instead of transferring valuables as a prelude to removing his bride from her family, the husband settles in temporarily with the family, hunts for them, and helps them clear their fields. From this situation it is but a small step to the kinds of marriages that are characteristic of matrilineal, matrilocal systems. Such marriages are easily broken liaisons in which husbands are in fact regarded as temporary sojourners with sexual privileges who can be asked to leave whenever their presence causes the slightest inconvenience. Among the matrilocal Pueblo Indians of Arizona and New Mexico, for example, inconvenient husbands were ejected by the simple expedient of placing their moccasins outside the front door. Iroquois women might at any moment decide to order a man to pick up his blanket and go elsewhere; as Lewis Henry Morgan noted of Iroquois marriage, "the most frivolous reasons, or the caprice of the moment, were sufficient for breaking the marriage tie." Among the Nayars, a militaristic matrilineal caste of the Malabar Coast in India, the insignificance of husbands reached the point where joint residence was limited to nightly visits.

Households that consist of a resident core of mothers, sisters, and daughters with men either away on war parties or other expeditions or temporarily installed with their wife's family are incompatible with the ideology and practice of patrilineal descent and inheritance. It is no longer to his own children—scattered among the various households in which he sojourned during his peripatetic liaisons—that a man can look for the continuity of his hearth and lands; rather, it is to his sisters' children, who will be brought up where he himself was reared. Or, to look at the same situation from the perspective of the children, it is not their father to whom they can turn for security and inheritance; rather it is their mother's brother.

Let me face one additional complication. Not all expansionist pre-state societies that engage in external warfare are matrilineally organized. In Africa, for example, pastoral societies such as the Nuer and the Massai engaged in external warfare but were patrilineal-patrilocal. These groups require separate consideration. Most nomadic or seminomadic pre-state pastoral societies are expansionist and extremely militaristic, but strongly patrilineal or patrilocal rather than matrilineal or matrilocal. The reason is that animals on the hoof rather than crops in the field are the pastoralists' main source of subsistence and wealth. When pre-state pastoralists intensify production and, as a result of population pressure, invade the territories of their neighbors, the male combatants do not have to worry about what's going on back home. Pastoralists usually go to war in order to lead their stock to better pasture, so "home" follows right along behind them. Hence the expansionist warfare of pre-state pastoral peoples is characterized not by seasonal long-distance raiding from a home base, as is the case among many agricultural matrilineal societies, but by the migration of whole communities—men, women, children, and livestock.

The discovery of the relationship between external warfare and the development of matrilineal institutions clears up a number of puzzles which have plagued anthropologists for over a hundred years. One can now see why patriarchy was never replaced by matriarchy, polygyny by polyandry, or bride-price by groom-price. Matriarchy is ruled out as long as males continue to monopolize the techniques and technology of physical violence. The reason residence with the mother's brothers—avunculocality—is so common in matrilineal societies is that men refuse to let their sisters dominate the allocation of their joint maternal estate. The reason amitalocality does not exist is that women—the father's sisters—are never able to exercise a degree of control over their paternal estate greater than that exercised by their brothers. The reason groom-price virtually does not occur is that husbands in matrilineal systems never occupy a position analogous to that of wives in patrilineal systems. They are not incorporated as dependents into the wife's domestic group and they do not surrender control over their domestic affairs to their sisters; therefore, wives do not pay groom-price to their husband's sisters in compensation for the loss of the man's productive and reproductive services. And the reason that matrilineal societies are not polyandrous as often as they are polygynous is that sex continues to be used as a reward for male bravery. No battle-hardened headhunter or scalp-taker is going to settle down to connubial bliss in the company of four or five of his boon companions under the tutelage of a single woman (although the sharing of concubines and gang rape are easily managed).

All of this is not to deny that the development of matrilineal institutions exerts a moderating influence on the severity of the male supremacist complex. For reasons associated with the explanation of the shift to external warfare, which I will discuss later on, matrilineality leads to a diminution of preferential female infanticide and even to a reversal of preference for the sex of the first-born child. An Iroquois man, for example, wanted his sisters to have daughters so that his matrilineage would not die out, and where strict matrilocality is observed a man who wants to have several wives must restrict himself to women who are each other's sisters. (Formal polygyny was often forgone in matrilineal societies as was true of the Iroquois.) And, as I've said, marriages in matrilineal societies are easily broken by the women. When a man is a guest in his wife's homestead, he cannot mistreat her and expect her to take it lying down. Yet this moderation of the sexist hierarchy should not be confused with the nullification of that hierarchy. In their eagerness to overturn common stereotypes of male supremacy, some anthropologists cite the moderating effect of matrilineal institutions on the degree of male control as if it were evidence of sexual parity. One should not make too much of the fact that Iroquois women "greatly resented being beaten by their husbands." And the fact that the women "might commit suicide to revenge themselves for the ill treatment" is not a sign of their equality with men, as one researcher has recently implied. The important point is that no Iroquois woman would dare to beat her husband. And if such a thing were ever to happen, the husband would certainly have "revenged" himself in a more convincing fashion than by committing suicide. I see no reason to doubt that Lewis Henry Morgan knew what he was talking about when he wrote that the Iroquois male "regarded women as the inferior, the dependent, and the servant of man, and from nurture and habit, she actually considered herself to be so." Early observers who expressed opinions contrary to Morgan's were completely befuddled by the difference between matrilineal descent and female supremacy.

The moderating effect of matrilineality upon the Iroquois was stronger and perhaps even more unusual in the sphere of politics than it was in marriage and domestic life. As far as I know, of all the village cultures about which we have any reliable information none came nearer to being a political matriarchy than the Iroquois. Yet the role of Iroquois women as political decision-makers did not establish political parity between the sexes. Iroquois matrons had the power to raise and depose the male elders who were elected to the highest ruling body, called the council. Through a male representative on the council they could influence its decisions and exercise power over the conduct of war and the establishment of treaties. Eligibility for office passed through the female line, and it was the duty of women to nominate the men who would serve on the council. But women themselves could not serve on the council, and the incumbent males had a veto power over the matrons' nominations. Judith Brown concludes her survey of the Iroquois sexual hierarchy with the remark that "the nation was not a matriarchy, as claimed by some." But she adds that "the matrons were an *éminence grise*." This is not the point. Women are always more influential behind the scenes than they seem to be out front. It is the fact that they are seldom out in front that is so puzzling and that, as I see it, can only be explained in relation to the practice of warfare.

Aside from the problems presented by warlike matrilineal societies, there is another reason that the influence of warfare on sex roles has been virtually ignored up to now. Modern theories about sex roles have been dominated by Freudian psychologists and psychiatrists.

Freudians have long been aware that some kind of link must exist between warfare and sex roles, but they have inverted the causal arrow and derived warfare from male aggressiveness rather than male aggressiveness from warfare. This inversion has penetrated to other disciplines and entered the popular culture, where it lies like a fog over the intellectual scene. Freud claimed that aggression is a manifestation of the frustrations of sexual instincts during childhood and that war is simply socially sanctioned aggression writ large in its most homicidal form. That men should dominate women followed automatically from the way in which the possessors of male sex organs and the possessors of female sex organs, respectively, experienced the pangs of childhood sexuality. According to Freud, boys compete with their father for sexual mastery of the same woman. They fantasize that they are omnipotent and that they can kill their rival, who in fact or fancy threatens to cut off their sex organs. This—the central scenario of Freudian psychodynamic theory—Freud called the Oedipus complex. Its resolution consists in the boy's learning to direct his aggression away from his father toward socially "constructive" activities (which may include warfare).

For the young girl, Freud envisioned a parallel but fundamentally different trauma. A girl's sexuality is also initially directed toward her mother, but at the phallic stage she makes a shocking discovery: she lacks a penis. The girl "holds her mother responsible for her castrated condition" and thus "transfers her love to her father because he has the valued organ which she aspires to share with him." But her love for her father and for other men "is mixed with a feeling of envy because they possess something she lacks." So while males must work out their Oedipus complex by learning how to express hostility against others, girls must learn to compensate for their lack of a penis by accepting a subordinate status and by having babies (which symbolically stand for the lost penis).

Although this scenario might seem sheer poppycock, anthropological research has shown that there is widespread if not universal occurrence of psychodynamic patterns that resemble Oedipal strivings—at least in the minimal sense of sexually charged hostility between older and younger generation males and penis envy among females. Bronislaw Malinowski pointed out that even among the matrilineal, avunculocal Trobriand Islanders, Oedipal rivalries exist—although not exactly in the form Freud had anticipated since the authority figure during childhood is the mother's brother rather than the father. Freud was definitely on to something, but unfortunately his causal arrows were running backwards. What is poppycock is the idea that the Oedipal situation is caused by human nature rather than by human cultures. No wonder the Oedipus situation is so widespread. All of the conditions for creating castration fears and penis envy are present in the male supremacy complex—in the male monopoly over weaponry and the training of males for bravery and combat roles, in female infanticide and the training of females to be the passive rewards for "masculine" performance, in the patrilineal bias, in the prevalence of polygyny, competitive male sports, intense male puberty rituals, ritual uncleanliness of menstruating women, in the brideprice, and in many other male-centered institutions. Obviously, wherever the objective of childrearing is to produce aggressive, "masculine," dominant males and passive, "feminine," subordinate females, there will be something like a castration fear between males in adjacent generations—they will feel insecure about their manliness—and something like penis envy among their sisters, who will be taught to exaggerate the power and significance of the male genitalia.

All of this leads to but one conclusion: The Oedipus complex was not the cause of war; war was the cause of the Oedipus complex (keeping in mind that war itself was not a first cause but a derivative of the attempt to control ecological and reproductive pressures). This may sound like a hopeless chicken and egg problem, but there are excellent scientific reasons for rejecting the Freudian priorities. Starting with the Oedipus complex, one cannot explain variations in the intensity and scope of warfare—why some groups are more warlike than others and why some practice external forms and others internal forms of raiding. Nor can one explain why the complex of male supremacist institutions varies in substance and strength. Nor, starting with the Oedipus complex, can one explain the origin of agriculture, the divergent paths of Old and New World intensifications and depletions, or the origin of the state. But by starting with reproductive pressure, intensification, and depletion, one can understand both the constant and variable aspects of warfare. And from a knowledge of the causes of the variations in warfare, one can reach an understanding of the causes of the variations in family organization, sex hierarchies, and sex roles, and thence of both the constant and variable features of the Oedipus complex. It is an established principle in the philosophy of science that if one must choose between two theories the theory that explains more variables with the least number of independent unexplained assumptions deserves priority.

This point is worth pursuing because different philosophical and practical consequences adhere to each theory. On the one hand, Freudian theory closely resembles the *war as human nature* approach. It makes homicidal aggression seem inevitable. At the same time it shackles both men and women with a biological imperative ("anatomy is destiny"), therewith clouding and constricting the movement to achieve sexual parity. Although I have argued that anatomy destines males for training to be fierce and aggressive if there is war, I have not said that anatomy or genes or instinct or anything else makes war inevitable. Merely because all human beings in the world today and in the known past have lived in warmaking sexist societies or societies affected by war-making sexist societies is not reason enough to cast human nature in the image of the savage characteristics which are necessary for waging successful war. The fact that warfare and sexism have played and continue to play such prominent roles in human affairs does not mean that they must continue to do so for all future time. War and sexism will cease to be practiced when their productive, reproductive, and ecological functions are fulfilled by less costly alternatives. Such alternatives now lie within our grasp for the first time in history. If we fail to make use of them, it will be the fault not of our natures but of our intelligence and will.

7
The Origin of Pristine States

In most band and village societies before the evolution of the state, the average human being enjoyed economic and political freedoms which only a privileged minority enjoy today. Men decided for themselves how long they would work on a particular day, what they would work at—or if they would work at all. Women, too, despite their subordination to men, generally set up their own daily schedules and paced themselves on an individual basis. There were few routines. People did what they had to do, but the where and when of it was not laid out by someone else. No executives, foremen, or bosses stood apart, measuring and counting. No one said how many deer or rabbits you had to catch or how many wild yams you had to dig up. A man might decide it was a good day to string his bow, pile on thatch, look for feathers, or lounge about the camp. A woman might decide to look for grubs, collect firewood, plait a basket, or visit her mother. If the cultures of modern band and village peoples can be relied upon to reveal the past, work got done this way for tens of thousands of years. Moreover, wood for the bow, leaves for the thatch, birds for the feathers, logs for the grubs, fiber for the basket —all were there for everyone to take. Earth, water, plants, and game were communally owned. Every man and woman held title to an equal share of nature.

Neither rent, taxes, nor tribute kept people from doing what they wanted to do.

With the rise of the state all of this was swept away. For the past five or six millennia, nine-tenths of all the people who ever lived did so as peasants or as members of some other servile caste or class. With the rise of the state, ordinary men seeking to use nature's bounty had to get someone else's permission and had to pay for it with taxes, tribute, or extra labor. The weapons and techniques of war and organized aggression were taken away from them and turned over to specialist-soldiers and policemen controlled by military, religious, and civil bureaucrats. For the first time there appeared on earth kings, dictators, high priests, emperors, prime ministers, presidents, governors, mayors, generals, admirals, police chiefs, judges, lawyers, and jailers, along with dungeons, jails, penitentiaries, and concentration camps. Under the tutelage of the state, human beings learned for the first time how to bow, grovel, kneel, and kowtow. In many ways the rise of the state was the descent of the world from freedom to slavery.

How did this happen? To answer, I shall have to draw a distinction between how it first happened in particular world regions and how it happened thereafter. I shall have to distinguish, in the terminology suggested by Morton Fried, between the origin of "pristine" and "secondary" states. A pristine state is one in which there is no preexisting state stimulating the process of state formation. To be sure, to the extent that no society exists in a vacuum, all developmental processes are influenced by interaction with other societies, but "there are situations in which none of the external cultures are any more complex than the one being considered, and these situations can be regarded as pristine."

Archaeologists are moving toward agreement that there were at least three centers of pristine state development, and possibly as many as eight. The three definite instances are Mesopotamia at about 3300 B.C., Peru about the time of Christ, and Mesoamerica about A.D. 100. It is virtually certain that in the Old World pristine states also arose in Egypt (about 3100 B.C.), in the Indus Valley (shortly before 2000 B.C.), and in the Yellow River Basin of northern China (shortly after 2000 B.C.). There is considerable doubt, however, about the claim made by some prehistorians that pristine states also developed in Crete and the Aegean at about 2000 B.C. and in the Lake Region of East Africa at about A.D. 200. Controversy also surrounds the question of whether in the New World the pristine Mesoamerican state arose first in the lowland Maya region or in the Mexican highlands—a question I shall explore in the next chapter.

The rise of pristine states would appear to be best understood as a consequence of the intensification of agricultural production. Like hunter-collectors, agricultural villages tended to intensify their food production efforts in order to relieve reproductive pressures. Unlike hunter-collectors however, agriculturalists in favored soil zones can intensify their efforts for a relatively long time without suffering sharp depletions and efficiency losses. Sedentary village agriculturalists therefore tend to develop special institutions which encourage intensification by conspicuously rewarding those who work harder than others. A key part of the process by which the state's structure of subordination developed involves the distinctive nature of the institutions responsible for rewarding production-intensifiers in sedentary pre-state agricultural villages.

Anthropologists refer to the intensifiers of agricultural production as "big men." In their purest, most egalitarian phase, known best from studies of numerous groups in Melanesia and New Guinea, "big men" play the role of hard-working, ambitious, public-spirited individuals who inveigle their relatives and neighbors to work for them by promising to hold a huge feast with the extra food they produce. When the feast takes place, the "big man," surrounded by his proud helpers, ostentatiously redistributes—parcels out—piles of food and other gifts but keeps nothing for himself. Under certain ecological conditions, and in the presence of warfare, these food managers could have gradually set themselves above their followers and become the original nucleus of the ruling classes of the first states.

Harvard University anthropologist Douglas Oliver carried out a classic study of "bigmanship" during his field work among the Siuai on Bougainville in the Solomon Islands. Among the Siuai a "big man" is called a *mumi* and to achieve *mumi* status is every youth's highest ambition. A young man proves himself capable of becoming a *mumi* by working harder than everyone else and by carefully restricting his own consumption of meat and coconuts. Eventually, he impresses his wife, children and near relatives with the seriousness of his intentions, and they vow to help him prepare for his first feast. If the feast is a success, his circle of supporters widens and he sets to work readying an even greater display of generosity. He aims next at the construction of a men's clubhouse in which his male followers can lounge about and in which guests can be entertained and fed. Another feast is held at the consecration of the clubhouse, and if this is also a success his circle of supporters—people willing to work for the feast to come—grows still larger and he will begin to be spoken of as a *mumi.* What do his supporters get from all this? Even though larger and larger feasts mean that the *mumi*'s demands on his supporters become more irksome, the overall volume of production goes up. So if they occasionally grumble about how hard they have to work, the followers nevertheless remain loyal as long as their *mumi* continues to maintain or increase his renown as a "great provider."

Finally the time comes for the new *mumi* to challenge the others who have risen before him. This is done at a *muminai* feast, where a tally is kept of all the pigs, coconut pies, and sago-almond puddings given away by the host *mumi* and his followers to the guest *mumi* and his followers. If the guest *mumi* cannot reciprocate in a year or so with a feast at least as lavish as that of his challengers, he suffers great social humiliation and his fall from "*mumi*hood" is immediate. In deciding on whom to challenge, a *mumi* must be very careful. He tries to choose a guest whose downfall will increase his own reputation but he must avoid one whose capacity to retaliate exceeds his own.

At the end of a successful feast, the greatest of *mumis* still faces a lifetime of personal toil and dependency on the moods and inclinations of his followers. "*Mumi*hood"—at least, as Oliver observed it—does not confer the power to coerce others into doing one's bidding, nor does it elevate one's standard of living above anyone else's. In fact, since giving things away is the lifeblood of "*mumi*hood," great *mumis* may even consume less meat and other delicacies than an ordinary, undistinguished Siuai. Among the Kaoka, another Solomon Island group reported on by H. Ian Hogbin, there is the saying: "The giver of the feast takes the bones and the stale cakes; the meat and the fat go to the others."

Moreover, a *mumi* cannot rest on his laurels but must constantly prepare for new challenges. At a great feast attended by 1,100 people on January 10, 1939, the host *mumi*, whose name was Soni, gave away thirty-two pigs plus a large quantity of sago-almond puddings. Soni and his closest followers, however, went hungry. "We shall eat Soni's renown," the followers said. That night, exhausted from weeks of feverish preparations, they talked about the rest they had earned now that the feast was over. But early the next morning they were awakened by the booming sound of wooden gongs being beaten in Soni's clubhouse. A handful of sleepy people straggled over to see who was making all the noise. It was Soni, and this is what he told them:

> "Hiding in your houses again; copulating day and night while there's work to be done! Why, if it were left up to you, you would spend the rest of your lives smelling yesterday's pig. But I tell you yesterday's feast was nothing. The next one will be really big."

Formerly, the *mumis* were as famous for their ability to get men to fight for them as they were for their ability to get men to work for them. Warfare had been suppressed by the colonial authorities long before Oliver carried out his study, but the memory of *mumi* war leaders was still vivid among the Siuai. As one old man put it:

> "In the olden times there were greater *mumi* than there are today. Then they were fierce and relentless war leaders. They laid waste to the countryside and their clubhouses were lined with the skulls of people they had slain."

In singing the praises of their *mumis*, the generation of pacified Siuai call them "warriors" and "killers of men and pigs."

Thunderer, Earth-shaker,
Maker of many feasts,
How empty of gong sounds will all the places be
when you leave us!
Warrior, Handsome Flower,
Killer of men and pigs,
Who will bring renown to our places
When you leave us?

Oliver's informants told him that *mumis* had more authority in the days when warfare was still being practiced. Some *mumi* war leaders even kept one or two prisoners who were treated like slaves and forced to work in the *mumi*'s family gardens. And people could not talk "loud and slanderously against their *mumis* without fear of punishment." This fits theoretical expectations since the ability to redistribute meat, plant food, and other valuables goes hand in hand with the ability to attract a following of warriors, equip them for combat, and reward them with spoils of battle. Rivalry between Bougainville's war-making *mumis* appeared to have been leading toward an island-wide political organization when the first European voyagers arrived. According to Oliver, "for certain periods of time many neighboring villages fought together so consistently that there emerged a pattern of war-making *regions*, each more or less internally peaceful and each containing one outstanding *mumi* whose war activities provided internal social cohesion." These regional *mumis* undoubtedly enjoyed some rudiments of coercive power. Nonetheless, the Siuai's approach toward classes based on differential power prerogatives remained incipient and evanescent. This is shown by the fact that *mumis* had to provide their warriors with prostitutes brought into the clubhouses and with gifts of pork and other delicacies. Said one old warrior:

> "If the *mumi* didn't furnish us with women, we were angry. . . . All night long we would copulate and still want more. It was the same with eating. The clubhouse used to be filled with food, and we ate and ate and never had enough. Those were wonderful times."

Furthermore, the *mumi* who wanted to lead a war party had to be prepared personally to pay an indemnity for any of his men who were killed in battle and to furnish a pig for each man's funeral feast. (As if, in the interest of keeping up a proper respect for ordinary human lives, we were to oblige our own political and military "big men" to pay the insured value of each combat death out of their own pockets.)

Let me give another illustration of how redistributor war chiefs could have evolved little by little into permanent rulers with coercive control over production and consumption. About 125 miles north of the eastern tip of New Guinea lies the Trobriand archipelago, a small group of low coral islands studied by the great Polish-born ethnographer Bronislaw Malinowski. Trobriander society was divided into several matrilineal clans and subclans of unequal rank and privilege through which access to garden lands was inherited. Malinowski reported that the Trobrianders were "keen on fighting" and that they conducted "systematic and relentless wars," venturing across the open ocean in their canoes to trade—or, if need be, to fight—with the people of islands over a hundred miles away. Unlike the Siuai *mumis*, the Trobriand "big men" occupied hereditary offices and could be deposed only through defeat in war. One of these, whom Malinowski considered to be the "paramount chief" of all the Trobrianders, held sway over more than a dozen villages containing several thousand people all told. (His actual status was somewhat less exalted since others claimed to be his equal.) Chieftainships were hereditary within the wealthiest and largest subclans, and the Trobrianders attributed these inequalities to wars of conquest carried out long ago. Only the chiefs could wear certain shell ornaments as the insignia of high rank, and it was forbidden for any commoner to stand or sit in a position that put a chief's head at a lower elevation than anyone else's. Malinowski tells of seeing all the people present in the village of Bwoytalu drop from their verandas "as if mowed down by a hurricane," at the sound of the drawn-out "*O guya'u!*" that announced the arrival of an important chief.

Despite such displays of reverence, a chief's actual power was limited. It rested ultimately upon his ability to play the role of "great provider," which depended on ties of kinship and marriage rather than on the control of weapons and resources. Residence among the Trobriand commoners was normally avunculocal. Adolescent boys lived in bachelor huts until they got married. They then took their brides to live in their mother's brother's household, where they jointly worked the garden lands of the husband's matrilineage. In recognition of the existence of matrilineal descent, at harvest time brothers acknowledged that a portion of the produce of the matrilineal lands was owed to their sisters and sent them presents of baskets filled with yams, their staple crop. The Trobriand chief relied on this custom to maintain his political and economic base. He married the sisters of the headman of a large number of sublineages. Some chiefs acquired as many as two dozen wives, each of whom was entitled to an obligatory gift of yams from her brothers. These yams were delivered to the chief's village and displayed on special yam racks. Some of the yams were then redistributed in elaborate feasts in which the chief validated his position as a "great provider," while the remainder were used to feed canoe-building specialists, artisans, magicians, and family servants who thereby fell under the chief's control and enhanced his power. Undoubtedly, in former times the yam stores also furnished the base for launching long-distance trading and raiding expeditions.

So, even though they feared and respected their "great provider" war chiefs, the Trobriand commoners were still a long way from being reduced to peasant status. Living on islands, the Trobrianders were not free to spread out, and their population density had risen in Malinowski's time to sixty persons per square mile. Nonetheless, the chiefs could not control enough of the production system to acquire great power. There were no cereal grains and yams rot after three or four months, which means that the Trobriand "great provider" could not manipulate people through dispensing food nor could he support a permanent police-military garrison out of his stores. An equally important factor was the open resources of the lagoons and ocean from which the Trobrianders derived their protein supply. The Trobriand chief could not cut off access to these resources and hence could never exercise genuine permanent coercive political control over his subordinates. But with more intense forms of agriculture and large harvests of grains, the power of "great providers" evolved far beyond that of the Trobriand chief.

As Colin Renfrew has pointed out, the writing of eighteenth-century naturalist William Bartram contains a graphic account of the importance of redistribution in the social structure of North American agricultural societies. Bartram's description of the Cherokee, the original owners of much of the Tennessee Valley, shows a redistributive system functioning in a manner roughly similar to that of the Trobrianders, despite the totally different "flavor" of Eastern Woodland and Melanesian cultures. The Cherokee, like the Iroquois, had matrilineal and matrilocal institutions and practiced external warfare. Their principal crops were maize, beans, and squash. At the center of the principal settlements was a large, circular "council house" where the council of chiefs discussed issues involving many villages and where redistributive feasts were held. The council of chiefs had a supreme chief, or *mico*, who was the central node in the Cherokee redistributive network. Bartram reported that at harvest time a large crib, identified as the "*mico*'s granary," was erected in each field. "To this each family carries and deposits a certain quantity according to his ability or inclination, or none at all if he so chooses." The *mico*'s granaries functioned as "a public treasury . . . to fly to for succor" in the case of crop failure, as a source of food "to accommodate strangers, or travellers," and as a military store "when they go forth on hostile expeditions." Although according to Bartram every citizen enjoyed "the right of free and public access," commoners clearly had to acknowledge that the store really belonged to the supreme chief since the "treasure is at the disposal of the king or *mico*," who had "an exclusive right and ability . . . to distribute comfort and blessings to the necessitous." The fact that the *mico*, like the Trobriand chief, was far from actually being a "king" shows up clearly in Bartram's comment that when outside the council "he associates with the people as a common man, converses with them, and they with him in perfect ease and familiarity."

Redistribution undoubtedly provides the key to the understanding of numerous ancient monuments and structures which for centuries have puzzled scholars and tourists. As we have seen, from *mumis* on up, "big men," headmen, and chiefs have the capacity to organize labor on behalf of communal enterprises. Among such enterprises was the construction, involving hundreds of workers, of large canoes, buildings, tombs, and monuments. Colin Renfrew has drawn attention to the rather striking similarity between the circular wooden Cherokee feast center council houses and the mysterious circular buildings whose wooden post holes have been found within the precincts of neolithic ceremonial enclosures, or "henges," in Great Britain and northern Europe. The increasingly elaborate burial chambers, earth mounds, and megalithic alignments characteristic of the period from 4000 B.C. to 2000 B.C. in Europe have rather precise parallels among the mounds erected by prehistoric inhabitants of the Ohio and Mississippi valleys, the stone burial platforms and monolithic statuary of Polynesia, and the monolithic tombs and memorials of modern Borneo. All of these constructions played a role in the smooth functioning of pre-state redistributive systems, serving as the locus for redistributive feasts, community rituals dedicated to controlling the forces of nature, and memorials to the generosity and prowess of deceased "big man" hero chiefs. They seem enigmatic only because they are the skeletons, not the substance, of redistributive systems. Since we cannot see the investment of extra labor in agricultural production, monument-building appears to be a kind of irrational obsession among these ancient peoples. But viewed within the living context of a redistributive system, tombs, megaliths, and temples appear as functional components whose costs are slight in comparison with the increased harvests which the ritualized intensification of agricultural production makes possible.

The larger and denser the population, the larger the redistributive network and the more powerful the redistributor war chief. Under certain circumstances, the exercise of power by the redistributor and his closest followers on the one side and by the ordinary food producers on the other became so unbalanced that for all intents and purposes the redistributor chiefs constituted the principal coercive force in social life. When this happened, contributions to the central store ceased to be voluntary contributions. They became taxes. Farmlands and natural resources ceased to be elements of rightful access. They became dispensations. And redistributors ceased to be chiefs. They became kings.

To illustrate these momentous transformations in the context of a small preindustrial state, I shall call upon John Beattie's description of the Bunyoro. Ruled over by a hereditary ruler called the *mukama*, the Bunyoro numbered about 100,000, occupied an area of 5,000 square miles of that portion of the central lake area of East Africa which is now known as Uganda, and earned their living primarily by raising millet and bananas. The Bunyoro were organized into a feudal but nonetheless authentic state society. Their *mukama* was a king, not a mere redistributor chief. The privilege of using all lands and natural resources was a dispensation granted by the *mukama* to a dozen or so chiefs, who then passed on the dispensation to the commoners. In return for this dispensation, quantities of food, handicrafts, and labor services were funneled up through the power hierarchy into the *mukama*'s headquarters. The *mukama* in turn directed the use of these goods and services on behalf of state enterprises. Superficially, the *mukama* appears to be just another "great provider" redistributor chief. In Beattie's words:

> The king was seen both as the supreme receiver of goods and services, and as the supreme giver. . . . The great chiefs, who themselves received tribute from their dependents, were required to hand over to the Mukama a part of the produce of their estates in the form of crops, cattle, beer or women. . . . But everyone must give to the king, not only the chiefs. . . . The Mukama's role as giver was, accordingly, no less stressed. Many of his special names emphasize his magnanimity and he was traditionally expected to give extensively in the form both of feasts and of gifts to individuals.

But a comparison of the *mukama* with the Trobriand or Cherokee supreme chief reveals that power relationships had become inverted. The Trobriand and Cherokee chiefs were dependent on the generosity of the food producers; the Bunyoro food producers were dependent on the generosity of the king. The *mukama* alone could grant or withhold permission for blood vengeance, and failure to contribute to the *mukama*'s income could result in the loss of one's lands, banishment, or corporal punishment. Despite his lavish feast-giving and reputation as a "great provider," the *mukama* used much of his income to bolster his monopoly over the forces of coercion. With his control over the central grain stores he maintained a permanent palace guard and heaped rewards on warriors who displayed bravery in combat and loyalty to his person. The *mukama* also spent a considerable portion of the state treasury on what we would today call "image-building" and public relations. He surrounded himself with numerous officials, priests, magicians, and such regalia keepers as the custodians of spears, of royal graves, of the royal drums, of royal thrones, and of royal crowns, as well as "putters-on" of the royal crowns, cooks, bath attendants, herdsmen, potters, bark-cloth makers, and musicians. Many of the officials had several assistants. Other advisers, diviners, and retainers hung around the court in the hope of being appointed to a chieftainship. Also present were the *mukama*'s extensive harem, his many children, and the polygynous ménages of his brothers and of other royal personages. To keep his power intact, the *mukama* and portions of his court made frequent trips throughout Bunyoro land, staying at local palaces maintained at the expense of the chiefs and commoners.

As Beattie points out, many features of Bunyoro kingship were also present in post-Roman feudal Europe. Like the *mukama,* William the Conqueror and his entourage traveled constantly about twelfth-century England, checking up on his "chiefs" and living off their hospitality. The English kings at that time still displayed evidence of their origins as "great providers" at the head of redistributive networks. William the Conqueror, for example, held three great feasts yearly at which he wore his crown and entertained great numbers of lords and subjects. As we shall see, however, the further evolution of state systems gradually led to the removal of all obligations on the part of rulers to act as "great providers" for their subjects.

Under what circumstances would the conversion of a redistributive chieftainship to a feudal state be likely to occur? To intensification, population growth, warfare, storageable grains, and hereditary redistributors, add one more factor: impaction. Suppose, as Robert Carneiro has suggested, a population being served by redistributors has been expanding inside a region that is circumscribed, or closed off, by environmental barriers.

These barriers need not be uncrossable oceans or unclimbable mountains; rather, they might merely consist of ecological transition zones where people who had broken away from overcrowded villages would find that they would have to take a severe cut in their standard of living or change their whole way of life in order to survive. With impaction, two types of groups might find that the benefits of a permanently subordinate status exceeded the costs of trying to maintain their independence. First, villages consisting of kinspeople forced to enter the transition zones would be tempted to accept a dependent relationship in exchange for continued participation in the redistributions sponsored by their parent settlements. And second, enemy villages defeated in battle might find it less costly to pay taxes and tribute than to flee into these zones.

Very little direct physical coercion would be needed to keep the emergent peasantry in line. Kinship would be used to justify the legitimacy of differential access to resources on the part of junior and senior lineages or of wife-giving, wife-taking alliance groups (those who gave wives would expect tribute and labor services in return). Access to the stored grains might be made contingent upon rendering craft or military services. Or the "big men" of the more powerful group could simply begin taxation by redistributing less than they took in. External warfare would increase and defeated villages would be regularly assimilated into the tax and tribute network. A growing corps of military, religious, and craft specialists would be fed out of the central grain stores, amplifying the image of the rulers as beneficent "great providers." And the social distance between the police-military-priestly-managerial elite and the emergent class of food-producing peasant drudges would widen still further as the scope of the integrated food production facilities increased, as trade networks expanded, as population grew, and as production was intensified still further through more taxation, labor conscription, and tribute.

How well does the theory of environmental circumscription and impaction accord with the evidence? The six most likely regions of pristine state development certainly do possess markedly circumscribed zones of production. As Malcolm Webb has pointed out, all of these regions contain fertile cores surrounded by zones of sharply reduced agricultural potential. They are, in fact, river valleys or lake systems surrounded by desert or at least very dry zones. The dependence of ancient Egypt, Mesopotamia, and India on the flood plains of the Nile, Tigris-Euphrates, and Indus is well-known. In ancient China conditions of climate, soil, and topography limited intensive forms of agriculture beyond the river margins of the Yellow River Basin. Central highland Mexico south to Tehuantepec is also dry and in addition "suffers from severe rain shadow effects in the highland basins and stream valleys that were the aboriginal population centers." And finally, the Peruvian coast is notable for the stark contrast between the lush vegetation bordering the short coastal rivers that flow down from the Andes and the desert conditions that prevail everywhere else. All of these regions present special difficulties to villages that might have sought to escape from the growing concentration of power in the hands of overly aggressive redistributor war chiefs.

Furthermore, there is no doubt that all of these regions were the scene of rapid population growth prior to the emergence of the state. I mentioned earlier that the population of the Middle East increased fortyfold between 8000 and 4000 B.C. Karl Butzer estimates that the population of Egypt doubled between 4000 and

3000 B.C. William Sanders estimates that population tripled or quadrupled in the highland zones of early state formation in Mexico, and similar estimates also apply to Peru, China, and the Indus Valley. "For all areas one receives the impression of an increase not only in the total number of sites but also in the density of distribution, size, and elaboration of sites."

Malcolm Webb has also reviewed the evidence for warfare. Egypt's legendary history begins with a tale of conquest, and specialized instruments of war and fortifications appear early in the archaeological record. In Mesopotamia weaponry and representations of slaves and battles are present in early predynastic times. Fortifications and documentary evidence indicate that Shang China, at the time of the emergence of the first Yellow River states, was an extremely militaristic society. Recent discoveries in the heartland of the earliest Indus River states have confirmed the existence of strongly fortified neolithic villages that were destroyed by conquest. In the New World "both coastal Peru and Mesoamerica show a long history of warfare"; archaeological "indications of fighting are present no later than the start of the first millennium B.C."

The kind of warfare that was conducive to the evolution of the state obviously must have involved long-distance external combat by large coalitions of villages rather than internal warfare of the Yanomamo variety. Matrilocality being a recurrent method of transcending the limited capacity of patrilineal village groups to form multi-village military alliances, it seems likely that societies on the threshold of statehood would frequently adopt matrilineal forms of social organization. According to Robert Briffault, there is a considerable body of literary evidence to support the view that ancient state societies did possess matrilineal institutions shortly before and shortly after their achievement of statehood. The great Egyptologist Flinders Petrie, for example, was of the opinion that the administrative divisions, or nomes, of early dynastic Egypt had once been matrilineal clans and that postmarital residence in earliest times was matrilocal. Strabo, the Greek historian, recorded that the ancient peoples of Crete worshiped predominantly female divinities, granted women a prominent role in public life, and practiced matrilocality. Plutarch says that in Sparta marriage was matrilocal and that "women ruled over men." The great classicist Gilbert Murray was convinced that in Greece during Homeric times "sons went off to foreign villages to serve and marry women in possession of the land there." Herodotus said of the Lycians at the eastern end of the Mediterranean, "They have one singular custom in which they differ from every other nation in the world: naming themselves by their mothers, not their fathers." And of the early Germans, Tacitus wrote that "the sons of a sister have the same position as regards their uncle as with their father" and "some even consider the former as the stronger tie."

To a modern-day anthropologist this emphasis upon the tie between mother's brother and sister's son strongly suggests the existence of an earlier matrilineal organization. Moreover, Tacitus' description of the relatively high status of women in ancient Germany is supported by discoveries of females dressed as warriors buried side by side with males dressed the same way. Livy reports that the *curiae*, or the earliest administrative divisions, were named after the Sabine women whom Romulus' followers were supposed to have raped. Finally, Briffault points out that Roman kinship nomenclature preserved a distinction between the father's brother and the mother's brother. The former was called *patruus;* the latter, *avunculus.* The Latin word for ancestor was *avus.* Hence, as would be the case in a matrilineal system, the mother's brother was designated by a term denoting common ancestry with the sister's son. (The fact that the English word "uncle" survives from the word for "mother's brother" suggests the former importance of mother's brother–sister's son relationships.)

Female figurines and statues found among many prestate cultures of Europe and Southwest Asia provide another line of evidence suggestive of matrilineal organizations. On Malta, for example, the Temple of Tarxien, built before 2000 B.C., contained a six-foot stone statue of a rotund seated woman. The theme of "fat ladies" is echoed in several smaller versions found in Maltese temples, all of which are associated with human burials, altars, and the bones of sacrificed animals—suggestive of a cult of female ancestors.

While most of this evidence pertains largely to the formation of secondary states in Europe, it is sufficiently consistent to warrant the inference that the pristine states had earlier passed through a similar matrilineal phase. But if there was such a phase, whether for pristine or secondary states, it must have been short-lived. What we glimpse through the writings of the classical Greek and Roman historians are the lingering traces of systems that had already reverted back to patrilineal descent. Very few ancient or modern state societies have matrilineal descent or practice matrilocality (which is why Herodotus described the Lycians as differing from "every other nation in the world"). With the rise of the state, women again lost status. From Rome to China they were legally defined as the wards of their fathers, husbands, or brothers. The reason for this, I believe, is that matrilocality was no longer functionally necessary for recruiting and training the armed forces. States wage war by means of military specialists whose solidarity and effectiveness depend on hierarchical ranks and strict discipline, not on common postmarital residence. The rise of the state, therefore, saw the old male supremacy complex reassert itself in full force. I do not think it is an accident that the pre-state Siuai, Trobrianders, and Cherokee engage in external warfare and have matrilineal institutions, while the Bunyoro state, which engages in even more external warfare, has patrilineal institutions and a strong male supremacy complex.

Once pristine states have formed in a given region, secondary states begin to develop under a variety of special conditions. Some secondary states form as a matter of defense against the predatory inroads made by their more advanced neighbors; others develop as a result of attempts to capture control over strategic trade routes and the increased volume of goods in transit which usually accompanies the growth of states in any region. Still others form as part of an attempt by nomadic peoples living on the margin of a state to plunder its wealth. States found in relatively low-density, unimpacted regions must always be examined with these possibilities in mind before concluding that intensification and reproductive pressures did not cause the evolution of the region's pristine states. For example, low-density pastoralist peoples—Turks, Mongols, Huns, Manchus, and Arabs—have repeatedly developed states but only by preying upon the preexisting Chinese, Hindu, Roman, and Byzantine empires. In West Africa secondary states developed as a result of Moslem and European attempts to control the slave, gold, and ivory trades, while in southern Africa the Zulu developed a state in the nineteenth century to meet the military threat posed by Dutch colonists invading their homeland.

What I find most remarkable about the evolution of pristine states is that it occurred as the result of an unconscious process: The participants in this enormous transformation seem not to have known what they were creating. By imperceptible shifts in the redistributive balance from one generation to the next, the human species bound itself over into a form of social life in which the many debased themselves on behalf of the exaltation of the few. To paraphrase Malcolm Webb, at the beginning of the lengthy process no one could foresee the end result. "Tribal equalitarianism would gradually vanish even as it was being appended, without awareness of the nature of the change, and the final achievement of absolute control would at that point seem merely a minor alteration of established custom. The consolidation of governmental power would have taken place as a series of natural, beneficial, and only slightly (if at all) extra-legal responses to current conditions, with each new acquisition of state-power representing only a small departure from contemporary practice." By the time the remnants of the old council finally sank into impotence before the rising power of the king, no one would remember the time when the king had been only a glorified *mumi* whose exalted status rested on the charity of his friends and relatives.

I urge those who feel that my explanation of the evolution of culture is too deterministic and too mechanical to consider the possibility that at this very moment we are again passing by slow degrees through a series of "natural, beneficial, and only slightly . . . extralegal" changes which will transform social life in ways that few alive today would consciously wish to inflict upon future generations. Clearly, the remedy for that situation cannot lie in the denial of a deterministic component in social processes; rather, it must lie in bringing that component into the arena of popular comprehension.

But more about the moral implications of this tale later on. The immediate task before us is to trace out the further consequences of the rise in the state in the context of different regional patterns of intensifications, depletions, and ecological crises. I turn first to the tragic history of Mesoamerica.

8
The Pre-Columbian States of Mesoamerica

Some archaeologists claim that ecology and reproductive pressure had little to do with the rise of the state in Mesoamerica. They believe that the transition to statehood occurred first among the Olmec and Maya, who lived in lowland swamps and jungles where there was neither an opportunity to practice intensive forms of agriculture nor barriers to the dispersion of population. Supposedly these jungle states evolved as a result of spiritual impulses peculiar to the Olmec and Maya conception of the world. Believing that the rains, crops, and continuity of life were dispensations of the gods, the Olmec and Maya felt the urge to build ceremonial centers and to house and provision a priestly class of non-food producers. Because they happened to be more religious than other pre-state village peoples, they built larger temples and showed uncommonly great respect and devotion to their priests and officials. Cost benefits were irrelevant. Their political organization did not result from population growth, declining efficiencies, warfare, impaction—or anything else so crass. Rather, it evolved from voluntary submission to a benevolent theocracy.

Archaeologists who advance this kind of explanation for the origin of the state of Mesoamerica seem to be exhilarated by the notion that human faith and ingenuity triumphed over adverse ecological conditions.

While I sympathize with the sentiment that lies behind this celebration of the creative achievements of cultures like the Olmec and Maya, I think it is far more urgent that we understand the limitations placed by ecological and reproductive factors on even the most inspired forms of human activity.

The Olmec are indeed a puzzling case. Described by the Mexican archaeologist Covarrubias as the "mother civilization" of the New World, the Olmec inhabited the humid lowlands and coastal plains of the Mexican Gulf Coast states of Vera Cruz and Tabasco. Between 1200 and 800 B.C. they erected a number of widely separated temple centers—the earliest in the New World—on top of artificial mounds two or three acres in extent. The best-known site is La Venta in Tabasco, on an island in the middle of a swamp. La Venta's most imposing structure is an earthen cone 420 feet in diameter and about 105 feet high. Monumental sculptures consisting of fifty-ton carved stone slabs called stelae, altars, and huge, round human heads that appear to be wearing football helmets lie strewn about the site.

While the Olmec ceremonial centers contain impressive evidence of the ability of redistributor-chiefs to organize cooperative projects and to support artisans skilled in sculpture, masonry, and the making of jade jewelry and fine ceramics, the scale of their endeavors falls short of what one would expect of a state-level polity. Each site could easily have been constructed by a population of no more than two or three thousand people and each is too far from the others to constitute a single interconnected political system.

To keep the Olmec in perspective, one must consider the scale of construction characteristic of sites that are historically known to have reached the threshold of state formation. When the first French explorers ascended the Mississippi Valley, for example, they found populous "towns" and huge earthen platforms supporting wooden temples and the houses of priests and nobles. A remnant of the largest of these structures, the Cahokia mound, still exists on the outskirts of east St. Louis. Before being chewed up by bulldozers, it was over a hundred feet high and covered fifteen acres, as compared with the two or three acres typical of the Olmec sites. Moreover, we know that impressive feats of construction can be carried out under the auspices of "big man" redistributor-chiefs who lack the capacity to tax, conscript, and punish their followers. Even the nonagricultural Kwakiutl and Haida of the Pacific Northwest, led by redistributor-chiefs, were capable of a certain amount of monument-making in the form of totem poles and carved house posts. At Stonehenge and other early ceremonial centers in Europe associated with the spread of farming, pre-state chieftainships managed to erect elaborate astronomically oriented monuments out of blocks of stone that weighed considerably more than those found at La Venta. And the Olmec sites are actually puny by comparison with the great highland centers of the central plateau of Mexico. At best they represent a stage of development which was arrested at the level of incipient statehood. Their failure to develop further was clearly related to the fact that because of ecological circumstances their regional population densities remained low and unimpacted.

I should also mention the possibility that ceremonial structures indicative of incipient statehood older than the Olmec may yet be discovered in the central plateau highlands. Recent excavations by Ronald Grennes-Ravitz and G. Coleman indicate that Olmec-type figurines found in Morelos and the Valley of Mexico are as old as those found in Vera Cruz and Tabasco. Moreover, at these highland sites Olmec artifacts occur above strata containing indigenous highland ceramic traditions that predate the Olmec period by as much as 400 years. Olmec temple centers may therefore yet be shown to have been partially dependent on the growth of the first highland states. It is even possible that the Olmec sites represent colonial outposts—perhaps pilgrimage centers, as Grennes-Ravitz and Coleman have suggested—around which trade between the tropical lowlands and the arid central plateau was organized.

To the east of the Olmec heartland lies the Yucatán Peninsula, another region in which the path toward statehood seems to flout ecological principles. Here lived the Maya, a people who invented a complex system of hieroglyphic writing and mathematical numeration, wrote their history in accordion-shaped books, made precise astronomical observations, developed a highly accurate solar calendar, and were masters of the arts of stone sculpture and masonry.

And yet the lower half of the Yucatán Peninsula is covered by a dense jungle region called the Petén. From A.D. 300 to A.D. 900 the Maya busied themselves with the construction of numerous ceremonial centers right in the middle of this region. Norman Hammond has counted eighty-three major sites in the southern portion of the Yucatán, separated by an average distance of only 15 kilometers (9.3 miles). In these centers are elaborately ornamented multi-room buildings grouped symmetrically about paved central plazas; ball courts for ritual games; stone slab stelae with commemorative dates, genealogies of the rulers, and other historical information not yet decoded; altars incised with additional hieroglyphic texts; and massive statues of the gods and the nobility. Towering over all are great truncated pyramids faced with cut stone and topped by stone temples. The largest site is Tikal, whose temple pyramids rise precipitously 190 feet above the plaza floor. At its maximum, during the 19th century A.D., Tikal may have had as many as 40,000 inhabitants in its rural perimeter while the overall regional density has been estimated at 250 people per square mile. This would make the Petén as thickly populated as modern-day Europe. There is no doubt that the largest of the Maya centers were the administrative capitals of small states. But there is no chance that the Maya achieved statehood entirely independently of preexisting states in the highland region. Teotihuacán, which I'll describe in a moment, already contained several tens of thousands of inhabitants when Tikal was just beginning to rise above the treetops. Teotihuacán is more than 600 miles from Tikal, but the military and economic shock waves sent out by the great highland empires regularly reached even more remote regions. We know that by A.D. 300 Kaminaljuyú, a Maya city in the Guatemalan highlands overlooking the Petén, had come under the influence of Teotihuacán. Kaminaljuyú probably contained a military garrison which controlled the trade routes between the Petén, the Pacific Coast, and the Central Mexican Plateau. After A.D. 300 trade goods, painting styles, and architectural motifs in the Petén centers themselves leave no doubt that the Maya were being affected by events in the central plateau highlands. Actual military engagements between late formative or early classic highland states and incipient Maya states in the Petén are not to be ruled out.

Trade between the Maya and their highland neighbors may also have moved the Maya closer to statehood. The Petén region lacks indigenous sources of rocks suitable for making *metates* and *manos* or knives and projectile points. These items were crucial for grinding corn and for military weaponry. Along with salt, they were obtained through trade with the highlands. This trade may have widened the distance between the early Maya redistributor-chiefs and commoners in two ways: more effective terms of trade could be obtained by more powerful individuals who were the equals of the state-level nobility with whom they had to deal, and the control over these additional strategic resources could have added to the potential for controlling the incipient peasant food producers. In general, the larger the volume of trade, the greater the flow through the redistributive system and the greater the power of the individuals who are in charge of the redistributive process.

The evidence allowing for an interpretation of the Maya centers as secondary states does not rule out the possibility that reproductive and ecological pressures generated within the Petén region itself might also have contributed to the process of state formation. The Petén "jungle," on close inspection, turns out to be full of surprises. The first aspect that needs to be clarified is its size—only 30,000 square miles, compared with 2 million square miles for the Amazon-Orinoco. Next, there is its peculiar pattern of rainfall. As one moves northward from the Petén to the tip of the Yucatán Peninsula, annual rainfall decreases and forests are replaced by thorny shrubs, cactus, and other drought-resistant plants. Within the central Petén forest itself, annual precipitation is only about half that of the Amazon-Orinoco. The Petén dry season is exceptionally severe, and both the annual and seasonal totals are subject to extreme variations. A single drop of rain may not fall during the months of March and April. Drought conditions frequently prevail during February and May, and even during the rainy season itself. In the words of C. L. Lundell:

> The vegetation does not have the luxuriance of true rain forest, hence it may be designated a quasi–rain forest. The rainfall averages less than 1800 mm. [71 in], a maximum not sufficient to maintain true rain forest in a region with a pronounced dry season.

Many of the Petén trees shed their leaves every dry season, a tendency that is accentuated during droughts. This "jungle," in fact, sometimes gets so dry that farmers don't even have to "slash" in order to clear next season's garden plots by setting fire to the underbrush. Preventing fires from spreading is the major preoccupation on such occasions.

And now we come to the fact that the Yucatán Peninsula has a peculiar geological structure. Its bedrock consists almost exclusively of porous limestone (hence the need to import rocks for grinding corn from the highlands). This results in there being few permanent rivers and lakes since most of the rainfall percolates rapidly down through the limestone and disappears entirely without any surface runoff. During the dry season there is even a shortage of drinking water except where there are natural clay-bottomed water holes in the limestone whose interior drainage has gotten clogged.

As one might expect, the earliest Maya villages were located near the only two permanent rivers on the Yucatán Peninsula: The Usumacinta on the southwest and the Belize on the southeast. Around 600 B.C. the region surrounding Tikal appears to have been uninhabited, suggesting that it was only after the favorable riverine locales had filled up that farmers began to colonize the interior of the forest. These colonists must have resembled the Yanomamo and other canoe-less "foot Indians" who live in the protein-deficient zones of the Amazon-Orinoco basin away from the main rivers. But in a short while the peculiar geomorphology and climate of the Petén region would have created a situation which has no parallel in Amazonia.

The early Petén farmers were not free to spread out evenly through the forest. Settlements would have had to be located near water holes which could be counted on not to dry up during a severe drought. We know that later on entirely artificial cisterns called *chultuns* were dug as deep as sixty-six feet into the limestone bedrock and plastered with lime cement in order to assure supplies of fresh water. Some *chultuns* were built under the paved plazas of ceremonial centers, which acted as catchment basins during rainstorms. At one modern village in Campeche, dry-season drinking water had to be obtained by descending 450 feet below the surface through an underground cavern. All of the classic Maya sites, including Tikal and other Petén centers, were built next to artificial or natural storage wells or reservoirs. The most famous of the natural water holes, or *cenotes*, is located next to Chichén Itzá, a late Maya center in northern Yucatán. Large quantities of human bones and gold artifacts dredged up from its bottom suggest that people and ritual objects were thrown into it to appease the water gods. And so the lively possibility exists that the early settlements in the Petén tended to increase beyond the normal breaking-up point of tropical forest villages. This theory removes the problem of the initial growth of Maya ceremonial centers from the realm of heaven to the realm of earth and water. The Maya farmers had a very practical reason for not fleeing into the forests when their redistributor-chiefs started acting like kings instead of like *mumis*.

The next question to be confronted is how the Maya under the direction of their redistributor-chiefs managed to raise their population density to a level that was 250 times greater than that achieved in the interfluvial zones of the Amazon-Orinoco. Archaeologists have generally assumed that the ancient Maya farmed the Petén the way their modern descendants do—by means of the system known as slash-and-burn. But this is clearly an impossibility.

Slash-and-burn is a form of agriculture that is well-suited for regions that have abundant forest cover and high rates of regeneration. The object of the slash-and-burn system is to use a section of forest for a few years, let it lie fallow long enough for trees to grow back, and then use it again. "Slash" refers to the practice of cutting down small trees, vines, and shrubs and letting them dry before setting fire to them. The burning, usually carried out just before the onset of the rainy season, creates a layer of ash that acts as fertilizer. Crops are planted directly into the ash-covered soil in holes or small mounds without the need for tillage. High yields of corn, beans, squash, and other crops can be obtained for two or three seasons. Thereafter weeds spread from the surrounding uncut forest and infest the field; at the same time the ash fertilizer is leached away by rainfall. Soon a new plot must be found. Slash-and-burn agriculture is capable of high returns per acre and man-hour provided that an interval sufficient to permit a substantial regrowth of trees and shrubs is maintained between successive burnings. The greater the quantity of ash, the higher the yields. The longer the interval during which a forest is left fallow, the more wood there is to make ashes with. For this reason, slash-and-burn farmers in Southeast Asia think of themselves as "the people who eat forests." The shorter the fallow period, the lower the yields. In tropical forests the decline can be precipitous not only because the concentrated heavy rainfall rapidly leaches away the soil nutrients but because weeds grow thicker each year the field remains in continuous use.

Slash-and-burn was undoubtedly the system used by the earliest farming peoples who entered the Petén, but it could not have remained the principal mode of subsistence during and after the transition to the state. By counting the ruins of house sites, Dennis Puleston of the University of Minnesota estimates that there were 2,250 persons per square mile in the residential zone around Tikal and 750 persons per square mile in the zone between Tikal and its neighbor, Uaxactun. It is impossible for slash-and-burn systems to support such densities. Considering the entire Petén area, Sherburne Cook shows that enough maize, beans, and squash could have been grown with slash-and-burn techniques to support the estimated overall population of 1.5 million. But these calculations assume that the farmers were evenly spread throughout the forest and that they were free to move to new clearings as the old ones were exhausted. Neither of these assumptions is valid since the limiting effect of the dry season on the availability of drinking water is not taken into account. Furthermore, during the rainy season low-lying areas face the opposite problems—too much water—and are too swampy to be used without digging drainage ditches.

On theoretical grounds, the picture of what must have happened seems clear. As the population of the Petén increased, the slash-and-burn cycle must have been intensified, resulting in shorter fallows between burning and hence declining efficiency. This set the stage for the adoption and spread of a more efficient system involving higher start-up costs, which in turn provided the basis for still higher population densities and the emergence of the first statelets. But what was the nature of the new and more productive system? I fear that my theory has run ahead of the archaeological facts, but there are some hopeful signs that the facts are about to catch up.

One of the measures taken by the Maya when the efficiency of slash-and-burn declined was to plant groves of breadnut trees *(Brosimum alicastrum)*. As C. L. Lundell pointed out back in the 1930's, the breadnut is the most common tree covering the ruins of the Petén ceremonial centers. When archaeologists speak dramatically of having to hack away the jungle in order to expose the wonders of Maya architecture and sculpture, they generally neglect to say that they were hacking away at an overgrown orchard. Tree crops, of course, do have high start-up costs—one must wait several years before they begin to return the labor invested in them—but they are highly productive per acre and per man-hour. Recently, Dennis Puleston, having discovered that each house site at Tikal was surrounded by a grove of breadnut trees, reached the conclusion that breadnuts provided 80 percent of the calories consumed by the people of Tikal during the ninth century A.D. There are other alternatives, however, which may simply have been overlooked by the generation of archaeologists who preferred to think the Maya temples were let down from heaven on golden threads rather than built on the backs of people who wanted to know where the next meal was coming from. In this connection, one of the most important discoveries ever made about the Maya may prove to be the one made in 1975 by Ray Mathenay at Edzná in Campeche. Working with aerial photographs taken during the rainy season (others had limited their aerial photography to the dry season, when conditions were "better"), Mathenay detected a network of canals, moats, and reservoirs radiating out from the ceremonial center. Because of the dense foliage covering them during the rainy season and the fact that the water in them dries up during the dry season, these constructions are difficult to detect from ground surveys alone.

The canals range up to a mile or so in length, a hundred feet in width and about ten feet in depth. Mathenay's suggestion is that they were used for drinking water, for hand-watering adjacent gardens, and as a source of mud for renewing the fertility of fallow fields. I would add the implication that they enabled some regions to grow two crops a year, one based on draining low-lying areas during the rainy season and the second planted on wet mud during the dry season. While Edzná lies outside the central Petén area, the fact that its water control system remained undetected for so long means that all judgments concerning the absence of intensive systems within the Petén itself must be held in abeyance.

And this brings us to the most spectacular aspect of the Petén Maya. After A.D. 800, in center after center, construction ceased, no more commemorative inscriptions were made, temples became littered with household rubbish, and all governmental and ecclesiastical activity in the Petén came to a more or less abrupt end. Authorities differ concerning how fast the population declined. But by the time of the arrival of the Spanish, the Petén area had long since returned to population densities at or below those characteristic of pre-state times and to this day the area remains virtually depopulated. Many other Mesoamerican pre-Columbian state systems, including Teotihuacán, suffered equally abrupt collapses at one time or another. What is unique about the Petén Maya is that not only did the states permanently disappear but so did their entire populations. In the central plateau highlands political collapse was usually followed by the rise of new and larger states and empires embracing the territory and population of their predecessors. The implication of the Maya collapse, therefore, is that the Petén state developed on an unusually vulnerable ecological base which could not be regenerated once it broke down.

Exactly how the Maya destroyed their ecological base cannot be known until we have a better understanding of how the various components in their agricultural system fitted together. The best one can do for the moment is to say that each component had a limit to which it could be pushed, after which it would push back with devastating consequences. Short-fallow slash-and-burn can turn jungles into permanent grasslands. At the very middle of the Petén area is a huge, grassy savanna that was probably created by excessive burning. Deforestation leads in turn to erosion on hillsides. In the Petén the upland soil cover is extremely shallow and readily lost when not protected by plant cover. Erosion can also damage lowland water control systems since it leads to the build-up of excessive silt in canals and reservoirs. Finally, tampering with forest cover over an area as large as that of the Petén can easily change the regional pattern of annual precipitation, lengthening the dry season and increasing the frequency and severity of droughts.

The actual demise of each Petén center may have involved a slightly different scenario—crop failure and famine in some, rebellion in others, military defeat in still others, or various combinations depending on local events. But the underlying process undoubtedly involved the depletion of fragile soil and forest resources to a point so low that centuries of disuse were required for their regeneration.

Whatever the precise cause of the Maya collapse, the reason for the preeminence of the highlands in Mesoamerica seems clear. The capacity of the semiarid valleys of the central plateau to undergo successive agricultural intensifications exceeded that of the Maya's quasi-tropical forest. Let me show how this process of intensification operated in the history of the Teotihuacán empire.

The Teotihuacán Valley is a branch of the Valley of Mexico lying some twenty-five miles northeast of downtown Mexico City. Like the Tehuacán Valley, where the earliest domesticated plants were found by Richard MacNeish, the Teotihuacán Valley had no permanent villages until the first millennium B.C. Between 900 B.C. and 600 B.C. villages were confined to the forested upper slopes of the valley, below the early frost line but high enough up to take advantage of the extra precipitation which falls on the hillsides. The kind of agriculture practiced by these first villagers was undoubtedly some form of long-fallow slash-and-burn. By 600–300 B.C. several larger villages had formed at lower altitudes at the edge of the valley floor, presumably to take advantage of the alluvial soils and to practice a rudimentary form of irrigation. During the next period, 300–100 B.C., settlements grew up squarely on the valley floor, and one of them—the nucleus of what was to become the city of Teotihuacán—already contained thousands of people. The movement from the slopes to the valley floor strongly suggests increasing reproductive pressures resulting from the intensification and depletion of the slash-and-burn system, especially from deforestation and erosion. As the labor efficiency of slash-and-burn farming declined, it became worthwhile to expend start-up and construction labor on irrigation facilities. Numerous large springs fed by water percolating through the porous volcanic hillside to the valley floor formed the basis for the Teotihuacán irrigation system and are still in use today. As the population of the central settlement increased, the network of river-sized spring-fed canals was eventually used to water about 14,000 acres of highly productive double-crop farmlands.

The city of Teotihuacán grew rapidly after A.D. 100, reaching a peak population of perhaps 125,000 people in the eighth century A.D. Careful mapping by René Millon of the University of Rochester shows that the city was divided into planned quarters and districts, each with its craft specialities, ethnic enclaves, temples, markets, palatial stone and plaster dwellings for the rich and powerful, and dark multi-family apartment houses for the populace—some 2,200 apartment houses in all. Millon has counted more than 400 workshops specializing in the manufacture of obsidian tools and more than 100 ceramic workshops. The largest and most ornamented buildings lined the huge stepped avenue which ran the length of the city almost two miles from north to south. The central monument—the so-called Pyramid of the Sun, built of stone-faced rubble—measures 700 feet to a side and rises to a height of 200 feet.

Around A.D. 700 Teotihuacán suffered a cataclysmic collapse, possibly due to burning and sacking, associated with the rise of a new imperial power—the Toltec, whose capital was located a scant twenty miles away in the Tula Valley. The evidence is incomplete, but I propose that environmental depletion was primarily responsible. The volume of water issuing from the springs fluctuates in relation to rainfall. A slight permanent drop in the volume of spring-fed water and in the water table underlying the valley floor would have compelled many people to move out of the city. We know that there was deforestation over an ever-widening perimeter as the city grew and consumed increasing quantities of wood for house beams and rafters, cooking fuel, and the manufacture of lime plaster. This deforestation was carried out on a sufficiently large scale to have altered the pattern of precipitation and runoff on the upper slopes of the valley.

There was one technical solution to the water problem which the people of Teotihuacán did not try except on a very limited basis. This consisted of using the shallow lake and swamplands that bordered the Teotihuacán Valley on the southwest and that in those days were probably linked to Lake Texcoco, a large, partly brackish body of water that filled most of the adjacent Valley of Mexico. To utilize the margins of the lake, it was necessary to dig drainage ditches and to pile up the excavated soil on ridges—a procedure which was much more costly than other forms of irrigation. Beginning about A.D. 1100 the high start-up costs of this form of agriculture could no longer be avoided by the people living in the Valley of Mexico. A network of drainage canals and highly productive ridges, whose fertility was constantly augmented by new dredgings, spread along the margin of the lake and provided the subsistence base for a half-dozen warring polities. One of these was the Aztec state, which would become the last American Indian imperial power in North America. Since the Aztec capital, Tenochtitlán, was located on an island connected to the shore by a causeway, the Aztecs enjoyed a military advantage over their neighbors and were soon in control of the entire lake region. As the population grew to unprecedented densities, the ridged mounds were extended out into the lake itself by dumping mud on top of brush, corn stalks, and tree branches, resulting in fabulously productive *chinampas*, or "floating gardens" (which, of course, did not float).

At first, only the freshwater arms of the lake were used in this manner. But as the areas occupied by the *chinampas* increased, Aztec engineers tried to reduce the salinity of the brackish portions by diking them off and flushing them with fresh water channeled through a complicated system of aqueducts and sluice gates.

Looking back, then, on the developmental sequence in the Teotihuacán Valley and the Valley of Mexico during the millennium from A.D. 200 to A.D. 1200, we can discern three broad phases of agricultural intensifications followed by three shifts in the mode of production: first, the intensification of hillside slash-and-burn farming; second, spring-fed canal irrigation; and third, *chinampa* construction. Each of these involved progressively greater start-up and construction outlays, but each ultimately sustained greater population densities and larger and more powerful states. In those thousand years the population of the Valley of Mexico rose from a few tens of thousands to 2 million, while the scope of political control grew from one to two valleys to a whole subcontinent. By the old onwards-and-upwards theory of progress, the steady augmentation of agricultural production should have meant that the Aztecs and their neighbors increasingly enjoyed the benefits of "high civilization"—a phrase anthropologists have not hesitated to apply to them. But the phrase is wildly inappropriate.

9
The Cannibal Kingdom

As well-trained, methodical butchers of the battlefield and as citizens of the land of the Inquisition, Cortés and his men, who arrived in Mexico in 1519, were inured to displays of cruelty and bloodshed. It must have come as no great surprise to them that the Aztecs methodically sacrificed human beings, inasmuch as the Spaniards and other Europeans methodically broke people's bones on the rack, pulled people's arms and legs off in tugs-of-war between horses, and disposed of women accused of witchcraft by burning them at the stake. Still, they were not quite prepared for what they found in Mexico.

Nowhere else in the world had there developed a state-sponsored religion whose art, architecture, and ritual were so thoroughly dominated by violence, decay, death, and disease. Nowhere else were walls and plazas of great temples and palaces reserved for such a concentrated display of jaws, fangs, claws, talons, bones, and gaping death heads. The eyewitness accounts of Cortés and his fellow conquistador, Bernal Díaz, leave no doubt concerning the ecclesiastical meaning of the dreadful visages portrayed in stone. The Aztec gods ate people. They ate human hearts and they drank human blood. And the declared function of the Aztec priesthood was to provide fresh human hearts and human blood in order to prevent the remorseless deities from becoming angry and crippling, sickening, withering, and burning the whole world.

The Spaniards first glimpsed the inside of a major Aztec temple as the invited guests of Moctezuma, the last of the Aztec kings. Moctezuma had not yet made up his mind concerning Cortés' intentions—an error which was shortly to prove fatal for him—when he invited the Spaniards up 114 steps to the twin temples of Uitzilopochtli and Tlaloc, which stood at the top of Tenochtitlán's tallest pyramid in the center of what is today Mexico City. As they mounted the steps, wrote Bernal Díaz, other temples and shrines "all gleaming white" came into view. In the open space at the top of the pyramid "the great stones stood on which they placed the poor Indians for sacrifice." Here also was "a bulky image like a dragon, and other evil figures and much blood shed that very day." Then Moctezuma let them see the image of Uitzilopochtli, with its "very broad face and monstrous and terrible eyes," before which "they were burning the hearts of three Indians whom they had sacrificed that day." The walls and floor of the temple "were so splashed and encrusted with blood that they were black" and the "whole place stank vilely." In Tlaloc's temple, too, everything was covered with blood, "both walls and altar, and the stench was such that we could hardly wait for the moment to get out of it."

The main source of food for the Aztec gods was prisoners of war, who were marched up the steps of the pyramids to the temples, seized by four priests, spread-eagled backward over the stone altar, and slit open from one side of the chest to the other with an obsidian knife wielded by a fifth priest. The victim's heart—usually described as still beating—was then wrenched out and burned as an offering. The body was rolled down the pyramid steps, which were built deliberately steep to accommodate this function.

Occasionally some sacrificial victims—distinguished warriors, perhaps—were given the privilege of defending themselves for a while before they were killed. Bernardino De Sahagún, the greatest historian and ethnographer of the Aztecs, described these mock battles as follows:

> . . . they slew other captives, battling with them—these being tied, by the waist, with a rope which passed through the socket of a round stone, as of a mill; and [the rope] was long enough so that [the captive] might walk about the complete circumference of the stone. And they gave him arms with which he might do battle; and four warriors came against him with swords and shields, and one by one they exchanged sword blows with him until they vanquished him.

Apparently in the Aztec state of two or three centuries earlier the king himself was not beyond the task of dispatching a few victims with his own hands. Here is an account by Diego Durán of the legendary slaughter of prisoners captured among the Mixtecs:

> The five priests entered and claimed the prisoner who stood first in the line. . . . Each prisoner they took to the place where the king stood and, when they had forced him to stand upon the stone which was the figure and likeness of the sun, they threw him upon his back. One took him by the right arm, another by the left, one by his left foot, another by his right, while the fifth priest tied his neck with a cord and held him down so that he could not move.
>
> The king lifted the knife on high and made a gash in his breast. Having opened it he extracted the heart and raised it high with his hand as an offering to the

sun. When the heart had cooled he tossed it into the circular depression, taking some of the blood in his hand and sprinkling it in the direction of the sun.

Not all the victims were prisoners of war. Substantial numbers of slaves were also sacrificed. In addition, certain youths and maidens were chosen to impersonate specific gods and goddesses. These were treated with great care and tenderness throughout the year preceding their execution. In the Florentine Codex, a sixteenth-century book written in Nahuatl, the language of the Aztecs, there is this account of the death of a woman who played the role of the goddess Uixtociuatl:

> And after they had slain the captives, only [then] Uixtociuatl['s impersonator] followed; she came only at the last. They came to the end and finished only with her.
>
> And when this was done, thereupon they laid her down upon the offering stone. They stretched her out upon her back. They laid hold of her; they pulled and stretched out her arms and legs, bending [up] her breast greatly, bending [down] her back, and stretching down her head taut, toward the earth. And they bore down upon her neck with the tightly pressed snout of a sword fish, barbed, spiny; spined on either side.
>
> And the slayer stood there; he stood up. Thereupon he cut open her breast.
>
> And when he opened her breast, the blood gushed up high; it welled up far as it poured forth, as it boiled up.
>
> And when this was done, then he raised her heart as an offering [to the god] and placed it in the green jar, which was called the green stone jar.
>
> And as this was done, loudly were the trumpets blown. And when it was over, then they lowered the

> body and the heart of [the likeness of] Uixtociuatl, covered by a precious mantle.

But such displays of reverence were few and far between. The great majority of victims did not walk joyfully up the steps of the pyramid, soothed by the prospect that they were about to make some god happy. Many of them had to be dragged by the hair:

> When the masters of the captives took their slaves to the temple where they were to slay them, they took them by the hair. And when they took them up the steps of the pyramid, some of the captives swooned, and their masters pulled them up and dragged them by the hair to the sacrificial stone where they were to die.

The Aztecs were not the first Mesoamericans to sacrifice human beings. We know that the Toltec and the Maya engaged in the practice, and it is a reasonable inference that all steep-sided, flat-topped Mesoamerican pyramids were intended to serve as a stage for the spectacle in which human victims were fed to the gods. Nor was human sacrifice an invention of state-level religions. To judge from the evidence of band and village societies throughout the Americas and in many other parts of the world, human sacrifice long antedated the rise of state religions.

From Brazil to the Great Plains, American Indian societies ritually dispatched human victims in order to achieve certain kinds of benefits. Virtually every element of Aztec ritual was foreshadowed in the beliefs and practices of band and village peoples. Even the preoccupation with the surgical removal of the heart had its precedents. The Iroquois, for example, vied with each other for the privilege of eating the heart of a brave prisoner so that they could acquire some of his courage. Everywhere, male prisoners were the chief victims. Before being killed, they were made to run a gauntlet, or were beaten, stoned, burned, mutilated, or subjected to other forms of torture and abuse. Sometimes they were tied to stakes and given a club with which to defend themselves against their tormentors. Occasionally one or two prisoners were kept for extended periods and provided with good food and concubines.

The ritual sacrifice of prisoners of war among band and village peoples was usually followed by the eating of all or part of the victim's body. Thanks to the eyewitness accounts provided by Hans Städen, a German sailor who was shipwrecked on the coast of Brazil early in the sixteenth century, we have a vivid idea of how one group, the Tupinamba, combined ritual sacrifice with cannibalism.

On the day of the sacrifice the prisoner of war, trussed around the waist, was dragged into the plaza. He was surrounded by women who insulted and abused him, but he was allowed to give vent to his feelings by throwing fruits or broken pieces of pottery at them. Meanwhile old women painted black and red and wearing necklaces of human teeth brought out ornamented vases in which the victim's blood and entrails would be cooked. The ceremonial club that would be used to kill him was passed back and forth among the men in order to "acquire the power to catch a prisoner in the future." The actual executioner wore a long feather cloak and was followed by relatives singing and beating drums. The executioner and the prisoner derided each other. Enough liberty was allowed the prisoner so that he could dodge the blows, and sometimes a club was put in his hands for protecting himself without being able to strike back. When at last his skull was shattered, everyone "shouted and whistled." If the prisoner had been given a wife during his period of captivity, she was expected to shed tears over his body before joining in the feast that followed. Now the old women "rushed to drink the warm blood," and children dipped their hands into it. "Mothers would smear their nipples with blood so that even babies could have a taste of it." The body was cut into quarters and barbecued while "the old women who were most eager for human flesh" licked the grease dripping from the sticks that formed the grill.

Ten thousand miles to the north, about two centuries later, Jesuit missionaries witnessed a similar ritual among the Hurons of Canada. The victim was an Iroquois man who had been captured along with several other companions while they were fishing on Lake Ontario. The Huron chief in charge of the ritual explained that the Sun and the God of War would be pleased by what they were about to do. It was important not to kill the victim before daybreak, so at first they should only burn his legs. Also, they ought not to have sexual intercourse during the night. The prisoner, his hands bound, alternately shrieking with pain and singing a song of defiance learned as a child for just this occasion, was brought indoors, where he was set upon by a crowd armed with brands of burning bark. As he reeled from one end of the room to the other, some people seized his hands, "breaking the bones thereof by sheer force; others pierced his ears with sticks they left in them." Whenever he seemed ready to expire, the chief intervened "and ordered them to cease tormenting him, saying it was important that he should see daylight." At dawn he was taken outside and forced to climb onto a platform built on a wooden scaffold so that the entire village could watch what was happening to him—the scaffold making do as a sacrificial platform in the absence of flat-topped pyramids reared for such purposes by the Mesoamerican states. Four men now took over the task of tormenting the captive. They burned his eyes, applied red-hot hatchets to his shoulders, and thrust burning brands down his throat and into his rectum. When it was apparent that he was about to die, one of the executioners "cut off a foot, another a hand, and almost at the same time a third severed the head from the shoulders, throwing it into the crowd where someone caught it" to carry to the chief, who later made "a feast therewith." The same day a feast was also made of the victim's trunk, and on their way home the missionaries encountered a man "who was carrying upon a skewer one of his half-roasted hands."

Let me pause here for a moment to discuss interpretations of these rituals which attribute them to innate human impulses. I am especially concerned with elaborate theories offered in the Freudian tradition which claim that torture, sacrifice, and cannibalism are intelligible as expressions of instincts for love and for aggression. Eli Sagan, for example, has recently argued that cannibalism is "the most fundamental form of human aggression" since it involves a compromise between loving the victim in the form of eating him and killing him because he frustrates you. Purportedly, this explains why the victims are sometimes treated with great kindness before their torture begins—the executioners are simply reenacting their love-hate relationship with their fathers. What this approach fails to make clear is that the torture, sacrifice, and eating of prisoners of war cannot take place without prisoners of war, and prisoners of war cannot be captured unless there are wars. I pointed out earlier that theories tracing warfare to pan-human instincts are useless for explaining variations in the intensity and style of intergroup conflict and that they are dangerously misleading because they imply that war is inevitable. Attempts to understand why prisoners are sometimes pampered, then tortured, sacrificed, and eaten in terms of conflicting universal instincts of love and hate are useless and dangerous for the same reason. Prisoners are not always pampered, tortured, sacrificed, and eaten, and any theory purporting to explain why this complex occurs must also be able to explain why it also does not occur. Since the activities in question are part of the process of armed conflict, their explanation must be sought first and foremost in military costs and benefits—in variables which reflect the size, political status, armament technology, and logistics of the combatants. The taking of prisoners, for example, is itself an act which depends on the capacity of a raiding party to avoid counterattacks and ambushes on its return home while encumbered with reluctant enemy captives. When the raiding party is small, and when it must travel considerable distances through regions where the enemy can retaliate before safe territory is reached, the taking of prisoners may be forgone entirely. Under such circumstances only pieces of the enemy can be brought back to validate the body count essential for establishing a claim on the social and material rewards reserved for excellence and bravery in combat. From this we get the widespread custom of bringing back heads, scalps, fingers, and other body parts in lieu of the whole live captive.

Once the prisoner has been brought back to the village, the treatment he can expect is determined largely by the capacity of his hosts to absorb and regulate servile labor, the decisive difference being that between pre- and post-state political systems. When prisoners are few and far between, their temporary treatment as honored guests is not surprising. Whatever deep psychological ambivalences may exist in the minds of the captors, the prisoner is a valuable possession—one for whom his hosts have literally risked their lives. Yet there is usually no way to absorb him into the group; since he can't be sent back to the enemy, he must be killed. And torture has its own gruesome economy. If to be tortured is, as we say, to die a thousand deaths, then to torture one poor captive is to kill a thousand enemies. Torture is also a spectacle—an entertainment—which has been time-tested for audience approval down through the ages. I have no intention of asserting that it is part of human nature to enjoy seeing people bruised, burned, and dismembered. But it is part of human nature to pay rapt attention to unusual sights and sounds such as blood spurting from wounds and loud shrieking and howling. (And even then, many of us turn away in horror.)

The point once again is not that we instinctively enjoy watching another person suffer but that we have the capacity to learn to enjoy it. The realization of that capacity was important for societies such as the Tupinamba and Huron. These were societies that had to teach their youths to be remorselessly brutal toward their enemies on the battlefield. Such lessons are more readily learned when you realize that the enemy will do unto you what you have done to him should you fall into his hands. Add to the prisoner's value his living body, standing to warriors in training as cadavers to doctors in training. Next we come to the rituals of the killing—sacrifice to please the gods, executioners with their sacred equipment, abstention from sexual intercourse. To understand all this is to understand that warfare in band and village societies is ritual murder, regardless of whether the enemy is killed on the battlefield or at home. Before leaving for battle, the warriors paint and decorate themselves, invoke the ancestors, take hallucinogenic drugs to contact tutelary spirits, and strengthen their weapons with magical spells. Enemies slain on the field of battle are "sacrifices" in the sense that their deaths are said to please the ancestors or the war gods, just as the ancestors or the war gods are said to be pleased by the torture and death of a prisoner. Finally, there is the question of cannibalism—a question which, when asked, in itself reveals a profound misunderstanding on the part of the asker. People can learn to like or dislike the taste of human flesh, just as they can learn to be amused or horrified by torture. Obviously, there are many circumstances under which an acquired taste for human flesh can be integrated into the motivational system that inspires human societies to go to war. Moreover, to eat the enemy is literally to derive strength from his annihilation. What has to be explained, therefore, is why cultures that have no scruples about killing enemies should ever refrain from eating them. But that is a puzzle we are not yet ready to face.

If this digression into military cost-accounting as an explanation for the torture-sacrifice-cannibalism complex seems a bit too mechanical, let me point out that I do not deny the existence of ambivalent psychological motivations such as those engendered by the Oedipal situation in militaristic male-supremacist societies. I expect warfare to produce contradictory emotions and to mean many different things simultaneously to the participants. And I do not deny that cannibalism may express both affection and hatred toward the victim. What I definitely reject is the view that specific patterns of intergroup aggression can be explained by vague and contradictory psychic elements boldly abstracted from the specific ecological and reproductive pressures that induced people to make war in the first place.

Returning to the Aztecs, we can see that the unique contribution of their religion was not the introduction of human sacrifice but its elaboration along certain destructive pathways. Most notably, the Aztecs transformed human sacrifice from an occasional by-product of luck on the battlefield to a routine in which not a day went by when someone was not spread-eagled on the altars of the great temples such as Uitzilopochtli and Tlaloc. And sacrifices also took place at dozens of lesser temples ranging down to what might be called neighborhood chapels. One such neighborhood facility —a low, circular, flat-topped structure about twenty feet in diameter was excavated during the construction of Mexico City's subway. It now stands, preserved behind glass, at one of the busiest stations. For the less-than-total enlightenment of the crowds of commuters who pass it every day, an accompanying plaque notes only that the ancient Mexicans were "very religious."

Since the Aztec armies were thousands of times bigger than those of the Huron or the Tupinamba, they could capture thousands of prisoners in a single battle. In addition to daily sacrifices of small numbers of prisoners and slaves at major and minor shrines, then, mass sacrifices involving hundreds and thousands of victims could be carried out to commemorate special events. The Spanish chroniclers were told, for example, that at the dedication in 1487 of the great pyramid of Tenochtitlán four lines of prisoners stretching for two miles each were sacrificed by a team of executioners who worked night and day for four days. Allotting two minutes per sacrifice, the demographer and historian Sherburne Cook estimated that the number of victims associated with that single event was 14,100. The scale of these rituals could be dismissed as exaggerations were it not for the encounters of Bernal Díaz and Andrés de Tápia with methodically racked and hence easily counted rows of human skulls in the plazas of the Aztec cities. Díaz writes that in the plaza of Xocotlan

> there were piles of human skulls so regularly arranged that one could count them, and I estimated them at more than a hundred thousand.
>
> I repeat again there were more than one hundred thousand of them.

Of his encounter with the great skull rack in the center of Tenochtitlán, Tápia wrote:

> The poles were separated from each other by a little less than a vara [approximately a yard's length], and were crowded with cross sticks from top to bottom, and on each cross stick there were five skulls impaled through the temples: and the writer and a certain Gonzalo de Umbría, counted the cross sticks and multiplying by five heads per cross stick from pole to pole, as I said, we found that there were 136 thousand heads.

But that was not all. Tápia also describes two tall towers made entirely out of skulls held together by lime in which there was an uncountable number of crania and jaws.

Traditional explanations of the vast scale of this slaughter depict the Aztecs as people obsessed with the idea that their gods needed to drink human blood and who piously proceeded, therefore, to wage warfare in order to fulfill their sacred duty. In the words of Jacques Soustelle:

> Where then were more victims to come from? For they were essential to provide the gods with their nourishment. . . . Where could one find the precious blood without which the sun and the whole frame of the universe was condemned to annihilation? It was essential to remain in a state of war. . . . War was not merely a political instrument: it was above all a religious rite, a war of holiness.

But holy wars among states are a dime a dozen. The Jews, the Christians, the Moslems, the Hindus, the Greeks, the Egyptians, the Chinese, the Romans—all went to war to please their gods or carry out god's will. Only the Aztecs felt it was saintly to go to war in order to supply vast numbers of human sacrifices. And while all of the other archaic and not so archaic states engaged in butchery and mass atrocities, none of them did so on the pretext that the heavenly rulers had an uncontrollable desire to drink human blood. (As we shall see, it is no accident that the gods of many Old World states drank mead or ambrosia, ate honeydew, or expressed no concern at all about where their next meal was coming from.) So intent were the Aztecs on bringing back prisoners to be sacrificed that they would frequently refrain from pressing a military advantage for fear that they would kill too many enemy troops before terms of surrender could be arranged. This tactic cost them dearly in their engagements with Cortés' troops, who from the Aztec point of view seemed to be irrationally intent upon killing everyone in sight.

Sherburne Cook was the first modern anthropologist to disavow a sentimentalist approach to the puzzle of Aztec sacrifice: "However powerful, no purely religious urge can maintain itself successfully for any material period of time counter to fundamental economic resistance." Cook proposed that Aztec war and sacrifice were part of a system for regulating population growth. He calculated that the combined effect of combat deaths and sacrifices produced an annual elevation of 25 percent in the death rate. Since "the population was reaching the maximum consistent with the means of subsistence . . . the effect of warfare and sacrifice would have been very effective in checking an undue increase in numbers." This theory was an improvement over its predecessors, but it is clearly defective at its central point. The Aztecs could not have controlled the population of the Valley of Mexico by warfare and human sacrifice. Since almost all the combat deaths and sacrificed victims were males, the 25 percent rise in death rates refers only to males and could easily be matched by a 25 percent rise in the birth rate. If the Aztecs were systemically intent upon cutting back on the rate of population growth, they would have concentrated on sacrificing maidens instead of grown men. Moreover, even if the function of their sacrifices was population control, why didn't the Aztecs simply kill their enemies during battle as imperial armies in other parts of the world have always found it expedient to do? Cook's explanation fails to get at the particularity of the Mesoamerican practice—to explain why the slaughter had to be carried out on top of a pyramid instead of on the battlefield.

Conventional descriptions of the Aztec ritual of sacrifice end with the victim's body tumbling down the pyramid. Blinded by the image of a still-beating heart held aloft in the hands of the priest, one can easily forget to ask what happened to the body when it came to rest at the bottom of the steps. Michael Harner of The New School has pursued this question with greater intelligence and courage than anyone else. Throughout the rest of this chapter I shall draw heavily upon his work. He alone deserves the credit for solving the riddle of Aztec sacrifice.

As Harner points out, there really is no mystery concerning what happened to the bodies since all the eyewitness accounts are in fundamental agreement. Anyone with a knowledge of how Tupinamba, the Huron, and other village societies disposed of their sacrificial victims should be able to come to the same conclusion: the victims were eaten. Bernardino De Sahagún's description leaves little room for doubt:

> After having torn their hearts from them and poured the blood into a gourd vessel, which the master of the slain man himself received, they started the body rolling down the pyramid steps. It came to rest upon a small square below. There some old men, whom they called Quaquacuiltin, laid hold of it and carried it to their tribal temple, where they dismembered it and divided it up in order to eat it.

De Sahagún makes the same points repeatedly:

> After they had slain them and torn out their hearts, they took them away gently, rolling them down the steps. When they had reached the bottom, they cut off their heads and inserted a rod through them, and they carried the bodies to the houses which they called *calpulli*, where they divided them up in order to eat them.

> . . . and they took out their hearts and struck off their heads. And later they divided up all the body among themselves and ate it. . . .

Diego Durán gives us a similar description:

> Once the heart had been wrenched out it was offered to the sun and blood sprinkled toward the solar deity. Imitating the descent of the sun in the west the corpse

was toppled down the steps of the pyramid. After the sacrifice the warriors celebrated a great feast with much dancing, ceremonial and cannibalism.

These descriptions clarify a number of points about the Aztec warfare-sacrifice-cannibalism complex. Harner notes that each prisoner had an owner—probably the officer in charge of the soldiers who actually made the capture. When the prisoner was brought back to Tenochtitlán, he was housed in the owner's compound. We know little about how long he was kept there or how he was treated, but one can guess that he was fed enough tortillas to keep him from losing weight. It even seems likely that a powerful military commander would have kept several dozen prisoners on hand, fattening them up in preparation for special feast days or important family events such as births, deaths, or marriages. When the time for sacrifice approached, the prisoners may have been tortured for the instruction and amusement of the owner's family and neighbors. On the day of the sacrifice, the owner and his soldiers no doubt escorted the prisoner to the foot of the pyramid to watch the proceedings in the company of other dignitaries whose prisoners were being sacrificed on the same day. After the heart was removed, the body was not tumbled down the steps so much as pushed down by attendants, since the steps were not steep enough to keep the body moving all the way from top to bottom without getting stuck. The old men, whom De Sahagún refers to as Quaquacuiltin, claimed the body and took it back to the owner's compound, where they cut it up and prepared the limbs for cooking—the favorite recipe being a stew flavored with peppers and tomatoes. De Sahagún states that they put "squash blossoms" in the flesh. The victim's blood, as De Sahagún notes, was collected in a gourd vessel by the priests and delivered to the owner. We know the heart was put into a brazier and burned along with copal incense, but whether or not it was burned to ashes remains unclear. There is also some question concerning the fate of the trunk with its organs and the head with its brains. Eventually, the skull ended up on display on one of the racks described by Andrés Tápia and Bernal Díaz. But since most cannibals relish brains, we can assume that these were removed—perhaps by the priests or spectators—before the skulls ended up on exhibit. Similarly, although according to Díaz the trunk was tossed to the carnivorous mammals, birds, and snakes kept in the royal zoo, I suspect that the zoo keepers—Tápia says that there were large numbers of them—first removed most of the flesh.

I have been pursuing the fate of the victim's body in order to establish the point that Aztec cannibalism was not a perfunctory tasting of ceremonial tidbits. All edible parts were used in a manner strictly comparable to the consumption of the flesh of domesticated animals. The Aztec priests can legitimately be described as ritual slaughterers in a state-sponsored system geared to the production and redistribution of substantial amounts of animal protein in the form of human flesh. Of course, the priests had other duties, but none had greater practical significance than their butchery.

The conditions that gave rise to the Aztecs' cannibal kingdom deserve careful study. Elsewhere, the rise of states and empires contributed to a withering away of the earlier patterns of human sacrifice and cannibalism. Unlike the Aztec gods, the high gods of the Old World tabooed the consumption of human flesh. Why in Mesoamerica alone did the gods encourage cannibalism? As Harner suggests, we must look for the answer both in the specific depletions of the Mesoamerican ecosystem under the impact of centuries of intensification and population growth and in the cost/benefits of using human flesh as a source of animal protein where cheaper options were available.

As I said earlier, Mesoamerica was left at the end of the ice age in a more depleted condition, as far as animal resources are concerned, than any other region. The steady growth of population and the intensification of production under the coercive managerial influence of the classic highland empires virtually eliminated animal flesh from the diet of ordinary people. The ruling class and their retainers naturally continued to enjoy such delicacies as dogs, turkeys, ducks, deer, rabbits, and fish. But, as Harner notes, the commoners—despite the expansion of the *chinampas*—were often reduced to eating the algae skimmed from the surface of Lake Texcoco. While corn and beans in sufficient quantity could provide all of the essential amino acids, recurrent production crises throughout the fifteenth century meant that protein rations were frequently depressed to levels which would have biologically justified a strong craving for meat. In addition, fats of all sorts were perennially in short supply.

Could the redistribution of meat from sacrificial victims actually have significantly improved the protein and fat content in the diet of the Aztec nation? If the population of the Valley of Mexico was 2 million and the number of prisoners available for redistribution per annum was only 15,000, the answer is no. But the question is ill-framed. The point should be not how much these cannibal redistributions contributed to the health and vigor of the average citizen but how much the cost/benefits of political control underwent a favorable shift as a result of using human flesh to reward selected groups at crucial periods. If an occasional finger or toe was all anyone could expect, the system would probably not have worked. But if the meat was supplied in concentrated packages to the nobility, soldiers, and their retainers, and if the supply was synchronized to compensate for deficits in the agricultural cycle, the payoff for Moctezuma and the ruling class might have been sufficient to stave off political collapse. If this analysis is correct, then we must consider its inverse implications, namely, that the availability of domesticated animal species played an important role in the prohibition of cannibalism and the development of religions of love and mercy in the states and empires of the Old World. Christianity, it may yet turn out, was more the gift of the lamb in the manger than the child who was born in it.

10
The Lamb of Mercy

I hope I have not created the impression that the sacrifice and eating of prisoners of war was a specialty peculiar to the American Indians. As recently as fifty or a hundred years ago, small-scale sacrifice of prisoners of war and the redistribution of their flesh were common practices in hundreds of pre-state societies scattered across Africa south of the Sahara, Southeast Asia, Malaysia, Indonesia, and Oceania. I have reason to believe, however, that the eating of human flesh was never an important aspect of the redistributive feasts in the cultures which immediately preceded the rise of states in Mesopotamia, Egypt, India, China, or Europe.

Human beings were ritually sacrificed in all of these regions, but they were seldom eaten. Authoritative Roman sources—Caesar, Tacitus, and Plutarch—assert that the sacrifice of prisoners of war was a commonplace among the so-called "barbarian" nations on the margins of the Greco-Roman world. The Greeks and Romans of late classical antiquity regarded any kind of human sacrifice as immoral and were disturbed that honest soldiers should be deprived of their lives for the benefit of the cults of such "uncivilized" peoples as the Britons, Gauls, Celts, and Teutons. During Homeric times, however, the Greeks themselves had not been averse to killing small numbers of prisoners to influence the gods. At the battle of Troy, for example, the hero

Achilles put twelve captured Trojans on the funeral pyre of his comrade-in-arms, Patroclus. And as late as the great naval battle of Salamis in 480 B.C. between the Greeks and the Persians, Themistocles, the Greek commander-in-chief, ordered the sacrifice of three Persian captives in order to assure victory. The Romans, too, had once practiced human sacrifice. About 226 B.C. two Gauls and two Greeks were buried alive in order to forestall the prophecy that the Gauls and the Greeks would soon occupy the city of Rome. Similar incidents occurred in 216 B.C. and in 104 B.C.

Seasoned Roman troops were unnerved by their first encounters with the Celts, who went into battle uttering weird chants, rushing stark-naked through the snow against the Roman lines. The existence of a Celtic "cult of the severed head" all across pre-Roman iron age Europe makes it clear that blacks and Indians are not the only contemporary Americans who are descendants of headhunters. Celtic warriors placed the freshly decapitated heads of their enemies on their chariots and brought them home to hang from the rafters. In the South of France the Celts exhibited skulls in niches carved into stone monoliths. Skulls adorned the Celtic hill forts and the gateways to their villages and towns. Whether some of these skulls were obtained from sacrificial victims is not known. What is known is that human sacrifice was an important part of Celtic ritual, and that it was carried out under the supervision of the priestly caste called the Druids. The Celts preferred to burn people, and for this purpose they wove life-size wickerwork baskets around the prisoners and then set them on fire. On other occasions the victims were disemboweled or stabbed in the back so that the Druids could foretell the future from the condition of the steaming entrails or from the position of the limbs when the writhing stopped.

Herodotus reports that another famous headhunting barbarian nation, the Scythians, who lived on the lower Danube and on the shores of the Black Sea, regularly sacrificed one out of each hundred prisoners taken on the battlefield. And in earliest Mesopotamia, according to Ignace Gelb of the University of Chicago, prisoners were sacrificed in temples. An inscription from Lagash written about 2500 B.C. refers to the piling up of thousands of enemy corpses in large heaps. Gelb also says that "POWs were often sacrificed" in early China.

As the Biblical story of Abraham and his son Isaac shows, the possibility of human sacrifice was clearly very much on the minds of the ancient Israelites. Abraham thinks he hears God asking him to kill his son, who is saved only at the last moment by a friendly angel. When Hiel of Bethel rebuilt Jericho, he "laid its foundation at the cost of Abiram his first born, and set up its gates at the cost of his youngest son Segub, according to the word of the Lord."

Early Brahmanic scriptures also reveal a lingering interest in human sacrifice. The goddess of death, Kali, bears a striking resemblance to the bloodthirsty Aztec deities. She is described in the *Kalika Purana*—the Holy Book of Kali—as a hideous figure garlanded with a string of human skulls, besmeared with human blood, and holding a skull in one hand and a sword in the other. Minute instructions are given concerning the manner in which human victims are to be killed.

> Having placed the victim before the goddess, the worshipper should adore her by offering flowers, sandal paste, and bark, frequently repeating the *mantra* appropriate for sacrifice. Then, facing the north

> and placing the victim to face east, he should look backward and repeat this *mantra*: "O man, through my good fortune thou has appeared as a victim; therefore I salute thee. . . . I shall slaughter thee today, and slaughter as a sacrifice is no murder." Thus meditating on that human-formed victim, a flower should be thrown at the top of its head with the *mantra:* "Om, Aim, Hriuh, Sriuh." Then, thinking of one's own wishes, and referring to the goddess, water should be sprinkled on the victim. Thereafter, the sword should be consecrated with the *mantra:* "O sword, thou art the tongue of Chandikā". . . . The sword, having thus been consecrated, should be taken up while repeating the *mantra:* "Am hum phat," and the excellent victim slaughtered with it.

Perhaps the most persistent form of human sacrifice found among early Old World states and empires was the slaughter of wives, servants, and bodyguards at the funerals of kings and emperors. The Scythians, for example, killed off all the old king's royal cooks, grooms, and butlers. The king's finest horses were also killed, as well as youths to ride them in the afterlife. Traces of retainer sacrifices have been found in early Egyptian tombs at Abydos and in the Sumerian royal tombs at Ur. Sacrifices of royal retainers had a double function. A king needed to take his court along with him after death in order to enjoy the style to which he had grown accustomed during life. But in a more down-to-earth vein the obligatory murder of a sovereign's wives, servants and bodyguards went a long way toward assuring him that his closest associates would value his life as much as they valued their own and hence would not conspire against his rule nor tolerate the least threat to his safety. The Chinese during the last part of the second millennium B.C. probably carried out the world's most extensive retainer sacrifices. Thousands of people were put to death at each royal funeral. This practice, along with the sacrifice of prisoners of war, was prohibited during Chou times (1023–257 B.C.). During the Ch'in dynasty pottery effigies were substituted for real people and animals. At the death in 210 B.C. of Ch'in Shih Huang Ti, the first ruler of a unified China, 6,000 life-size realistic ceramic statues of men-at-arms and cavalry horses were buried in a subterranean hall as big as a football field near the emperor's tomb.

What stands out in this rapid survey of ritual human sacrifice in the nuclear regions of Old World state formation is the lack of any strong association between human sacrifice and the eating of human flesh. Nowhere is there a trace of a system in which the redistribution of human flesh constituted a major preoccupation of the state or its ecclesiastical and military branches. Pausanius of Lydia says that the Gauls under the command of Combutis and Orestorios killed the whole male population of Callieas, then drank their blood and ate their flesh. Similar accusations were later made against the Tartars and the Mongols, but these reports all seem more like war-atrocity stories than ethnographic descriptions of Aztec-like cannibal cults. Reports of cannibalism in Egypt, India, and China are associated either with the preparation of exotic dishes for jaded upper-class palates or with famines, when the poor people fed on each other to stay alive. In post-Roman Europe cannibalism was regarded as so great a crime that only witches, werewolves, vampires, and Jews were deemed capable of it.

From Europe to China it was animal not human flesh that was brought to the altars, ritually sacrificed, dismembered, redistributed, and consumed in communal feasts. The Norse saga of Hakon the Good, for example, contains a clear description of the role played by animal sacrifice in the redistributions carried out by Celtic and Teutonic kings and princes.

> It was an old custom that when there was to be sacrifice all the bonders should come to the spot where the temple stood, and bring with them all that they required while the festival of the sacrifice lasted. To this festival all the men brought ale with them. All kinds of cattle, as well as horses, were slaughtered . . . and the flesh was boiled into savoury meat for those present. The fire was in the middle of the floor of the temple, and over it hung the kettles. The full goblets were handed across the fire, and he who made the feast, and was chief, blessed all the full goblets, and the meat of the sacrifice.

Generosity and communion are the prevailing themes of these rites, as epitomized in a nineteenth-century ballad about Sigurd (known in Germany as Siegfried), whom the sagas depict as an "open-handed man":

> *Of cup or platter need has none*
> *The guests who seek the generous one,—*
> *Sigurd the Generous, who can trace*
> *His lineage from the giant race . . .*
> *He loves the gods,—his liberal hand*
> *Scatters his sword's gains o'er the land.*

From Tacitus we learn that "it is the custom that each tribesman shall give the chieftain presents either of cattle or of part of his harvests," and that cattle "are in fact the most highly prized, indeed the only riches of the people." As Stuart Piggott points out, the ancient Irish tale "The Cattle-Raid of Cooley" begins with a scene in which Alill, chieftain of Cruachan, and Medb, his wife, boast of their wealth, beginning with iron cauldrons and moving up through gold ornaments, clothing, flocks of sheep, horses, and herds of pigs until finally they reach the epitome—their cattle. Among the ancient Irish, as among the Germans, Homeric Greeks, and earliest Latins, cattle were the most important measure of wealth and therefore, by inference, the most important item in the redistributive feasting upon which rested the organization of these chieftainships and incipient states.

The classical Greeks and Romans were also great sacrificers of animals at religious festivals, and various temples specialized in animals that were relevant to their deities. Goats, for example, were deemed appropriate gifts to Bacchus, the god of the vine, possibly because they were a menace to the vineyards. Some Greek cities treated their bulls the way the impersonators of gods were treated among the Aztecs—they were garlanded and feted throughout the year preceding their execution.

As every reader of the Old Testament knows, animal sacrifice was a major preoccupation of the ancient Israelites. The Book of Leviticus sets forth minute prescriptions about where, when, and how animals are to be offered. The Book of Numbers states that, during the dedication of the first tabernacle, 36 oxen, 144 sheep and lambs, and 72 goats and kids were sacrificed in a twelve-day period. As the Israelites moved from pastoral chieftainship to statehood, the scale of the redistributions increased. At the dedication of Solomon's temple in Jerusalem, 22,000 oxen and 120,000 sheep were slaughtered. The most important of the Israelite sacrifices was that of a lamb at the feast of Passover. While in bondage in Egypt, the Israelites sacrificed a lamb, smeared its blood on the lintels and doorposts of their houses, then roasted and ate it with bitter herbs and unleavened bread. That night the Lord smote all the first-born in the unmarked houses, convincing Pharaoh that the time had come to let the Israelites leave the country.

Levites, who constituted a priestly caste analogous to the Druids, held a monopoly over the slaughter of animals for food. Meat had to pass through their hands—literally, since they supervised or actually carried out the butchering of the animals and the redistribution of animal flesh, returning the largest share to the owner and his guests while holding back selected morsels for themselves and Jaweh.

W. Robertson Smith long ago pointed out in his important book *Religion of the Semites* that in old Israel all slaughter of animals was sacrifice: "People could never eat beef or mutton except as a religious act." Anthropologists who have studied modern pastoral peoples in East Africa have seen the same situation from a slightly different perspective. East African pastoralists generally live not from the meat of the herds but from their milk and blood. As among the Pakot studied by Harold Schneider, herd animals can only be slaughtered on "ritual and ceremonial occasions." The number of animals slaughtered per occasion and the number of occasions, however, are regulated by the availability of the animals. Anything as costly as an ox is too valuable not to be made part of some ceremonial. Americans who barbecue steaks for honored guests have much in common with the Pakot and the beef-loving peoples of the ancient world. (Incidentally, the word "barbecue" has an interesting history. It comes from the Carib word *barbricot*. The Caribs—whence the word "cannibal"—used the *barbricot*, a grill made of green boughs, to prepare their cannibal feasts.)

Returning to the Israelites, there is no doubt that at one time animals were sacrificed primarily to be eaten at redistributive feasts sponsored by "great provider" headmen and chiefs. "Open-handed generosity" was as important for the ancient Israelites as it was for the Teutons:

> As early as the time of Samuel we find religious feasts of clans or towns. . . . the law of the feast was open-handed generosity; no sacrifice was complete without guests; and portions were freely distributed to rich and poor within the circle of a man's acquaintances.

By the time of Christ, the Levites' slaughter monopoly had been given a monetary value. The faithful brought their animals to the temple priests, who slit throats at so much per head. Passover pilgrims traveled great distances to the temple at Jerusalem to have their lambs slaughtered. The famous temple moneychangers whose tables Jesus overturned ensured payment in coin of the realm. The Jewish rabbinate gave up the practice of animal sacrifice after the fall of Jerusalem in A.D. 70—but not quite, since Orthodox Jews to this day insist on having animals slaughtered by a slitting of the throat under the supervision of religious specialists.

Because the crucifixion of Jesus occurred in association with the celebration of Passover, his death was readily assimilated to the imagery and symbolism of both animal and human sacrifice. John the Baptist called the coming messiah "the lamb of god." Meanwhile, the Christians maintained tokens of the original redistributive functions of animal sacrifice in their rites called "communion." Jesus broke the Passover bread and poured the Passover wine, and distributed the bread and wine to his disciples. "This is my body," he said of the bread. "And this is my blood," he said of the wine. In the Roman Catholic sacrament of the Eucharist these redistributive activities are repeated as ritual. The priest eats the bread in the form of a wafer and drinks the wine while the members of the congregation eat only the wafer. Appropriately enough, this wafer is called the "host," a word derived from the Latin *hostis,* meaning "sacrifice."

Protestants and Catholics have spilled much blood and ink over the question of whether the wine and wafer are actually "transubstantiated" into the corporeal substance of Christ's blood and body. But theologians and historians have up to now generally failed to see the real evolutionary significance of the Christian "mass." By spiritualizing the eating of the paschal lamb and by reducing its substance to a nutritionally worthless wafer, Christianity long ago unburdened itself of the responsibility of seeing to it that those who came to the feast did not go home on an empty stomach. It took a while for this to happen. During the first two centuries of Christianity the communicants pooled their resources and actually held a communal meal known as the agape, or love feast. After Christianity became the official religion of the Roman Empire, the Church found that it was being used as a soup kitchen and in A.D. 363 the holding of love feasts on church premises was forbidden at the Council of Laodicea. The point that really merits attention is that the nutritive value of the communion feast is virtually zero, whether there is transubstantiation or not. Nineteenth-century anthropologists saw in the line of development which led from human sacrifice to animal sacrifice to the wafer and wine of the Eucharist a vindication of the doctrine of moral progress and enlightenment. I cannot share their optimism. Before we congratulate Christianity for its transcendence of animal sacrifice, we should note that corporeal protein supplies were also being transcended by a rapidly expanding population. What the end of animal sacrifice really signified was the end of ecclesiastical redistributive feasting.

Christianity was only one of several religions that opted for generosity after death when generosity in life ceased to be practiced or necessary. I do not think it detracts from the acts of mercy and kindness performed in the name of such religions to point out that it was a great convenience for the rulers of India, Islam, and Rome to humble themselves before gods to whom heaven was more important than earth, and a former or future life more important than this one. As the imperial systems of the Old World grew larger and larger, they chewed up and depleted resources on a continental scale. When the globe had filled with tens of millions of ragged sweating drudges, the "great providers" were unable to act with the "open-handed generosity" of the barbarian chiefs of yore. Under Christianity, Buddhism, and Islam they became "great believers" and built cathedrals, mosques, and temples where nothing at all was served to eat.

But let's get back to the time when there were still enough animals around so that meat could occasionally be part of everyone's diet. Persians, Vedic Brahmans, Chinese, and Japanese all at one time or another ritually sacrificed domesticated animals. In fact, it would be difficult to find a single society in a belt across Eurasia and North Africa in which domesticated animal sacrifice was not part of state-supported cults. The entire repertory of herbivores and ruminant species was drawn upon for the purpose of these redistributive sacrifices, although some regions displayed preferences dictated by special ecological considerations. North Africa and Arabia, for example, were noted for camel sacrifices; horses were sacrificed among the central Asian pastoralists; bulls were given special attention throughout the Mediterranean area. Meanwhile, across the same vast belt stretching from Spain to Japan, cannibalism was generally practiced on a very small scale, if at all. The Eurasian state religions prohibited the eating of human flesh and though this proscription was not sufficient to prevent sporadic outbreaks of cannibalism during times of hunger brought on by sieges or crop failures, such lapses had nothing to do with ecclesiastical policy and were usually discouraged rather than promoted by the governing classes.

Much of what I have said thus far has been commented on by previous authors. I am certainly not the first to discover the relationship between the scarcity of domesticated stock in Mesoamerica and the peculiar intensity of the cult of human sacrifice among the Aztecs. Yet it was not until Michael Harner linked the scale of human sacrifice among the Aztecs to the depletion of protein resources that a scientific theory of the divergent trajectories of early Old and New World state religions could be formulated. Others had previously reasoned that it was the lack of animals "suitable" for sacrifice that set the Mesoamericans off on their ghastly career. Allegedly, the Old World had a supply of animals whose demeanor was "suitable" for sacrificial rites. Hence there was no need to employ prisoners of war for such purposes and human sacrifice was replaced by animal sacrifice. Reay Tannahill, to name one recent adherent of this view, aptly notes that the native American horse had been wiped out, that caribou and bison were not found so far south as Mexico, and that other game was scarce. But as to why the dog and turkey—"the only domesticated livestock"—were not used instead of people, her answer is: "These were too contemptible to be worthy of the Gods."

I feel that this kind of explanation is as defective as the explanations the Aztecs themselves gave for eating their prisoners of war. What people think or imagine is contemptible to the gods cannot be taken as an explanation of their religious beliefs and practices. To do so is to rest the explanation of all social life ultimately on what people arbitrarily think or imagine—a strategy doomed to nullify all intelligent inquiry since it will always come down to one useless refrain: People think or imagine what they think or imagine. Why should dogs and turkeys be deemed unsuitable for the majesty of supernatural appetites? The members of some cultures find it easy to imagine that the gods dine on ambrosia or nothing at all. Surely a people who were capable of imagining what the face of Tlaloc looked like were capable of imagining that their gods were passionately fond of turkey giblets and dog hearts. It was the Aztecs, not their gods, who felt that it wasn't worth their while to wrench out the beating hearts of turkeys and dogs. And the reason they felt that way had nothing to do with the inherent dignity of dogs, turkeys—or, for that matter, domesticated ducks. Rather, it had to do with the cost of obtaining large quantities of meat from these species. The trouble with dogs as a source of meat is not that they are contemptible but that they thrive best when they themselves are fed on meat. And the trouble with turkeys and other fowl is that they thrive best when they are fed on cereal grains. In both cases it is enormously more efficient to eat the meat or the grain directly than to pass it through another link in the food chain. On the other hand, the great advantage of the Old World domesticated species is that they are herbivores and ruminants and thrive best when they feed on grass, stubble, leaves, and other plant foods which human beings cannot digest. Because of the pleistocene extinctions, the Aztecs lacked such species. And it was this lack, together with the extra costs involved in using carnivores and birds as a source of animal protein, that tipped the balance in favor of cannibalism. Of course, the meat obtained from prisoners of war is also costly—it is very expensive to capture armed men. But if a society lacks other sources of animal protein, the benefits of cannibalism may outweigh these costs. On the other hand, if a society already has horses, sheep, goats, camels, oxen, and pigs to eat, the cost of cannibalism may outweigh its benefits.

No doubt my story would be more inspirational if I could set aside this cost/benefit approach to cannibalism and return to the old theory of moral progress. Most of us would prefer to believe that the Aztecs remained cannibals simply because their morals were mired in primitive impulses while the Old World states tabooed human flesh because their morals had risen in the great onwards-and-upwards movement of civilization. But I'm afraid this preference arises from provincial if not hypocritical misconceptions. Neither the prohibition of cannibalism nor the decline of human sacrifice in the Old World had the slightest effect on the rate at which the Old World states and empires killed each other's citizens. As everyone knows, the scale of warfare has increased steadily from prehistoric times to the present, and record numbers of casualties due to armed conflict have been produced precisely by those states in which Christianity has been the major religion. Heaps of corpses left to rot on the battlefield are no less dead than corpses dismembered for a feast. Today, hovering on the brink of a third world war, we are scarcely in a position to look down on the Aztecs. In our nuclear age the world survives only because each side is convinced that the moral standards of the other are low enough to sanction the annihilation of hundreds of millions of people in retaliation for a first strike. Thanks to radioactivity the survivors will not even be able to bury the dead, let alone eat them.

I see two ways to add up the cost/benefits of cannibalism in the early phases of state formation. First of all, there is the question of the use of enemy soldiers as producers of food rather than as meals in themselves. Ignace Gelb points out in his discussion of the evolution of the state in Mesopotamia that at first men were killed either on the battlefield or in sacrificial rites, while only captive women and children were incorporated into the labor force. This implies that it was "relatively easy to exert control over foreign women and children" and that "the state apparatus was still not strong enough to control the masses of unruly male captives." But as the power of the state apparatus increased, male POW's were "marked or branded, tied with ropes or kept in neck stocks" and later "freed and resettled or used for specialized purposes of the crown, such as the personal guard of the king, mercenaries, or a movable force."

> The change of status of POWs represents the main factor in the creation of the second most important source (after the native impoverished classes) of productive labor in Mesopotamia.

Gelb emphasizes the fact that POW's in Mesopotamia, India, and China were not used as slaves but were deported from their homelands and established as more or less free peasants throughout the kingdom. It was clearly advantageous in a cost/benefit sense for these early Old World state systems to use their domesticated animals as a source of milk and meat and to use their captives as agricultural laborers and cannon fodder. And underlying this adaptation was the fact that the presence of domestic animals made it possible to expand and intensify the productive and reproductive base of the ancient Old World states and empires far beyond the level to which the Aztecs could go without suffering severe cuts in their standard of living (although the wages of the sins of intensification were shortly to catch up with them also).

The second dimension that must be considered in assessing the cost/benefits of cannibalism is more political than economic, even though it too ultimately boils down to a question of maintaining standards of living in the face of population growth, intensification, and environmental depletion. As I've shown, states emerged from band and village societies through the enlargement and stratification of leadership responsible for economic redistributions and the conduct of external warfare. The earliest kings, such as Sigurd the Generous, cultivated the image of the "great provider" which "big men" everywhere have always used to justify their preeminence: "His liberal hand scattered his sword's gains o'er the land." Continued generosity in the face of rapid population growth and environmental depletions, however, demanded continued expansion into new territories and the progressive absorption of additional masses of peasant producers. Not only did the eating of prisoners of war represent a great waste of manpower under the ecological conditions characteristic of the early Old World states, but it was the worst possible strategy for any state that had imperial ambitions. Empire building is not facilitated by the promise that those who submit to the "great provider" will be eaten. Rather, the fundamental principle guiding all successful imperial expansion is that those who submit to the "great provider" will not be eaten—literally or figuratively—but in fact their lives will be preserved and their diet improved. Cannibalism and empire don't mix. Throughout history people have been duped again and again into believing that enormous inequalities in the distribution of wealth are necessary for their own welfare. But the one thing no "great provider" has ever been able to do is convince people that there is some kind of parity in the relationship between eating and being eaten. To opt for a cannibal kingdom, in other words, is to opt for perpetual war with one's neighbors and for a revolt-ridden realm in which people are literally treated as being good for nothing but stew meat. Such a choice made sense only for a state which—like the Aztecs'—had already so depleted its environment that the imperial phase of politics could not be attained.

I should also point out that there was an internal counterpart to the policy of mercy toward prisoners of war. The growth of empire promoted the image of rulers as divine figures who protect the meek from overexploitation at the hands of other members of the ruling class. Imperial governments had to tread a fine line between too much and too little taxation. If the power of local officials to tax the peasantry was not restrained by the emperor, the people would become disorderly, the cost of maintaining law and order would soar, and the survival of the empire would be jeopardized. The natural outcome of the "great provider" image spread over a canvas of continental dimensions was that of the great dispenser of justice and mercy and divine protector of the meek. Here lies the origin of the Old World's universalistic religions of love and mercy. In the earliest law code known 1,700 years before the birth of Christ, Hammurabi made the protection of the weak against the strong a fundamental principle of Babylonian imperial rule. Hammurabi pictured himself as the greatest of "great providers": "shepherd," "giver of abundant riches," "bringer of overflowing wealth," "provider of abundant waters for his people," "giver of plentiful abundance . . . who enlarges the tilth" . . . "heaps the granaries of grain" . . . "bountiful provider of holy feasts" . . . "giver of the waters of abundance" . . . "who has firmly laid the foundations of habitations and supplies them with abundance and good things." Then he declared himself to be divine: "the sun-god of Babylon who makes the light to rise on the land." And finally the great protector: "destroyer of the evil and the wicked so that the strong may not oppose the weak."

The same imperial calculus lies at the heart of the political religion known as Confucianism. The early Chinese kings kept a kind of "brain trust" at court from whom they sought expert advice on how to stay rich and powerful without being overthrown. The most famous of these advisers were Confucius and Mencius, both of whom never tired of telling their royal majesties that the prescription for a long and prosperous reign was to see to it that the common people were well-fed and not taxed too much. Of the two, Mencius was the more daring; he even went so far as to say that the sovereign was relatively unimportant. Only the emperor who was good to his people could expect to endure:

> The people are the most important element in a nation, the spirits of the land and grain are the next; the sovereign is the lightest. Therefore to gain the peasantry is to become sovereign. If your majesty will indeed dispense a benevolent government to the people, being sparing in the use of punishments and fines, and making the taxes and levies light, so causing that the fields shall be plowed deep, and the weeding of them carefully attended to . . . you will then have a people who can be employed with sticks

> which they have prepared, to oppose the strong mail and strong weapons of the troops of Ch'in and Ch'u. . . . The rulers of those two states rob their people of their time so that they cannot plough and weed their fields. . . . Those rulers as it were, drive their people into pit falls or drown them. In such a case who will oppose your majesty? In accordance with this is the saying, "the benevolent have no enemy" and I beg your majesty not to doubt what I say.

Between these pragmatic doctrines and the emergence of a full-blown religion of love, charity, and the sacredness of human life, there was no great gulf. Already in Mencius' philosophy, "Benevolence is the distinguishing characteristic of man."

This balance of the cost/benefits of state-sponsored cannibalism explains, I think, why human sacrifice and cannibalism remained unimportant features of the ancient Old World state religions. Moreover, as Michael Harner has suggested, it may also provide an answer for the first time to the question why political development along the Pacific Coast and highlands of South America culminating in the appearance of the Inca Empire followed the Mesopotamian and Chinese rather than the Aztec pattern. At its prime the Inca Empire embraced a region which extended 1,500 miles from northern Chile to southern Columbia and contained a population of perhaps 6 million people. This vast realm, unlike Mesoamerica under the Aztecs, had an overall political structure of villages, districts, and provinces. Officials appointed by the supreme Inca were responsible for law and order and for the maintenance of high levels of production. Village lands were divided into three parts, the largest of which was the peasant's own subsistence plot; harvests from the second and third parts were turned over to ecclesiastical and political officials, who were in charge of provincial granaries. These granaries operated on the ever-normal principle. They were used to compensate for annual ups and downs as well as for regional crises. During times of drought their contents were rushed over a network of government roads and suspension bridges to needy provinces. The political philosophy of the Incas, like that of Hammurabi and Confucius, embraced the lingering impulse of generous "bigmanship." Enemy states were urged to submit to Inca rule in order to enjoy a higher standard of living. Defeated troops, as in early Mesopotamia, were resettled in different parts of the empire and fully incorporated into the peasant work force, while enemy leaders were taken to the capital at Cuzco and indoctrinated with the Incas' political religion. The Inca army did not march upon its foes under the banner WE WILL EAT YOU. As in early China and Mesopotamia, the Inca priests did occasionally sacrifice human beings—for the glory of the creator Viracocha and the sun god Inte—but these sacrifices were not an integral part of the war system. Only one or two soldiers from a defeated province were chosen. More often the principal victims appear to have been boys and girls who were primed for the occasion with food, drink, and special privileges. Most important, there is no evidence that the victims were dismembered and eaten.

The Inca priests functioned as redistributors of meat, and sacrifice was a daily event. But the high priests in Cuzco expended their surgical skills on llamas, while at lesser shrines guinea pigs were so honored. Both of these animals, as I pointed out earlier, were absent from the food production inventory of the Aztecs. Of the two, the llama is the more important in the context of the present discussion because it is a member of the camel family, whose natural pasture consists of high-altitude grasses which cannot be eaten by human beings. Recent excavations by J. and E. Pires-Ferreira and Peter Kaulicke of the University of San Marcos in Peru have traced the origin of llama domestication to hunters who invaded the puna of Junin at the end of the last ice age. Domestication was not completed until sometime between 2500 and 1750 B.C.—late by Old World standards but early enough to have played a role at the very beginning of the process of state formation in South America.

Inca llamas and guinea pigs were not inherently less contemptible than Aztec dogs and turkeys; they were simply better sources of meat. Llamas made it possible for the Incas to stop sacrificing human beings because llamas made it possible for the Incas to stop eating human beings. The lesson seems plain: the flesh of the ruminants tamed the appetites of the gods and made the "great providers" merciful.

nality where nature's peculiar chances of [illegible] [illegible] [illegible] [illegible] [illegible] [illegible] [illegible] [illegible] [illegible] of the [illegible] [illegible] [illegible] [illegible] [illegible] [illegible] [illegible] [illegible] [illegible] [illegible] [illegible] [illegible] [illegible] of the [illegible] [illegible] was not complete [illegible] between 2200 and [illegible] date of [illegible] dates apparently changed [illegible] beginning of the process of state formation in South Asia.

[illegible] were no [illegible] contemporary than [illegible] [illegible] [illegible] [illegible] [illegible] [illegible] [illegible] [illegible] [illegible] [illegible] [illegible] [illegible] [illegible] [illegible] [illegible] [illegible] [illegible] [illegible] [illegible] the [illegible] produce [illegible]

11
Forbidden Flesh

Earlier I showed that animal domestication originated as a conservation effort triggered by the destruction of the pleistocene megafauna. But what began as an attempt to guarantee meat rations to village populations ended in the usual paradox that we have come to expect whenever a mode of production is intensified to allay reproductive pressures. Sheep, goats, pigs, cattle, and other domestic species originally could be raised primarily for their meat because during early neolithic times villages were surrounded by ample reserves of forests and grazing lands which were not needed for the planting of wheat, barley, and other crops destined for direct consumption by human beings. Yet as human population density soared in response to the expansionist political economies of the early states and empires the area of forests and unplowed grasslands available per capita for animal husbandry grew smaller. Wherever a farming population possessing domesticated animals increased rapidly, a choice had to be made between growing more food plants or raising more animals. Ancient states and empires invariably gave priority to the raising of more food plants since the net calorie return on each calorie of human effort invested in plant production is on the average about ten times greater than the net calorie return obtainable from animal production. In other words, it is energetically much more efficient for human beings themselves to eat food plants than to lengthen out the food chain by interposing animals between plants and people. Grains convert about .4 percent of each unit of photosynthetically active sunlight to humanly edible matter. Feeding grain to cattle yields meat containing only 5 percent of this percentage, that is, .02 percent of the original unit of sunlight. The decision to increase the acreage devoted to farm crops at the expense of the acreage devoted to animal pasture thus represents a strategy aimed at raising and feeding people rather than raising and feeding animals.

But domesticated species are valuable for other products and services. To raise and slaughter them for their meat alone is to destroy their value as traction machines, as producers of fibers, and as providers of fertilizer. Since some of the domesticated species can also be made to yield a continuous supply of animal protein in the form of milk and milk products, one can readily understand why domesticated animals were used with steadily decreasing frequency as a source of meat: they were worth more alive than dead. Therefore, meat gradually disappeared from the daily diet of the common folk of the ancient states and empires, who after thousands of years of "progress" found themselves on the average consuming almost as little animal protein as the common citizens of Tenochtitlán. Over a vast region of the Old World corresponding to the former zones of greatest meat and grain production, animal flesh soon became a luxury whose consumption was increasingly restricted to occasions involving ritual sacrifice and ecclesiastical redistributions. Eventually, the consumption of the flesh of the most expensive species came to be forbidden altogether, while in the regions suffering the greatest depletions meat itself became ritually unclean. Before long there rose for the first time in history ecclesiastical doctrines aimed at inculcating the belief that eating plants was more godlike than eating flesh.

The decline in the per capita consumption of animal flesh represented a decline in nutritional standards. Since this may not seem obvious to modern-day vegetarian enthusiasts, who argue that meat-eating is a noxious habit, let me clarify this point before going on to ask why the flesh of certain animal species rather than others became taboo in the ancient Middle East. Vegetarians are perfectly correct when they claim that we human beings can satisfy all our nutritional needs by consuming nothing but food plants. All twenty amino acids, the building blocks of proteins, are present in plants. But no one food plant contains all twenty amino acids. The full complement of amino acids can be obtained from food plants only by eating large amounts of bulky nitrogenous foods, such as beans and nuts, plus still larger amounts of starchy grains or root crops on a daily basis. (Beans and nuts are expensive foods in themselves.) Eating meat is therefore a much more efficient way for the body to obtain all the amino acids needed for health and vigor. Meat provides the essential nutrients in highly concentrated packets. As a source of protein, it is physiologically more efficient than food plants and this fact is reflected in the virtually universal preference exhibited by pre-state village peoples for meat over vegetable foods as items in redistributive feasts.

The first domesticated species to become too expensive to serve as a source of meat was probably the pig. We know from the Old Testament that the Israelites were commanded to abstain from the eating of pork early in their history. Since the meat of cattle, sheep, and goats played an important role in the ancient Israelite "great provider" redistributions, prohibition of the consumption of such an excellent source of animal flesh seems difficult to understand. Remains of domesticated pig appear in the neolithic villages of Palestine, Syria, Iraq, and Anatolia almost as early as those of sheep and goats. Moreover, unlike other domesticated species, the pig was domesticated primarily for its flesh. Pigs can't be milked or ridden, can't herd other animals, pull a plow, or carry a cargo, and don't catch mice. Yet as a supplier of meat the pig is unrivaled; it is one of the most efficient converters of carbohydrates to proteins and fat in the entire animal kingdom. For every 100 pounds of feed consumed, a pig will produce about 20 pounds of meat, while from the same amount of feed cattle produce only about 7 pounds. In terms of calories produced per calorie of food, pigs are over three times more efficient than cattle and about two times more efficient than chickens. (Pound for pound, pork has more calories than beef.)

Before I attempt to explain why it was pork that first became the object of supernatural interdictions, let me say something about the general principles governing the establishment of taboos on animal flesh. As suggested by Eric Ross, who has studied the problem of animal taboos among the Indians of the Amazon Basin, the most important general point to be kept in mind is that the ecological role of particular species is not fixed for all time but is part of a dynamic process. Cultures tend to impose supernatural sanctions on the consumption of animal flesh when the ratio of communal benefits to costs associated with the use of a particular species deteriorates. Cheap and abundant species whose flesh can be eaten without danger to the rest of the system by which food is obtained seldom become the target of supernatural proscriptions. Animals that have high benefits and low costs at one time, but that become more costly later on, are the principal targets of supernatural sanctions. The most severe restrictions tend to develop when a nutritionally valuable species not only becomes more expensive but its continued use endangers the existing mode of subsistence. The pig is such a species.

Pig raising incurred costs that posed a threat to the entire subsistence system in the hot, semiarid lands of the ancient Middle East. And this threat increased sharply as a result of intensification, depletion, and population growth linked to the development of pristine and secondary states throughout the region after 4000 B.C. The pig is essentially a creature of forests, riverbanks, and the edges of swamps. It is physiologically maladapted to high temperatures and direct sunlight because it cannot regulate its body temperature without external sources of moisture—it cannot sweat. In its natural forest habitat the pig eats tubers, roots, and fruits and nuts that have fallen to the ground. If it is fed on plants with a high cellulose content, it completely loses its advantage over ruminant species as a converter of plants to meat and fat. Unlike cattle, sheep, goats, donkeys, and horses, hogs cannot metabolize husks, stalks, or fibrous leaves; they are no better than people when it comes to living on grass.

When the pig was first domesticated, there were extensive forests covering the hilly flanks of the Taurus and Zagros mountains and the other upland zones of the Middle East. But beginning in 7000 B.C. the spread and intensification of mixed farming and herding economies converted millions of acres of Middle Eastern forests to grasslands. At the same time, millions of acres of grasslands were converted to deserts.

Agricultural and pastoral intensification fostered the spread of arid-land plants at the expense of formerly lush tropical and semitropical vegetation. Authorities estimate that the forests of Anatolia were reduced from 70 percent to 13 percent of total surface area between 5000 B.C. and the recent past. Only one-fourth of the former Caspian shorefront forest remains, one-half of the mountain humid forest, one-fifth to one-sixth of the oak and juniper forests of the Zagros, and one-twentieth of the juniper forests of the Elburg and Khorassan ranges. The regions that suffered most were those taken over by pastoralists or former pastoralists. The history of the Middle East has always been dominated by the ephemerality of the boundary between farm and desert, as epitomized in Omar Khayyám's verse:

Along some strip of herbage strown
that just divides the desert from the sown.

Today, as R. D. Whyte has noted, "The bald mountains and foothills of the Mediterranean shorelines, the Anatolian plateau, and Iran stand as stark witnesses of millennia of uncontrolled utilization."

The ancient Israelites arrived in Palestine during the early to middle iron age, about 1200 B.C., and took possession of mountainous terrain which had not previously been cultivated. The woodlands in the Judean and Samaritan hills were rapidly cut down and converted into irrigated terraces. Areas suitable for raising pigs on natural forage were severely restricted. Increasingly, pigs had to be fed grains as supplements, rendering them directly competitive with human beings; moreover, their cost increased because they needed artificial shade and moisture. And yet they continued to be a tempting source of protein and fat.

Pastoralists and settled farmers living in regions

undergoing deforestation might be prompted to rear the pig for short-term benefits, but it would be extremely costly and maladaptive to raise pigs on a large scale. The ecclesiastical prohibition recorded in Leviticus had the merit of finality: by making even a harmless little bit of pig raising unclean, it helped put down the harmful temptation to raise a lot of pigs. I should point out that some of my colleagues have challenged this explanation on the ground that if pig raising was really so harmful there would have been no need for special ecclesiastical sanctions against it. "To require a taboo on an animal which is ecologically destructive is cultural overkill. Why use pigs if they are not useful in a stated context?" But it is the role of pigs in an evolving system of production that is under consideration here. To prohibit raising pigs was to encourage raising grains, tree crops, and less costly sources of animal protein. Moreover, just as individuals are often ambivalent and ambiguous about their own thoughts and emotions, so whole populations are often ambivalent and ambiguous about aspects of the intensification processes in which they are participating. Think of the pros and cons of offshore drilling and the ongoing debate about the taboo on abortions. It was not a matter of "cultural overkill" to invoke divine law against the pig any more than it is "cultural overkill" to invoke divine law against adultery or bank robberies. When Jahweh prohibited homicide and incest, he did not say, "Let there be only a little bit of homicide" or "Let there be only a little bit of incest." Why, then, should he have said, "Thou shalt eat of the swine only in small amounts"?

Some people feel that ecological cost/benefit analysis of pig raising is superfluous because the pig is simply an exceptionally unappetizing creature that eats human excrement and likes to wallow in its own urine and feces. What this approach fails to cope with is that if everyone naturally felt that way the pig would never have been domesticated in the first place, nor would it continue to be eagerly devoured in so many other parts of the world. Actually, pigs wallow in their own feces and urine only when they are deprived of alternative sources of the external moisture necessary for cooling their hairless and sweatless bodies. Moreover, the pig is scarcely the only domesticated animal that will, given the chance, gobble up human excrement (cattle and chickens, for example show little restraint in this regard).

The notion that the pig was tabooed because its flesh carried the parasite that causes trichinosis should also be laid to rest. Recent epidemiological studies have shown that pigs raised in hot climates seldom transmit trichinosis. On the other hand, naturally "clean" cattle, sheep, and goats are vectors for anthrax, brucellosis, and other human diseases that are as dangerous as anything the pig can transmit, if not more so.

Another objection raised against an ecological explanation of the Israelite pig taboo is that it fails to take into account the fact that the flesh of many other creatures is prohibited in the Old Testament. While it is true that the pig taboo is but one aspect of a whole system of dietary laws, the inclusion of the other interdicted creatures can also be explained by the general cost/benefit principles summarized earlier in this chapter. The majority of the forbidden species were wild animals which could only be obtained by hunting. To a person whose subsistence depended primarily on flocks, herds, and grain agriculture, the hunting of animals—especially of species that had become scarce or which did not live in the local habitat—was a poor cost/benefit bargain.

Let us start with the four-footed beasts with "paws" (Lev. XI:27). Though not identified by species, the "pawed" animals must have consisted primarily of carnivores such as wildcats, lions, foxes, and wolves. The hunting of such animals as a source of protein epitomizes low-benefit/high-cost meat production. Such animals are scarce, skinny, hard to find, and difficult to kill.

The taboo on animals with paws probably also included the domesticated cat and dog. Cats were domesticated in Egypt to serve the highly specialized function of rodent control. Eating them, except in emergencies, would not have made life better for anyone except mice and rats. (As for eating mice and rats, cats do that more efficiently.) Dogs were used primarily to herd and hunt. To produce meat, anything (other than bones) fed to a dog would be better spent put into the mouth of a cow or a goat.

Another category of forbidden flesh in Leviticus consists of water dwellers without fins or scales. By inplication, these include eels, shellfish, whales, porpoises, sturgeons, lampreys, and catfish. Most of these species, of course, were unlikely to be encountered in significant numbers on the edge of the Sinai Desert or in the Judean hills.

"Birds" constitute the largest group of specifically identified forbidden creatures: the eagle, ossifrage, osprey, kite, falcon, raven, sea gull, hawk, owl, cormorant, ibis, water hen, pelican, vulture, stork, heron, hoopoe, and bat (the last erroneously classified as a bird, Lev. XI:13–20). All of these are also either highly elusive, rare, or nutritionally trivial species—their nutritional value is about what you would expect to get from a mouthful of feathers.

Turning to the category "insect," it is written that

"all winged insects that go upon all fours" are forbidden with the exception of locusts, crickets, and grasshoppers, "which leap upon the earth." The exceptions are highly significant. Locusts are large, meaty insects; they occur in vast numbers and are easily gathered for food during what is likely to become a hungry period as a result of the damage they inflict on fields and pastures. They have a high benefit-to-cost ratio.

There is also the prohibition of animals that "chew the cud" but are not "cloven footed": "camel, rock badger and hare." And animals that are "cloven footed" but "do not chew the cud," of which the sole example is the pig.

The rock badger is a nondomesticated creature which seems to conform to the general pattern of the other interdicted feral animals. Though the hare is also a feral species, I am reluctant to pass judgment on its cost/benefit status. After a lapse of so many thousands of years it is difficult to assign this species a definite role in the local ecosystem. But I don't think I have to show that 100 percent of the interdicted feral creatures conform to the pattern of high costs and low benefits. I am not opposed to the idea that one or two of the species mentioned in Leviticus may have been interdicted not for ecological reasons but to satisfy random prejudices or to conform to some obscure principle of taxonomic symmetry intelligible only to the priests and prophets of ancient Israel. I should like these remarks to apply also to the category of animals that are called "swarming things": weasel, mouse, lizard, gecko, crocodile, and chameleon. Some of these species—crocodiles, for example—would seem to be quite useless as a source of food for the Israelites, yet one cannot be certain about others on the list without a detailed study of their ecological status.

Although the camel is the only domesticated animal specifically mentioned among the non-cloven footed cud-chewers, rabbinical authorities have always included horses and donkeys in the same category. What these three domesticated species really have in common (none of them "chew the cud") is that they are large high-cost/high-benefit animals kept by the Israelites for their contribution to transport and traction. Neither camels nor horses were kept in significant numbers. The horse was used primarily for aristocratic and military purposes, while camels were specialized for deep desert caravans. Neither could have supplied significant amounts of animal protein without interfering with their primary function. Donkeys were the Israelites' principal pack animal, but these too could not be slaughtered for food except at great economic loss. In other words, the domesticated non-cloven-footed "cud-chewers" were just too valuable to be eaten.

To sum up: There is nothing about the list of species interdicted in Leviticus that runs counter to the ecological explanation of the pig taboo. If anything, the whole pattern seems to be one of banning inconvenient or expensive sources of meat.

The confusion surrounding the question of animal taboos appears traceable to an overly narrow preoccupation with the unique history of particular cultures abstracted from their regional settings and from general evolutionary processes. To take the case in point, the ancient Israelite pig taboo can never be satisfactorily explained in terms of values and beliefs that were peculiar to the Israelites. The fact is that the Israelites were only one among many Middle Eastern peoples who found the pig increasingly troublesome.

The pig taboo recurs throughout the entire vast zone of Old World pastoral nomadism—from North Africa across the Middle East and Central Asia. But in China, Southeast Asia, Indonesia, and Melanesia the pig was and still is a much-used source of dietary proteins and fats, as it is in modern Europe and the Western Hemisphere. The fact that the pig was tabooed in the great pastoral zones of the Old World and in several of the river valleys bordering these zones suggests that the Biblical taboos must be seen as an adaptive response valuable over a wide area in relation to recurrent ecological shifts brought about by the intensification and depletions associated with the rise of ancient states and empires.

The ancient Israelites even shared their abhorrence of the pig with their mortal enemies, the Egyptians. In the words of H. Epstein, one of the outstanding authorities on the history of animal domestication in Africa,

> from a position of extreme importance at the beginning of the neolithic period [the pig] gradually declined in significance, and records from the dynastic period reveal the development of an increasing prejudice against it.

During Middle Dynastic times (2000 B.C.) the Egyptians began to identify pigs with Set, the god of evil. Although pig raising survived into post-Dynastic times, the Egyptians never lost their prejudice against pork. Egyptian swineherds were members of a distinct caste. They used their herds to tread seeds into the Nile flood plain as part of the planting process, and this useful function—together with the availability of permanent wetlands and swamps in the Nile Delta—may help to account for the occasional eating of pork in Egypt up to the time of the Islamic conquest. Still, according to Herodotus, the swineherds constituted the most despised caste in Egypt and, unlike all others, were forbidden to enter the temples.

Something similar seems to have happened in Mesopotamia. Archaeologists have found clay models of domesticated pigs in the earliest settlements of Lower Mesopotamia in the fifth and fourth millennia B.C. About 30 percent of the animal bones excavated from Tell Asmar (2800–2700 B.C.) belonged to pigs. Pork was eaten in Ur in pre-Dynastic times. In the earliest Sumerian dynasties there were specialist swineherds and pork butchers. After 2400 B.C., however, pork evidently became taboo and was no longer eaten.

The disappearance of the pig from the Mesopotamian diet coincides with severe ecological depletion and declining productivity in lower Sumeria, the cradle of the earliest Middle Eastern states. For 1,500 years Sumerian agriculture underwent continuous intensifications involving the construction of irrigation canals fed from the silt-laden waters of the Tigris and Euphrates rivers. The percentage of salt in the irrigation waters was harmless when the water was applied directly to the surface. However, the continuous irrigation of fields raised the level of the ground water. Through capillary action the accumulated salts were brought to the surface, rendering millions of acres unsuitable for growing wheat. Barley, more salt-resistant than wheat, was planted in zones that suffered less damage. But Sumeria became progressively weakened economically, leading to the collapse of the last Sumerian Empire, the Third Dynasty of Ur. By 1700 B.C. wheat had completely disappeared in the south. Thereafter, the center of population shifted to the north as Babylon began to emerge under Hammurabi. And even that great "giver of abundant riches" could not afford to keep his people fed on pork.

With the rise of Islam, the ancient Israelite pig taboo was incorporated directly into still another set of supernaturally sanctioned dietary laws. The pig was singled out for special opprobrium in the Koran, and today Moslems are as opposed as Orthodox Jews are to eating pork. Incidentally, the Koran contains an important bit of evidence in support of the ecological cost/benefit interpretation of animal taboos. The prophet Mohammed retained the Israelite taboo on the pig, but he explicitly released his followers from the taboo on eating camel flesh. The Arabian pastoralists, Mohammed's earliest supporters, were camel nomads who inhabited true desert oases and who were often obliged to make long journeys across barren wastes where the camel was the only domesticated creature that could survive. While the camel was too valuable to be eaten regularly, it was also too valuable not to be eaten at all. Under emergency conditions associated with military campaigns and long-distance caravan trade, its flesh often meant the difference between life and death.

At this juncture I would like to clarify one point which I am eager not to see misrepresented. By tracing the origin of religious ideas to the cost/benefits of ecological processes, I do not mean to deny that religious ideas themselves may in turn exert an influence on customs and thoughts. The authors of Leviticus and the Koran were priests and prophets interested in developing a coherent set of religious principles. Once these principles were formulated, they became part of Jewish and Islamic culture down through the ages and undoubtedly influenced the behavior of Jews and Moslems who lived far from their middle Eastern homelands. Food taboos and culinary specialties can be perpetuated as boundary markers between ethnic and national minorities and as symbols of group identity independently of any active ecological selection for or against their existence. But I don't think such beliefs and practices would long endure if they resulted in the sharp elevation of subsistence costs. To paraphrase Sherborne Cook's remarks about Aztec rituals, no purely religious urge can run counter to fundamental ecological and economic resistance for a long period of time. I doubt that modern-day observant Jews or Moslems suffer protein deficits as a result of spurning pork. Were this the case, I would expect them to begin to change their beliefs—if not at once, then in a generation or so. (Millions of Moslems do suffer from acute protein deficits, but no one has ever suggested a causal link between the taboo on pork and underdevelopment and poverty in Egypt or Pakistan.) I do not claim that the analysis of ecological costs and benefits can lead to the explanation of every belief and practice of every culture that has ever existed. Many alternative beliefs and alternative courses of action have no clear-cut advantages or disadvantages with respect to raising or lowering standards of living. Moreover, I admit that there is always some feedback between the conditions that determine ecological and economic costs and benefits and religious beliefs and practices. But I insist that on the evidence of prehistory and history the force they have hitherto exerted on each other has not been equal. Religions have generally changed to conform to the requirements of reducing costs and maximizing benefits in the struggle to keep living standards from falling; cases in which production systems have changed to conform to the requirements of changed religious systems regardless of cost/benefit considerations either do not exist or are extremely rare. The link between the depletion of animal proteins on the one hand, and the practice of human sacrifice and cannibalism, the evolution of ecclesiastical redistributive feasting, and the tabooing of the flesh of certain animals on the other, demonstrates the unmistakable causal priority of material costs and benefits over spiritual beliefs—not necessarily for all time, but almost certainly for the cases in question.

One more link in this chain remains to be examined: namely, how it happened that in India the neolithic promise of meat for all culminated in the Hindu prescription of meat for none.

12
The Origin of the Sacred Cow

In India today only untouchables freely partake of red meat. Observant high-caste Hindus limit their diets to vegetable foods and dairy products. To eat meat is always undesirable, but the worst of all is to eat beef. High-caste Hindus feel about eating beef as an American feels about eating the family poodle. And yet there was a time when meat, especially beef, appealed to the inhabitants of India as much as steak and hamburgers now appeal to the inhabitants of North America.

Village life in India during the neolithic period was based on the production of domestic animals and grain crops. Much like Middle Eastern villagers, the earliest Indians raised cattle, sheep, and goats in combination with wheat, millet, and barley. At about 2500 B.C., when the first large settlements began to appear along the Indus River and its tributaries, vegetarianism was still a long way off. Among the ruins of the earliest cities—Harappa and Mohenjo-Daro—half-burned bones of cattle, sheep, and goats are mixed in with the kitchen debris. In the same cities, archaeologists have also found bones of pigs, water buffalo, hens, elephants, and camels.

The cities of Harappa and Mohenjo-Daro, notable for their fired-brick buildings and their extensive baths and gardens, seem to have been abandoned sometime after 2000 B.C., partly as a result of ecological disasters involving changes in the course of the river channels upon which they depended for irrigation. In their weakened condition they became vulnerable to "barbarian tribes" moving into India from Persia and Afghanistan. These invaders, known as Aryans, were loosely federated, semimigratory pastoralist-farmers who first settled in the Punjab and later fanned out into the Ganges Valley. They were late bronze-age peoples who spoke a language called Vedic, the parent tongue of Sanskrit, and whose way of life strongly resembled that of the pre-Homeric Greeks, Teutons, and Celts beyond the pale of the centers of state formation in Europe and Southwest Asia. As Harappa and Mohenjo-Daro declined, the invaders took over the best lands, cleared the forests, built permanent villages, and founded a series of petty kingdoms in which they set themselves up as rulers over the region's indigenous inhabitants.

Our information about what the Aryans ate comes largely from the holy scriptures written in Vedic and Sanskrit during the second half of the first millennium B.C. This literature shows that during the early Vedic period—up to 1000 B.C.—they dined on animal flesh, including beef, frequently and with considerable gusto. Archaeological investigations at Hastinapur also strongly suggest that cattle, buffalo, and sheep were among the animals eaten by these earliest settlers of the Gangetic plain.

Om Prakash, in his authoritative study *Food and Drinks in Ancient India*, sums up the situation in the early Vedic period as follows:

> Fire is called the eater of ox and barren cows. The ritual offering of flesh implied that the priests would eat it. A goat is also offered to fire to be carried to forefathers. A barren cow was also killed at the time of marriage obviously for food. . . . A slaughter

house is also mentioned. The flesh of horses, rams, barren cows, and buffaloes was cooked. Probably flesh of birds was also eaten.

In the later Vedic period,

> it was customary to kill a big ox or a big goat to feed a distinguished guest. Sometimes a cow that miscarried or a sterile cow was also killed. *Atithigva* also implies that cows were slain for guests. Many animals—cows, sheep, goats, and horses continue to be killed at sacrifices and the flesh of those sacrificial animals was eaten by the participants.

The later Vedic and early Hindu texts contain many inconsistencies concerning the consumption of beef. Along with numerous descriptions of cattle being used for sacrifice are passages indicating that cows must never be slaughtered and that beef eating should be abandoned altogether. Some authorities—A. N. Bose, for example—claim that these inconsistencies can best be explained by the hypothesis that orthodox Hindu scholars interpolated the anti-beef-eating, anti-cow-slaughtering passages at a later date. Bose feels that "beef was the commonest flesh consumed" throughout most of the first millennium B.C. Perhaps a less controversial solution to the contradictions in the sacred texts is that they reflect gradual changes of attitudes over an extended period during which more and more people came to regard the eating of domesticated animals—especially cows and oxen—as an abomination.

What emerges with crystal clarity is that the late Vedic–early Hindu Ganges Valley kingdoms had a priestly caste analogous to the Levites among the ancient Israelites and the Druids among the Celts. Its members were called Brahmans. The duties of the Brahmans are described in the Sanskrit works known as

Brahmanas and *sutras*. There is no doubt that early Brahman ritual life, like that of the Druids and Levites (and the earliest religious specialists of every chiefdom and statelet between Spain and Japan), centered on animal sacrifice. Like their counterparts all over the Old World, the early Brahmans enjoyed a monopoly over the performance of those rituals without which animal flesh could not be eaten. Brahmans, according to the *sutras*, were the only people who could sacrifice animals.

The *sutras* indicate that animals should not be killed except as offerings to the gods and in extending "hospitality to guests" and that "making gifts and receiving gifts" were the special duties of Brahmans. These prescriptions precisely duplicate the regulatory provisions for the consumption of meat characteristic of societies in which feasting and animal sacrifice are one and the same activity. The "guests" honored by early Vedic hospitality were not a handful of friends dropping by for dinner but whole villages and districts. What the *sutras* are telling us, in other words, is that the Brahmans were originally a caste of priests who presided over the ritual aspects of redistributive feasts sponsored by "open-handed" Aryan chiefs and war lords.

After 600 B.C. the Brahmans and their secular overlords found it increasingly difficult to satisfy the popular demand for animal flesh. Like priests and rulers in the Middle East and elsewhere, they were unable to maintain high rates of animal slaughter and bountiful redistributions without the wasteful eating of animals needed to plow and manure the fields. As a result, meat eating became the privilege of a select group comprised of Brahmans and other high-caste Aryans, while the common peasants, lacking the power to tax or confiscate other people's animals, had no choice but to preserve their own domestic stock for traction, milk, and dung production. Thus the Brahmans gradually came to be part of a meat-eating elite whose monopoly over the privilege of slaughtering animals for redistributive feasts had been transformed into a monopoly over the privilege of eating them. Long after ordinary people in northern India had become functional vegetarians, the Hindu upper castes—later the most ardent advocates of meatless diets—continued to dine lustily on beef and other kinds of meat.

I base my argument for this widening gulf between a pampered meat-eating aristocracy and an impoverished meatless peasantry partly on the fact that toward the middle of the first millennium B.C. a number of new religions began to challenge the legitmacy of the Brahman caste and its sacrificial rituals. Of these reformist religions, the best-known are Buddhism and Jainism. Founded in the sixth century B.C. by charismatic holy men, both Buddhism and Jainism outlawed caste distinctions, abolished hereditary priesthoods, made poverty a precondition of spirituality, and advocated communion with the spiritual essence of the universe through contemplation rather than through the sacrifice of animals. In their condemnation of violence, war, and cruelty, and their compassion for human suffering, both of these movements anticipated key elements of Christianity.

For the Buddhists, all life was sacred, although it could exist in higher and lower forms. For the Jains, not only was all life sacred but it shared a common soul: there were no higher and lower forms. In either case, priests who sacrificed animals were no better than murderers. Buddhists tolerated the eating of animal flesh, provided the eater had not participated in the killing. The Jains, however, condemning the killing of all animals, insisted on a pure vegetarian diet. The members of some Jainist sects even deemed it necessary to employ sweepers to clear the path in front of them in order to avoid the calamity of accidentally extinguishing the life of a single ant.

As I suggested earlier, the end of animal sacrifice coincided with the growth of universalistic, spiritualized religions. With the erstwhile "great providers" increasingly unable to validate their majesty through popular displays of open-handed generosity, people were encouraged to look for "redistributions" in an afterlife or in some new phase of being. I have also pointed out that the image of the ruler as great protector of the weak against the strong arose as a matter of practical statecraft during periods of imperial expansion. Buddhism, like Christianity, was ideally suited, therefore, for adoption as an imperial religion. It dematerialized the obligations of the emperor at the same time that it obligated the aristocracy to show compassion to the poor. This explains, I think, why Buddhism became an official religion under Asoka, one of the most powerful emperors in the history of India. Asoka, grandson of the founder of the north Indian Maurya Dynasty, converted to Buddhism in 257 B.C. He and his descendants forthwith set about creating the first and still the largest ever of Indian empires—a shaky realm stretching briefly from Afghanistan to Ceylon. Asoka was thus possibly the first emperor in history to set out to conquer the world in the name of a religion of universal peace.

Meanwhile, Hinduism was profoundly affected by the new religions and began to adopt some of the reforms which had made its Buddhist rival politically successful. Eventually, the widespread opposition to animal sacrifice came to be represented within Hinduism by the doctrine of *ahimsa*—nonviolence based on the sacredness of life. But this change did not come all at once nor did it proceed in a single direction. After the collapse in 184 B.C. of the Maurya Dynasty, Brahmanism revived and meat eating among the elite flourished once more. As late as A.D. 350, according to Prakash, "flesh of various animals" was served to Brahmans at Sraddhas, the redistributive ceremonies commemorating the dead. "The Kurma Purana goes to the extent of saying that one who does not take flesh in a Sraddha is born again and again as an animal."

No one is able to say precisely when cows and oxen became distinct objects of veneration among Brahmans and other high-caste Hindus. It is impossible to assign precise dates to changes in Hindu ritual because Hinduism is not a single organized religion but an immense number of loosely affiliated congregations centering on independent temples, shrines, deities, and castes, each with its own doctrinal and ritual specialties. One authority, S. K. Maitz, claims that the cow had already become the most sacred of animals by A.D. 350, but his evidence is a single canto in an epic poem which describes a certain king and his queen as "worshipping cows with sandal paste and garlands." There is also the inscription of King Chandragupta II, dated to A.D. 465, which equates the killing of a cow with the killing of a Brahman. But the modern Hindu point of view may be intruding. The Gupta emperors issued royal decrees aimed at preventing the consumption of various animals by commoners. Hindu royalty fussed over horses and elephants as well as cows. They garlanded their animals, bathed them, provided them with carpeted stalls, and set them free to roam in protected reserves. It may have been only after A.D. 700 and the Islamic conquest of India that the sacred cow complex acquired its familiar modern form. The followers of Islam had no compunctions about eating beef. Hence under the Moguls, the Islamic emperors of India, cow protection may have become a political symbol of Hindu resistance against beef-eating Moslem invaders. At any rate, the Brahmans—for centuries the sacrificers and consumers of animal flesh—gradually come to regard it as their sacred duty to prevent the slaughtering or eating of any domestic animals, especially cows and oxen.

To the best of my knowledge, no one has previously been able to offer a rational explanation as to why India, unlike the Middle East or China, became the center of a religion that forbade the consumption of beef and venerated the cow as the symbol of life. Let us see if the general principles concerning the establishment of animal taboos that I suggested in the previous chapter are applicable. Ancient Indian beliefs and practices were initially similar to beliefs and practices common to most of Europe, Asia, and North Africa. As predicted, the general transformation from redistributive animal sacrifice to the taboo on the consumption of previously valuable and abundant species followed upon the intensification of agriculture, depletion of resources, and growth of population density. But these generalities do not explain the particular emphasis on cattle and vegetarianism in India or the particular religious complexes associated with animals in other regions.

The place to start, I think, is in the Ganges Valley, where the rate of population growth appears to have been much greater than in the Middle East—or, indeed, than anywhere else in the ancient world. During the Vedic period population was scanty and spread out in small villages. As late as 1000 B.C. population density was low enough to permit each family to own many animals (the Vedic texts mention twenty-four oxen harnessed to a single plow), and as in pre-Roman Europe cattle were regarded as the principal form of wealth. Less than 700 years later the Ganges had probably become the most populous region in the world. Estimates by Kingsley Davis and others give India a population of between 50 and 100 million in 300 B.C. At least half of that total must have been living in the Ganges Valley.

We know that during the early Vedic period the Gangetic plain was still covered with virgin forests. Scarcely a tree remained by 300 B.C. While irrigation provided a secure base for many farm families, millions of peasants received either insufficient flows of water or none at all. Because of fluctuations in monsoon rains, it was always risky to depend on rainfall alone. Deforestation undoubtedly increased the risk of drought. It also increased the severity of the floods which the Holy River Ganges unleashed when the monsoons dumped too much rain all at once onto the Himalayan foothills. Even today droughts that endure in India for two or three consecutive seasons endanger the lives of millions of people who depend on rainfall to water their crops. From the *Mahabharata*, an epic poem composed sometime between 300 B.C. and A.D. 300, we know of one drought that lasted twelve years. The poem tells how lakes, wells, and springs dried up, and how agriculture and cattle rearing had to be abandoned. Markets and shops were left empty. The sacrifice of animals came to a halt, and the very stakes for tying up the animals disappeared. There were no festivals. Everywhere heaps of bone could be seen and cries of creatures could be heard. People left the cities. Hamlets were abandoned and set on fire. People fled from one another. They feared each other. Places of worship were deserted. Old people were driven from their houses. Cattle, goats, sheep, and buffalo turned into ferocious beasts that attacked one another. Even the Brahmans died without protection. Herbs and plants withered. The earth looked like a crematorium and "in that dreadful age when righteousness was at an end, men began to eat one another."

As population density grew, farms became increasingly smaller and only the most essential domesticated species could be allowed to share the land. Cattle were the one species that could not be eliminated. They were the animals that drew the plows upon which the entire cycle of rainfall agriculture depended. At least two oxen had to be kept per family, plus one cow with which to breed replacements when the oxen wore out. Cattle thus became the central focus of the religious taboo on meat eating. As the sole remaining farm animals, they were potentially the only remaining source of meat. To slaughter them for meat, however, constituted a threat to the whole mode of food production. And so beef was tabooed for the same reason that pork was tabooed in the Middle East: to remove temptation.

The respective interdictions against beef and pork, however, reflect the different ecological roles of the two species. The pig was abominated; the cow was deified. Why this should have been the case seems obvious from what I've said about the importance of cattle in the agricultural cycle. When pork became too costly to be raised for meat, the whole animal was rendered useless—worse than useless—because it had only been good as something to eat. But when cattle became too costly to be raised for meat, their value as a source of traction did not diminish. Hence they had to be protected rather than abominated, and the best way to protect them was not only to forbid the eating of their flesh but to forbid their slaughter. The ancient Israelites had the problem of preventing the diversion of grains to the production of pork. The solution was to stop raising pigs. But the ancient Hindus could not stop raising cattle since they depended on oxen to plow the land. Their main problem was not how to refrain from raising a certain species but how to refrain from eating it when they got hungry.

The conversion of beef into forbidden flesh originated in the practical life of individual farmers. It was the product neither of a superhuman culture hero nor of a collective social mind brooding over the cost/benefits of alternative resource management policies. Culture heroes express the preformed sentiments of their age and collective minds don't exist. The tabooing of beef was the cumulative result of the individual decisions of millions and millions of individual farmers, some of whom were better able than others to resist the temptation of slaughtering their livestock because they strongly believed that the life of a cow or an ox was a holy thing. Those who held such beliefs were much more likely to hold onto their farms, and to pass them on to their children, than those who believed differently. Like so many other adaptive responses in culture and nature, the "bottom line" of the religious proscriptions on the use of animal flesh in India cannot be read from short-term cost/benefits. Rather, it is the long term that counted most—performance during abnormal rather than normal agricultural cycles. Under the periodic duress of droughts caused by failures of the monsoon rains, the individual farmer's love of cattle translated directly into love of human life, not by symbol but by practice. Cattle had to be treated like human beings because human beings who ate their cattle were one step away from eating each other. To this day, monsoon farmers who yield to temptation and slaughter their cattle seal their doom. They can never plow again even when the rains fall. They must sell their farms and migrate to the cities. Only those who would starve rather than eat an ox or cow can survive a season of scanty rains. This human forbearance is matched by the fantastic endurance and recuperative powers of the Indian zebu breeds. Like camels, Indian cattle store energy in their humps, survive for weeks without food or water, and spring back to life when favored with the slightest nourishment. Long after other breeds have expired from disease, hunger, and thirst, zebus continue to pull plows, bear calves, and give milk. Unlike European cattle breeds, zebus were selected not for their strength, beefiness, or copious flow of milk, but largely for their ability to survive severe dry seasons and droughts.

And this brings us to the question why the cow rather than the ox has come to be the most venerated animal. The flesh of either sex is equally taboo, but in ritual and art Hinduism emphasizes the sacredness of cows far more than that of male cattle. Yet practice belies theory. Oxen outnumber cows two to one in the Gangetic plain —a sex ratio which can be accounted for only by the existence of systematic selection against female calves through malign neglect and indirect "bovicide" (exactly paralleling the sub rosa treatment of female human infants). This lopsided ratio reflects the greater value of oxen over cows as a source of traction for plowing the fields. Despite all the fuss made over the holy mother cow, under normal circumstances oxen are, in fact, treated much better. They are kept in stalls, fed by hand, and given grain and oil cake supplements to make them strong and healthy. Cows, on the other hand, are treated in everyday rural life the way American Indians treated their dogs or the way European farmers used to treat their pigs. They are the village scavengers. They are not kept in stalls and fed on fodder crops. Instead, they are let loose to roam around the village to pick up whatever scraps of garbage they can find. Having licked the village clean, they are permitted to wander off in search of a few blades of grass that somehow survived their last tour of a roadside ditch or that have sprouted in the spaces between the railroad ties. Because cows are treated as scavengers, they are likely to show up in such inconvenient places as the gutters of busy thoroughfares and the edges of airport runways, giving rise to the foolish charge that India has been overrun by millions of "useless" cattle.

If the cow more than the ox is the symbol of *ahimsa*, the sacredness of life, perhaps it is because the cow more than the ox is endangered by the sentiment that it is "useless." During times of hunger the cow stands more in need of ritual protection than the draft oxen. Yet from the point of view of the resumption and continuity of the agricultural cycle the cow is actually more valuable than the male draft animal. Although it is not as strong as an ox, it can in emergencies pull the plow as well as someday produce replacements for animals that succumb to thirst and hunger. Under duress, therefore, the cow must be treated as well as—if not better than—the ox, and that is probably why it is the principal object of ritual veneration. Mohandes Gandhi knew what he was talking about when he said Hindus worshiped the cow not only because "she gave milk, but because she made agriculture possible."

Why beef came to be forbidden flesh in India cannot fully be explained unless one can also account for its not becoming taboo in the other early centers of state formation. One possibility is that Indian farmers were more dependent on irregular monsoon rainfall than were farmers in other regions. This may have made it more urgent to protect cows and oxen during times of hunger. In Egypt and Mesopotamia, where cattle were venerated and their sacrifice prohibited in late dynastic times, beef continued to be eaten. But both Egypt and Mesopotamia, unlike India, were totally dependent on irrigation agriculture and never had large numbers of farmers who relied on drought-resistant cattle to get through the dry season.

China presents a more difficult problem. Although they also need ox-drawn plows, the Chinese never developed a cow-love complex. On the contrary, female cattle in China have long been held in rather low esteem. This is reflected in Chinese cooking. Whereas in northern India the traditional cuisine relies heavily on milk or milk products and the basic cooking fat is clarified butter, or ghee, Chinese recipes never call for milk, cream, or cheese and the basic cooking fat is lard or vegetable oil. Most adult Chinese have a strong dislike for milk (although ice cream has gained increasing popularity in recent years). Why are the Indians milk-lovers and the Chinese milk-haters?

One explanation for the Chinese aversion to milk is that they are physiologically "allergic" to it. Adult Chinese who drink quantities of milk generally get severe cramps and diarrhea. The cause is not really an allergy but a hereditary deficiency in the ability of the intestines to manufacture the enzyme lactase. This enzyme must be present if the body is to digest lactose, the predominant sugar found in milk. Between 70 and 100 percent of Chinese adults have a lactose deficiency. The trouble with this explanation is that many Indians —between 24 and 100 percent, depending on the region —also have a lactase deficiency. And so do most human populations, Europeans and their American descendants being the exception. Moreover, all the unpleasant consequences of lactase deficiency can easily be avoided if milk is drunk in small quantities or if it is consumed in any one of a number of soured or fermented forms such as yogurt or cheese, in which the lactose is broken down into less complex sugars. In other words, lactase deficiency is only a barrier to the drinking of large quantities of milk American-style. It can't explain the aversion to butter, sour cream, cheese, and yogurt—all of which are conspicuously absent from Chinese cuisine.

What stands out in the comparison of Chinese and Indian ecosystems is the virtual absence in China of the cow as a farm animal. John Lasson Buck's authoritative survey of pre-Communist Chinese agriculture showed that in northern China there were on the average .05 oxen but less than .005 cows per farm. This indicates a cattle sex ratio of more than 1,000 males to 100 females, as compared with a ratio of between 210:100 and 150:100 in the Central Gangetic Plain and 130:100 for all of India. This difference reflects the fact that the cow had virtually no role in the northern Chinese domestic economy other than to breed oxen, which explains at least one aspect of the Chinese distaste for milk: there were no cows around the typical northern Chinese village. No cows, no milk, no chance to acquire a taste for milk products.

The livestock picture in China was always characterized by considerable regional variation in the use of large draft and pack animals. In the north central and northeastern provinces the sum of all the horses, donkeys, and mules was almost as great as the number of cattle. This contrasts with the states of Uttar Pradesh, Bihar, and West Bengal in the Ganges Valley, where horses, donkeys, and mules occur in insignificant numbers.

The greatest difference between the Chinese and Indian livestock situations, however, lies in the vast number of pigs in China and the virtual absence of pigs from most of the Gangetic Plain. Buck estimated that on the average each farm in northern China had .52 pigs. A member of a recent delegation to China, G. F. Sprague of the Department of Agronomy of the University of Illinois, estimates that China produced between 250 to 260 million swine in 1972. This is more than four times the amount produced in the United States, "a nation noted for extensive swine production." If the Chinese produced these animals the way they are produced in the United States, Sprague writes, they "would represent a severe drain on the available food supply." But there is little resemblance between the production practices in the two countries. Swine production in the United States depends upon providing the animals with corn, soya meal, vitamin and mineral supplements, and antibiotics. In China swine are raised primarily as a household enterprise and, like cows in India, are "fed on waste materials not suitable for human food; vegetable refuse, ground and fermented rice hulls, sweet potato and soya bean vines, water hyacinths and so forth." Just as Indian cows are valued for their manure, so Chinese swine are valued "almost as much for manure as for their meat." In other words, the pig is and was the main village scavenger for the Chinese. It provided them with crucial supplements of fats and proteins and much-needed fertilizer just as the Indians derived essentials from their village scavenger, the cow. With one big difference: since the pig cannot be killed, it has to be eaten if it is to serve as a source of dietary fats and proteins. This means that as long as swine filled the niche of village scavenger, the Chinese would never accept a religion such as Islam, which specifically prohibits the consumption of pork.

But why did the Chinese adopt the pig as the village scavenger while the Indians adopted the cow? Several factors were probably involved. First of all, the Gangetic Plain is less desirable as a habitat in which to rear pigs than is the Yellow River Basin. The fierce spring heat and the recurrent droughts to which the zebu cattle breeds have adapted render the moisture-loving pig a risky investment. In Uttar Pradesh, India's largest food-producing state, 88 percent of the rainfall occurs in four months, while average daily high temperatures in May and June hover well over 100 degrees Fahrenheit. Northern China, on the other hand, has cool springs, moderate summers, and no marked dry season.

Another important factor is the comparative availability of grazing lands on which traction animals can be reared. China, unlike India, has a large area that is suitable for pasturing traction animals and that cannot be used for growing food crops. In China only 11 percent of the total land area is under cultivation, while in India almost 50 percent of the total area is cropland. According to Buck, the northern spring wheat region of China contains "considerable public grazing land where low rainfall and broken topography make cultivation difficult." By contrast, less than 2 percent of the total cropland area of the Central Gangetic Plain is permanent pasture or grazing land. Thus in India the breeding of the basic traction animal had to take place in zones that were already tightly packed with human beings—zones lacking nonarable lands suitable for forage. The traction animal, therefore, had to be fed primarily on waste products such as those available to a village scavenger. In other words, the traction animal and the scavenger had to be one and the same species. And it had to be cattle, because neither horses, donkeys, nor mules could perform satisfactorily in the blistering heat and aridity of the monsoon climate, while water buffalo were useless to farmers who lacked irrigation.

Perhaps the best way to view the treatment of animals in India as opposed to China is in terms of different phases of a single great convergent process of intensification. Neither China nor India could afford large-scale exploitation of animals primarily for flesh or dairy products because of the immense human population densities and the severe caloric losses entailed in animal husbandry carried out on arable lands. In pre-Communist China the rural population lived on a diet that derived 97.7 percent of its calorie ration from farm plant foods and only 2.3 percent from animal products —mainly pork. The species used primarily as draft animals were seldom eaten in rural China, any more than they were eaten in India. Why, then, wasn't beef prohibited by a religious taboo?

In fact, there was such a taboo in some regions. No less an authority than Mao Tse-tung made the following observations when he was in Hunan:

> Draught-oxen are a treasure to the peasants. As it is practically a religious tenet that "Those who slaughter cattle in this life will themselves become cattle in the next," draught oxen must never be killed. Before coming to power, the peasants had no way of stopping the slaughter of cattle except the religious taboo.

And T. H. Shen writes:

> The butchering of cattle for beef is against Chinese tradition. It is only near the large cities that any cattle are butchered to furnish meat, and then it is done when they are no longer needed on the farms.

While both China and India have suffered the effects of millennia of intensification, the process seems to have been carried to the greater extreme in India. Chinese agriculture is more efficient than Indian agriculture primarily because of the greater area cultivated under irrigation—40 percent of Chinese croplands versus 23 percent of Indian croplands. Average yields per acre of rice are therefore twice as high in China as in India. Given the viability of the pig, donkey, mule, and horse in China, and the topographical and climatic factors of production, intensification did not reach levels necessitating a total ban on the slaughter of animals for meat. Instead of milking their traction animals, the Chinese slaughtered their pigs. They settled for a little less animal protein in the form of meat than they could have gotten in the form of milk—had they used the cow rather than the pig in the scavenger niche.

Hindus and Westerners alike see in the meat-eating taboos of India a triumph of morals over appetite. This is a dangerous misrepresentation of cultural processes. Hindu vegetarianism was a victory not of spirit over matter but of reproductive over productive forces. The very same material process that promoted the spread of empty-handed religions in the West, the end of animal sacrifice and redistributive feasts, and the interdiction of the flesh of such domestic species as the pig, horse, and donkey led India inexorably in the direction of religions that condemned the eating of all animal flesh. This did not happen because the spirituality of India surpassed the spirituality of other regions; rather, in India the intensification of production, the depletion of natural resources, and the rise in the density of population were pushed further beyond the limits of growth than anywhere else in the preindustrial world except for the Valley of Mexico.

[illegible] which China and India have enjoyed the [illegible] [illegible] of [illegible] the process [illegible] [illegible] [illegible] greater [illegible] [illegible] [illegible] [illegible] [illegible] [illegible] [illegible] [illegible] [illegible] greater [illegible] with [illegible] [illegible] [illegible] of [illegible] [illegible] [illegible] [illegible] [illegible] [illegible] [illegible] [illegible] [illegible] [illegible] [illegible] are the [illegible] [illegible] [illegible] [illegible] [illegible] the [illegible] of the [illegible] [illegible] [illegible] and [illegible] in [illegible] and [illegible] [illegible] [illegible] [illegible] of [illegible] [illegible] [illegible] [illegible] [illegible] [illegible] [illegible] [illegible] [illegible] [illegible] [illegible] [illegible] [illegible] [illegible] of [illegible] their [illegible] [illegible] [illegible] [illegible] [illegible] [illegible] [illegible] [illegible] [illegible] [illegible] [illegible] the [illegible] of [illegible] [illegible] they [illegible] [illegible] [illegible] [illegible] [illegible] [illegible] [illegible] [illegible] the [illegible] [illegible] [illegible] in the [illegible] [illegible]

[illegible] [illegible] [illegible] [illegible] [illegible] [illegible] [illegible] [illegible] [illegible] [illegible] [illegible] [illegible] [illegible] [illegible] [illegible] of [illegible] [illegible] [illegible] [illegible] [illegible] [illegible] [illegible] [illegible] of [illegible] [illegible] [illegible] of [illegible] [illegible] [illegible] The very same [illegible] [illegible] [illegible] [illegible] [illegible] [illegible] [illegible] [illegible] the [illegible] of animal sacrifice and [illegible] [illegible] [illegible] of the [illegible] [illegible] of the [illegible] [illegible] [illegible] [illegible] [illegible] [illegible] [illegible] [illegible] [illegible] of [illegible] that [illegible] the [illegible] of [illegible] animal [illegible] [illegible] [illegible] because [illegible] [illegible] [illegible] [illegible] [illegible] [illegible] [illegible] [illegible] [illegible] [illegible] [illegible] [illegible] [illegible] [illegible] [illegible] natural resources, and [illegible] [illegible] [illegible] [illegible] population were [illegible] [illegible] beyond the limits of [illegible] [illegible] [illegible] [illegible] [illegible] [illegible] the [illegible] [illegible].

13
The Hydraulic Trap

In the 4,000 years between the appearance of the first states and the beginning of the Christian era, world population rose from about 87 million to 225 million. Almost four-fifths of the new total lived under the dominion of the Roman, Chinese Han, and Indian Gupta empires. This world total conceals the fact that the density of population in the core area did not continue to rise without check during that 4,000-year period. The demographic history of the early empires does not support the crude Malthusian notion that human population growth is an ever-present historical trend. Stationary populations were as much the rule in ancient empires as they were during the paleolithic era. There was a limit to how many people and animals could be packed into the great river valleys of Egypt, Mesopotamia, India, and China. After the stage of functional vegetarianism had been reached, population density remained constant or even declined. Of course, outside the core areas population continued to increase as larger empires and more secondary states came into existence. But one by one the core regions seem to have reached their ecological limit of growth.

According to Kingsley Davis, the population of India as a whole had leveled off by 300 B.C. and did not begin to expand until the eighteenth century. Karl Butzer estimates that in Egypt the population of the Nile

Valley quadrupled between 4000 B.C. and 2500 B.C., the apex of the period in Egyptian history known as the Old Kingdom. Then it remained virtually stationary for over a thousand years. In 1250 B.C. it rose to a new peak, which was only about 1.6 times the mark set in the Old Kingdom, and just before the beginning of the Greco-Roman period it fell back once more to the Old Kingdom level. Under Roman rule it peaked again at a point slightly more than twice that of the Old Kingdom, but by the end of the Roman Empire in 500 B.C. it had fallen below the figure for 3,000 years earlier. Our best information comes from China, where census data covering a span of over 2,000 years can be consulted. Hans Bielenstein's authoritative study shows that for the period A.D. 2 to A.D. 742 China's overall population remained close to 50 million, with a maximum of 58 million and a minimum of 48 million. More significantly, there were marked declines in the original core areas of the Han Dynasty. The Great Plain of the Yellow River, for example, had a population of 35 million in A.D. 2. This fell to 25 million in A.D. 140, rose to 31 million in 609 and fell again to 23 million in 742. Discounting increments brought about by the conquests of new territories, China's rate of population growth remained close to zero for the better part of two millennia. (After 1450 the introduction of new varieties of rice, sweet potatoes, and American Indian maize made it possible for Chinese agricultural methods to support much denser populations than in earlier periods.)

Century after century the standard of living in China, northern India, Mesopotamia, and Egypt hovered slightly above or below what might be called the threshold of pauperization. When population density in a particular region climbed too high, standards of living dipped below the threshold. This led to wars, famines, and population decline. With lower densities, the standard of living would rise more to a point slightly above the long-term average.

Western observers have always been astonished by the static or "stationary" nature of these ancient dynastic systems. Pharaohs and emperors came and went decade after decade; dynasties rose and fell; the life of the coolies, ryots, and fellahin, however, went on as always, just a notch above barest subsistence. The ancient empires were warrens full of illiterate peasants toiling from morning to night only to earn protein-deficient vegetarian diets. They were little better off than their oxen and were no less subject to the commands of superior beings who knew how to keep records and who alone had the right to manufacture and use weapons of war and coercion. The fact that societies providing such meager rewards endured thousands of years—longer than any other system of statehood in the history of the world—stands as a grim reminder that there is nothing inherent in human affairs to ensure material and moral progress.

Each ancient empire developed its own integrated pattern of social life. From cookery to art styles, each was a universe unto itself. And yet for all their differences, ancient China, India, Mesopotamia, and Egypt possessed fundamentally similar systems of political economy. Each had a highly centralized class of bureaucrats and hereditary despotic overlords who claimed heavenly mandates or were said to be gods in themselves. Excellent networks of government-maintained roadways, rivers, and canals linked every hamlet and village to provincial and national administrative centers. Each village had at least one important person who served as a link between the village and the central administration. Political lines of force ran in one direction only: from top to bottom. While peasants might sometimes own their land, as in China, the bureaucracy tended to regard private property as a gift of the state. Production priorities were set by state tax policies and by regular call-ups of village men and women for work on state-sponsored construction projects. The "state was stronger than society." Its right to collect taxes, confiscate materials, and conscript labor was virtually unlimited. It carried out systematic censuses village by village to determine the available labor power and the tax revenue base. It deployed antlike armies of workers wheresoever the lords of the realm decreed and undertook the construction of tombs, pyramids, defense works, and palaces whose dimensions are stupendous even by modern industrial standards. In Egypt seasonal employment of as many as 100,000 able-bodied men was needed to carry out the monumental projects of the Old Kingdom, a labor force of 84,000 men employed eighty days a year worked for twenty years to construct the Great Pyramid of Cheops. In China construction on the Great Wall required a million workers at a time; another million toiled on the Grand Canal; over two million each month were put to work in the construction of the Sui Dynasty's Eastern capital and imperial palace during the reign of Emperor Yang (A.D. 604–617).

Despite the development of philosophies and religions advocating justice and mercy, the rulers of these vast realms frequently had to rely on intimidation, force, and naked terror to maintain law and order. Total submissiveness was demanded of underlings, the supreme symbol of which was the obligation to prostrate oneself and grovel in the presence of the mighty. In China a commoner had to kowtow—fall forward, strike the ground with his head, and kiss the dust. In Hindu Indian commoners embraced the sovereign's feet. In Pharaonic Egypt underlings crawled on their bellies. In all of these ancient empires there were ruthless systems for routing out and punishing disobedient persons. Spies kept the rulers informed about potential troublemakers. Punishments ranged from beatings to death by torture. In Egypt the tax collectors beat recalcitrant peasants and threw them, bound hand and foot, into the irrigation ditches; the foremen on all state projects carried clubs and whips. In ancient India the magistrates condemned disobedient subjects to eighteen different kinds of torture, including beatings on the soles of the feet, suspension upside down, and burning of finger joints: for mild offenses, they ordered a fresh variety eighteen days in a row; for severe offenses, they sentenced the condemned to receive all eighteen on the same day. In China the emperor punished those who expressed incautious opinions by having them castrated in a darkened cell.

These ancient empires shared one other feature: each was what the great institutional historian Karl Wittfogel has called a "hydraulic society." Each developed amid arid or semiarid plains and valleys fed by great rivers. Through dams, canals, flood control, and drainage projects, officials diverted water from these rivers and delivered it to the peasants' fields. Water constituted the most important factor in production. When it was applied in regular and copious amounts, high yields per acre and per calorie of effort resulted.

Among modern scholars, Wittfogel has done the most to clarify the relationship between hydraulic production and the emergence of unchanging agro-managerial despotisms. My own view of that relationship borrows heavily from Wittfogel's but does not correspond precisely with his formulation. I hold that preindustrial hydraulic agriculture recurrently led to the evolution of extremely despotic agro-managerial bureaucracies because the expansion and intensification of hydraulic agriculture—itself a consequence of reproductive pressures—was uniquely dependent on massive construction projects which, in the absence of machines, could only be carried out by antlike armies of workers. The larger the river, the greater the food production potential of the region through which it flowed. But the larger the river, the greater the problems in making use of its potential. On the one hand, the state undertook the construction of extensive networks of diversionary and feeder canals, ditches, and sluice gates to ensure that there would be enough water at the right time; on the other hand, the state undertook the construction of dams, levees, and drainage ditches to avoid the damaging effects of too much water all at once. The scale of the activities in question literally demanded changing the face of the earth: moving mountains, reshaping riverbanks, digging out whole new riverbeds. Recruiting, coordinating, directing, feeding, and housing the brigades of workers needed for these monumental undertakings could only have been carried out by cadres obedient to a few powerful leaders pursuing a single master plan. Hence the larger the hydraulic networks and facilities, the greater the overall productivity of the system, the greater the tendency of the agro-managerial hierarchy to become subordinate to one immensely powerful person at its top.

The peculiar capacity of hydraulic societies to restore themselves despite frequent dynastic upheavals and recurrent conquests by barbarian invaders arises from the interplay between their political structures and their basic ecological adaptation. Though the concentration of total power in the supreme ruler and his family meant that all lines of political force ran in one direction only, the sheer size and complexity of the state apparatus gave high officials and lesser bureaucrats the opportunity to satisfy their own ambitions at the expense of the people under them. Despite the value placed by the wise ruler on moderation and justice, the bureaucracy tended to fatten itself at the expense of peasant welfare. Corruption tended to increase geometrically with the number of years a dynasty remained in power. Soon public works were neglected, the dikes began to leak, the canals filled up with silt, and production declined. Sheer incompetence, human error, and natural disasters added to the subversive forces at work. Recurrently, therefore, a reigning dynasty would find that it was no longer capable of protecting and providing for the peasant masses. Torn by dissension, it would become vulnerable to the "barbarians" outside the walls, to the armies of neighboring empires, or to its own rebellious people. The dynasty would then collapse. This happened again and again in the history of Egypt, Mesopotamia, India, and China. But the new leaders—whether internal or external foes—had only one choice if they wanted to enjoy the wealth of empire: to repair the dikes, clean out the canals, rebuild the levees, and restore the hydraulic mode of production. A new cycle would then begin. Production would increase, the depauperized peasantry would lower its rate of infanticide and abortion, and population density would rise. But as density rose, productivity would decline, and corrupt officials would become more and more immoderate in their attempt to line their own pockets. Finally, as the peasants slipped back into pauperdom, the struggle for dynastic control would break out once again.

As Wittfogel has insisted, the kernel of the hydraulic

theory was anticipated by Karl Marx in a number of works that were either disguised or ignored by Lenin and Stalin. Marx attributed the peculiar political economies of India and China to what he called the "Asiatic Mode of Production." He wrote:

> There have been in Asia, generally, from immemorial times, but three departments of Government: that of Finance, or the plunder of the interior; that of War, or the plunder of the exterior; and, finally, the department of Public Works. In Egypt and India, Mesopotamia, Persia, etc., advantage is taken of a high level for feeding irrigation canals. This prime necessity of an economical and common use of water . . . necessitated, in the Orient, where civilization was too low and territorial extent too vast to call into life voluntary associations, the interference of the centralizing powers of government.

One reason this part of Marx's scheme of world evolution fell into disrepute under Lenin and Stalin is its implication that state communism or the "dictatorship of the proletariat" may actually be nothing more than a new and more highly developed form of managerial despotism reared on an industrial rather than an agricultural base. Another reason is that Marx referred to the Asiatic societies as "stagnant" or "stationary" and saw no prospect for their further evolution through purely internal processes. This was at odds with other aspects of Marx's theories, for he held that the contradictions within society gave rise to class struggle and that class struggle was the key to the understanding of all history. Hydraulic societies had plenty of contradictions and class struggle, but they seem to have been remarkably resistant to fundamental change.

Some critics of the hydraulic theory contend that

the bureaucratic features of the ancient empires had already come into existence before the irrigation networks and flood control projects reached the stage of requiring huge numbers of laborers and centralized control. Robert McC. Adams of the University of Chicago, for example, argues that in early dynastic Mesopotamia "irrigation, on the whole, was conducted on a small-scale basis, which involved little alteration of the natural hydraulic regime and the construction of only small-scale feeder canals" and that therefore "there is nothing to suggest that the rise of dynastic authority in southern Mesopotamia was linked to the administrative requirements of a major canal system." In rebuttal I would point out that Wittfogel's theory is one not of the origin of the state but of the origin of the highly despotic and enduring nature of certain kinds of imperial state systems. Adams does not deny that during the maturity of the Mesopotamian empires construction and management of colossal hydraulic enterprises was a constant and salient preoccupation of highly centralized agro-managerial cadres. The dynastic history of Mesopotamia fully confirms Wittfogel's basic contention that as the scope and complexity of the waterworks increased, so did the "interference of the centralizing power of government."

Karl Butzer has recently rejected the applicability of Wittfogel's theory to the hydraulic and managerial features of ancient Egypt. Like Adams, Butzer claims that the dynastic phase had already been reached before there was any large-scale investment in hydraulic construction. But he seems to go further in insisting that "competition for water was never an issue except at the local level"; that "there is no evidence for a centralized bureaucratic apparatus that might have served to administer irrigation at the national, regional, or local level"; and finally that "ecological problems were handled at the local level."

Butzer attributes the permanently decentralized nature of the dynastic Egyptian irrigation system to the fact that the Nile flood plain is broken into a series of natural basins which fill up sequentially when the river rises and overflows the levees along its main channel. Before the construction of the Aswan dam in the 1960's across the whole width of the main channel and flood plain, there was no way for districts to cut off the water of districts further downstream, as there was in Mesopotamia. Artificial constructions, according to Butzer, were small-scale and consisted primarily of attempts to strengthen and enlarge the preexisting natural levees and dikes separating each basin from the river and one basin from another.

Butzer's critique of Wittfogel's theory is contradicted by much of the data provided by Butzer himself. It appears that he has not understood what Wittfogel is saying. For example, the mace head of the Scorpion King pictures a 3100 B.C. predynastic ruler either opening a levee or initiating construction of a canal. Butzer accepts this and other evidence as an indication that "artificial irrigation including deliberate flooding and draining by sluice gates, and water contained by longitudinal and transverse dikes, was established by the 1st Dynasty." He also admits that the central government engaged in vast hydraulic projects beginning in the Middle Kingdom (2000 B.C.) aimed at regulating the level of the Fayum lake and at draining large portions of the Delta region, though he regards these monumental undertakings as exceptions and therefore insignificant for an understanding of dynastic political organization. Further, despite his claim that local officials could regulate and administer the distribution of water, he describes formidable technical requirements:

> conversion of the natural to higher and stronger artificial levees; enlarging and dredging of natural diverging overflow channels; blocking off of natural, gathering or drainage channels by earthen dams and sluice gates; subdivision of the flood basin by dams into manageable, in part special-purpose, units; controlling water access to an retention in the basin subunits by temporary cuts in the levees and dikes or by a network of short canals and masonry gates.

Butzer admits that these operations would frequently require the "mass input of the total able-bodied rural population of a basin unit," but supposedly of only one unit at a time. This conclusion is clearly false since each "basin unit" had at least two neighbors—one upstream and one downstream. At high water, failure to maintain the between-basin dikes and the return drainage channels in proper condition could result in the uncontrolled flooding of the downstream basin. When the Nile flood was higher than usual, a break in an upstream levee would threaten not only the adjacent basin, but the next basin as well, since the uncontrolled pressure could easily sweep away the between-basin dikes. The need for coordinating the response of several basins was equally great when the Nile flood failed and the amount of water diverted by the upstream basins affected the amount that reached those further downstream. Butzer himself paints a stark picture of the "famines . . . poverty . . . mass burials . . . rotting corpses . . . suicide . . . cannibalism . . . anarchy . . . mass dislocations . . . civil war . . . mass plundering . . . roving bands of marauders . . . as well as looting of cemeteries" that resulted from a failure of the annual flood. While there were occasions when the crests were either so high or so low that no power on earth could render assistance, a government capable of putting 100,000 men to work building artificial mountains out of stone blocks in the desert surely did not refrain from attempting to moderate the effect of too much or too little water under emergency conditions.

As in so many other long-term natural and cultural processes, emergency or extreme rather than normal conditions shaped the political adaptation to the hydraulic mode of production. In China as in Egypt, when the major irrigation and flood control facilities were functioning properly, irrigation farming could flourish without any need for a highly centralized government. But when the great dams and levees on the major rivers were threatened by floods or earthquakes only a central administration could muster resources and labor power on a sufficiently grand scale. During the Han period, for example, population density was highest on the Great Plain of the Yellow River in the Shan-Si and Ho-Nan provinces. Periodically, the Yellow River overflowed its banks and flooded huge areas of the plain. In order to prevent these disasters, the central government supervised the construction of dikes and levees. This had the effect of increasing the amount of impounded water and of raising its level during flood seasons, thereby adding to the damage that the river could inflict when it broke through its containments. In 132 B.C. the river breached the dikes, flooded sixteen districts, and sent a whole new branch across the plain. Tens of millions of peasants were affected. The break remained open for twenty-three years until Emperor Wu-ti himself visited the scene and personally supervised its repair. In A.D. II another breach occurred near the same point, but now the whole river changed its course and found a new path to the sea—a hundred miles away from its former mouth. Repair work was again delayed, this time for several decades.

These facts warrant two conclusions. First, no effort on a village, county, or even provincial level was adequate to the enormity of the undertaking; otherwise, so many years would not have elapsed between the breaking and the repair. Second, whoever possessed the means to control the river literally possessed the means to control the life span and well-being of vast numbers of people.

In my opinion, the actual record of discoveries made by archaeologists has consistently favored the hydraulic theory. When the theory was first formulated, almost nothing was known about the conditions that had given rise to the agro-managerial states and empires of the New World. Wittfogel stimulated the first attempt by archaeologists in the late 1930's to detect the presence of irrigation during the formative phases of native states in South America. Recent work by archaeologists at Columbia University and Harvard continue to support the view that the growth of cities, states, and monumental architectures in the pre-Columbian cultures of highland and coastal Peru grew step by step with an increase in the size and complexity of their irrigation systems. Excavations carried out in Mesoamerica by William Sanders and Richard MacNeish have also tended to confirm the importance of irrigation. As I showed in an earlier chapter, hydraulic agriculture was the basic source of subsistence for Teotihuacán and for the Aztecs' cannibal kingdom.

According to Wittfogel, the hydraulic theory has ominous implications for our own times. While he traces the origin of the agro-managerial form of despotism to specific ecological conditions, he emphasizes that once in existence it was spread by conquest far beyond its semiarid riverine homelands. He insists, for example, that the Mongols transplanted the agro-managerial form of despotism from China to Russia in the aftermath of the Mongol conquest of Central Asia and the eastern part of Europe. In czarist Russia the same system of "Oriental despotism" lingered on into the twentieth century. The Bolshevik Revolution and Lenin's "dictatorship of the proletariat" were not, in Wittfogel's view, transient steps along the way toward the restoration of liberties that human beings enjoyed before the evolution of the state; rather they led to the restoration of the centralizing powers of government and an increase in czarist tyranny through the development of industrial means of exploitation and control. Turning to China, Wittfogel sees the Communist revolution there as the restoration of the ancient imperial system, the founding of one more dynasty after one more collapse and brief interlude under foreign control. Because of the continuing agrarian and hydraulic structure of modern China, this analysis seems to me much more apt in the case of China than of Russia, where an industrial mode of production now prevails.

In either case, Wittfogel seems to have short-circuited the kind of analysis that is needed if we are to assess the true nature of the threat to liberty in our times. I do not believe that we are endangered by despotic traditions that have acquired a life of their own and that are transferred from one mode of production to another or from one ecosystem to another. What Wittfogel's theory suggests to me is that when certain kinds of state-level systems of production undergo intensification, despotic forms of government may arise which can neutralize human will and intelligence for thousands of years. This implies further that the effective moment for conscious choice may exist only during the transition from one mode of production to another. After a society has made its commitment to a particular technological and ecological strategy for solving the problem of declining efficiency, it may not be possible to do anything about the consequences of an unintelligent choice for a long time to come.

14
The Origin of Capitalism

The hydraulic theory not only suggests an explanation for the remarkable convergences among the social institutions of Egypt, Mesopotamia, India, China, and Inca Peru; it also opens up promising avenues of inquiry relevant to the question of why capitalism and parliamentary democracy evolved in Europe before they appeared anywhere else in the world. North of the Alps, where there is no Nile or Indus or Yellow River and where winter snows and spring rains provide sufficient moisture for field crops and pastures, population remained more dispersed than in the hydraulic regions. Long after the great river valleys were packed from horizon to horizon with human settlements, northern Europe stood to the Mediterranean and the Orient as America was later to stand to Europe: a frontier still covered by virgin forests. (Yet population density was higher than in temperate-zone North America, where the absence of domesticated animals served to slow population growth even more.)

The appearance of the first states in northern Europe was not caused by the concentration of people in a circumscribed habitat. All were secondary states called into existence to cope with the military threat of the Mediterranean empires and to exploit the possibilities of trade and plunder provided by the great wealth of Greece and Rome.

Although most scholars refer to the political organization of the iron age Gauls, Franks, Teutons, and Britons as "chiefdoms," these were societies that had obviously crossed the threshold into statehood. They should be compared with feudal states such as that of the Bunyoro rather than with redistributive chiefdoms such as those of the Trobianders and the Cherokee. By 500 B.C. the social life of the peoples of Europe had become highly stratified. Like the Vedic invaders of the Indus Valley, the Franks, Gauls, Teutons, and Britons were divided into three hereditary castes: a warrior chief aristocracy; a priesthood, the Druids, in charge of rituals, record keeping, and time reckoning; and commoners living in farm villages or dispersed pastoral homesteads that were part of a local chief's domain. At the apex of society was a hereditary or semihereditary warrior king who was a member of a ruling house or lineage.

While the king and his warrior chiefs sought to retain the image of open-handed generosity characteristic of egalitarian "big man" redistributors, they held a monopoly over the possession of the equipment essential for maintaining law and order and for waging military campaigns. The items over which they exercised their monopoly were war chariots, horses, body armor, and iron swords. Commoners were obliged to provide ritual gifts of grain and cattle and to render labor services when summoned by the chiefs or the king. If they knew what was good for them, they were prompt and courteous in their response to requests from their headhunting overlords. Society had passed beyond the point at which the redistributors had to rely on the spontaneous generosity of their followers, though there were still uninhabited forest lands into which commoners and disaffected chiefs could flee if the "gift-giving" became too one-sided.

It certainly was not for want of suitable personalities that the northern European statelets failed to develop into monolithic despotisms. The Irish hero tales, *Beowulf*, the Nordic sagas, and Homer's *Iliad* are filled with frustrated chieftains whom Marc Bloch has called "odd little potentates." Hurtling themselves into battle, sacking cities amid screams and the sound of trumpets, slaughtering men and boys and carrying girls and women off in chariots hung with fresh heads, the Celtic kings and their chiefs are among the most ruthless figures in history. In Piggott's words, they were a swaggering, belching, touchy, impossible crew—"hands twitching to the sword hilt at the imagined hint of an insult . . . wiping the greasy moustaches that were a mark of nobility."

Yet the Celtic kingdoms remained small and disjointed. Commoners slipped from the protection of one chief to another. New coalitions of warriors signaled the rise of new ruling houses and the fall of old ones. Whole segments of kingdoms detached themselves from their homelands and migrated en masse from one region to another—the Belgae to Britain, the Helvetii to Switzerland, the Cimbri, Teutons, and Ambroni into Gaul, the Scythians into Transylvania. The Romans consolidated these loose, mobile feudal kingdoms into imperial provinces, constructed the first large masonry buildings and the first decent roads, and established systems of coinage, regular tax collection, and law courts. Much of this was a thin veneer laid over a countryside which was still barely prepared for statehood. Outside the provincial capitals the Romanized descendants of the Franks, Gauls, Celts, and Teutons practiced small-scale subsistence agriculture in isolated villages. Trade in manufactured items and agricultural products remained rudimentary compared with the circum-Mediterranean portions of the empire. Virtually everyone remained illiterate. Hence with the collapse of Rome in the fifth century A.D. transalpine Europe did not lapse back into the "Dark Ages," never having gotten out of them in the first place. What it lapsed back into was feudalism.

Through force of arms the ethnic chiefs and kings, ex-Roman governors, generals, war lords, peasant leaders, and bandits carved the former Roman provinces into a new set of feudal kingdoms. Of course, the restoration was not complete. Population had grown under Roman rule and many of the semimigratory pastoral peoples had been obliged to settle down and to practice a completely sedentary form of mixed farming. The new feudalism was more rigid and more formalized than its pre-Roman variety. Peasants were permanently assigned as serfs to the "manorial estates" controlled by the new aristocracy. They were promised protection against being routed or robbed in return for providing sufficient quantities of food, labor, and material to support the lord of the realm and his knights and artisans. Oaths of loyalty exchanged between knights and lords and between less powerful and more powerful princes and kings formalized the political hierarchy.

Despite the rigidities introduced by serfdom into the feudal system, the post-Roman political organization of Europe continued to contrast with that of the hydraulic empires. Central bureaus of internal and external plunder and of public works were conspicuously absent. There was no national system for collecting taxes, fighting wars, building roads and canals, or administering justice. The basic units of production were the independent, self-contained rainfall-farming manorial estates. There was no economical way for the more powerful princes and kings to interrupt or facilitate the production activities that took place in each separate little manorial world.

Unlike the hydraulic despots, Europe's medieval kings could not furnish or withhold water from the fields. The rains fell regardless of what the king in his castle decreed, and there was nothing in the productive process to necessitate the organization of vast armies of workers. In Wittfogel's words, "the scattered operations of rainfall farming did not involve the establishment of national patterns of cooperation as did hydraulic agriculture." And so the feudal aristocracy was able to resist all attempts to establish genuinely national systems of government. The king, instead of turning into an "Oriental" despot, remained merely "the first among equals." Like John of England at Runnymede in 1215, Europe's feudal kings generally had to refrain from interfering with the nobility's right to tax commoners. The Magna Carta extracted from John by the English barons prevented the rise of a centralized despotism, not by guaranteeing parliamentary representation—there was no parliament as yet—but by guaranteeing that each baron would remain a "king" in his own castle.

Despite its reputation for being a "dark age," the early medieval period was a time of population growth and of expansion and intensification of agricultural production. Around A.D. 500 there were probably only about nine persons per square mile in transalpine Europe, but by A.D. 1086 England had reached a density of thirty persons per square mile. It was only after A.D. 500 that iron axes and saws became cheap enough to be used by the average farmer. Settlements expanded into the remaining forest lands and the edges of moors and swamps. Lumbering, house building, and fence construction were intensified. The invention of the horseshoe increased the utility of the horse as a traction animal. And the development of blacksmithing led to the introduction of a new kind of plow—a heavy iron-tipped instrument mounted on wheels and capable of cutting deep furrows in the wet clays and loams characteristic of rainy, forested regions. Because the furrows were cut deep, cross-plowing was unnecesary and the most economical field under cultivation became the one whose shape required the least number of turnarounds per unit area, that is, a field longer than it was broad. This new shape facilitated an improved method of crop rotation, which reduced the need for letting fields lie fallow. The whole system was admirably suited to the relations of production characteristic of the manor. Each peasant family had access to the manor's blacksmith facilities, heavy plow, teams of draft animals, and contiguous fields which a farmer could not have afforded on an independent basis. Why, then, did this system not endure beyond the fourteenth century?

Explanations for the collapse of feudalism usually begin by noting that trade and manufacture increased in the tenth and eleventh centuries, and that the search for profits transformed all the customary feudal obligations into demand-and-supply market relationships. But as Immanuel Wallerstein points out, "Feudalism as a system should not be thought of as something antithetical to trade." Feudal lords had always encouraged the growth of towns and the development of town-based artisans and merchants who could facilitate the conversion of the manor's agricultural products into a multitude of goods and services that the manor could not provide. They were never ideologically opposed to buying and selling and making profits. What has to be explained, therefore, is why it took over 500 years for the towns and markets to begin to subvert the feudal order.

The answer, I think, is that towns and markets grew slowly as long as the serfs and free peasants could maintain a relatively high standard of living from their traditional agricultural activities. The development of commercial life to the point where it threatened the feudal status quo had to wait for the build-up of population density. As density rose, efficiency declined, and so did agricultural profitability from the point of view both of the peasants and of the feudal lords. This encouraged the feudal lords to seek supplementary sources of income, the most important of which was the raising of sheep for wool, which in turn restricted the amount of land available for food crops, reduced the size of peasant holdings, pauperized much of the rural population, and stimulated migrations to the towns and wool production centers.

My account of this process owes a great deal to the work of Richard G. Wilkinson. In his book *Poverty and Progress* Wilkinson indicates that the fertility of arable land and the yield from seed were in decline in England during the thirteenth century:

> The balanced system of medieval agriculture has been upset. The expansion of the arable acreage had not been matched by sufficient expansion of pasture and animals to provide manure. . . . Fallow periods had been shortened . . . and poorer quality land had been brought into cultivation.

Attempts were made to increase yields per acre through liming, marling, plowing in straw ash, sowing more intensively, and experimenting with new seeds. But to no avail. Although overall production went up, population went up even further. The price of wheat almost trebled between the late twelfth and early fourteenth centuries at the same time that English exports of wool rose by 40 percent. A rise in grain prices meant that families who lacked sufficient lands to feed themselves were pushed down close to or below the pauperization threshold.

As I pointed out in the discussion of population growth among the Yanomamo, the period immediately before and shortly after the overloading and depletion of a preindustrial ecosystem should be characterized by peak rates of female infanticide. Although this proposition could not be tested in the Yanomamo case, the data are available for late medieval England. According to Josiah Russel, the junior age sex ratio rose to a peak of 130:100 between 1250 and 1358, and remained drastically imbalanced for another century. Of course, since infanticide in the Judeo-Christian tradition was considered murder, every effort was made by parents to make it seem as if the deaths of unwanted babies was purely accidental. Barbara Kellum's study of infanticide in thirteenth- and fourteenth-century England suggests that the coroner would be called in if a child was scalded to death by a pot of water that tipped off a stove, or was drowned in a pan of milk, or fell down a well. But suffocation, the most frequent cause of "accidental" infant death, was handled by the parish priest. Death by suffocation was routinely attributed to "overlaying," and the mother was rarely punished with anything more severe than public remonstrance and penitence—restriction to a diet of bread and water.

The theory behind "overlaying" was that a mother had the right to nurse her child in her own bed, keeping it at her side during the night, but that she was obligated to exercise care in not falling asleep and rolling over on it. When a baby died under these circumstances, homicidal intent was impossible to prove. Obviously, however, mothers who were strongly motivated to rear their babies would seldom roll over on them. Selective infanticide, not accident, is the only explanation for the huge imbalance in the late medieval juvenile sex ratios.

Despite the high rate of female infanticide, the population of England continued to increase until 1348, when the most devastating plague in the history of Europe—the Black Death—carried off between one-quarter and one-half of the population. From what is known about the relationship between malnutrition and resistance to disease, I think it is reasonable to suppose that a significant percentage of the mortality rate in the Black Death pandemic was related to the deterioration of nutritional standards. Certainly, the shift in population from countryside to towns and the increase in the overall density of settlements were causally related to the outbreak.

In the aftermath of the plague, Europe entered a period of intense political and economic unrest. The feudal kingdoms were shaken from top to bottom by massive peasant uprisings, messianic movements, an outbreak of cults that practiced self-flagellation, massacres of Jews, schisms within the Catholic Church, crusades to suppress heretics, the founding of the Inquisition, and a ceaseless round of wars, one of which is known appropriately enough as the Hundred Years' War (1337–1453). What all this adds up to, I suggest, is that the intensification of the manorial mode of production had reached its ecological limits and that the crisis preceding the emergence of the new mode of production which we call capitalism was at bottom similar to the crises preceding the neolithic "revolution" and the rise of pristine states. Let me make this point clearer. I am not claiming that ecology and reproductive pressures alone are capable of accounting for the crisis of feudalism in the fourteenth century. Other factors such as the exploitation of peasants by feudal lords and the rise of new classes of merchants and bankers also exerted an influence. The pressure from the feudal nobility and from the rising mercantile interests played a role in producing the crisis just as surely as the corrupt ambitions of China's managerial bureaucracy played a role in destroying numerous dynasties. Moreover, I find it conceivable that had there been less pressure from the feudal ruling class to get the peasants to intensify production, population might have stopped growing temporarily at a point low enough to avert a crisis and to keep the standard of living above the pauperization threshold. Perhaps the Church's opposition to infanticide also played a role in accelerating the growth of population and in precipitating the crisis.

But the ecological factors cannot be ignored. The consequences of enclosing lands for wool production would have been insignificant had the capacity of the unenclosed lands to produce additional food crops not already been pushed beyond the limit of marginal returns. And I see no reason to doubt that eventually, because of some climatic perturbation, reproductive pressures would have been sufficient to set the stage for a shift to a new mode of production. After all, the cycle of intensifications, depletions, and new modes of production started in classless, pre-state band and village societies. I think we must conclude, therefore, that the manorial system was inherently unstable for both political-economic and ecological reasons and must not attempt in our present state of knowledge to assign greater causal significance to one or the other.

One question that remains is why the decline in population after the Black Death did not become part of a cycle of demographic and economic ups and downs similar to the rise and fall of living standards that lay behind the dynastic changes in hydraulic society. Why, in other words, was feudalism replaced by an entirely new system instead of being restored when the crisis had passed? Here, too, I believe Wittfogel's theory provides the key by drawing attention to the contrasting ecologies of the feudal and hydraulic worlds—although again I want to stress the existence of an interplay between ecological and political-economic factors.

In hydraulic societies pauperization and dynastic collapse were typically associated with the decay and disrepair of the waterworks. The first order of business was to restore the hydraulic infrastructure. This was up to the new dynasty, which acted not out of altruism but out of attention to the maximization of its own political and economic welfare. In committing itself to the restoration of the hydraulic infrastructure, the new dynasty was automatically committing the entire society to the restoration of the political economy of agro-managerial despotism. In the crisis of European feudalism, on the other hand, the problem lay in the landlessness of the victims of enclosures and the raising of animals on lands that were needed to raise food crops. The first order of business of the manorial lords turned merchants and manufacturers could not be to drive out the sheep, restore the peasants to the land, and stop manufacturing woolens. The maximization of their own immediate political and economic welfare lay not in going backward but in going forward into larger and more uninhibited attempts to make money and accumulate capital by raising more sheep and manufacturing more woolens. In short, the manorial system was not restored; rather, it was replaced by a system based on scientific technology, machine production, capitalism, and parliamentary democracy.

Under capitalism the distribution of most goods and services is carried out by "companies" which control or have access to accumulated supplies of money or "capital." The object of such companies is to accumulate more capital and to do it as quickly and efficiently as possible by maximizing the rate of making profits. A company can increase its rate of profit if it gains a technological advantage over its competitors and lowers its unit costs. Technological innovation, therefore, soon becomes the key to the accumulation of capital and business success. Science, in turn, provides the key to technological innovation. Hence capitalism, science, and scientific technologies form a distinctive mutually reinforcing complex that originated in Europe as the resolution of the crisis of feudalism.

Many features of this complex were also present in the hydraulic societies. The Chinese, for example, had private property in land, price-making markets for agricultural and manufactured goods, rich merchants, and a network of banks and merchant associations. Peasant families bought and sold in local markets with the intent of maximizing profits. Moreover, the Chinese emperors encouraged scientific and technological innovations. In fact, we now know that until the fourteenth century China's rate of scientific and technological advance was as great as that of Europe. Modern historical research has demonstrated that the Chinese were responsible for developing a crucial element of the watch—namely, the escapement, the part that prevents the spring from unwinding faster when it is tightly wound. Ironically, it was the Chinese who invented gunpowder, which the Europeans used in their conquest of the Orient. Because of investment in government-controlled dams, canals, and irrigation systems, Chinese water mills were superior to those in Europe. Joseph Needham, the great historian of Chinese science and technology, regards the Chinese water-powered metallurgical blowing machine as the direct ancestor of the steam engine. Needham also credits the Chinese with the invention of the first computer, the canal lock gate, the iron chain suspension bridge, the first true mechanical crank, the stern-post rudder, and the man-lifting kite. And as long ago as A.D. 1313 the Chinese were experimenting with water-driven spinning machines that were the direct prototypes of the European spinning jennies.

Despite these great experiments, one may reasonably doubt that China would ever have developed an industrial mode of production without the threat and stimulus of the European example. In China technological advantage over one's competitors never became the key factor in raising profits and accumulating capital. The key variable in Chinese commercial life was the support of the agro-managerial bureaucracy—Marx's "bureau of internal plunder." Without proper imperial connections, profits could be dissipated by corrupt officials. Licenses to trade could be arbitrarily suspended, and businesses that proved too lucrative were in constant danger of being swallowed up by the government. In other words, in China the growth of private trade and manufacture followed the growth of the agro-managerial state and remained an important but dependent aspect of the centralized political economy. "At best," writes Wittfogel, the masters of hydraulic society "treated what capitalist enterprise there was like a useful garden. At worst, they clipped and stripped the bushes of capital-based business to a stalk." In post-medieval Europe, by contrast, private industry and commerce accompanied or even preceded the emergence of the European parliamentary monarchies. The power of Europe's kings and merchants emerged from a common substratum of feudal restrictions and limitations, and both kings and merchants competed for control over the post-feudal political economy.

While the English, French, and Spanish monarchs were capable of brutal interventions in the lives of their subjects, their tyranny was always limited by the opposition of big property owners and wealthy merchants. "The rulers of European absolutism," says Wittfogel, "schemed as ruthlessly and killed as mercilessly as did their Eastern confreres. However, their power to persecute and appropriate was limited by the landed nobles, the Church, and the cities whose autonomy the autocratic overlords could restrict, but not destroy." When Europe's kings claimed divine mandates and absolute authority, the bourgeoisie in France and England balked. Would-be European Pharaohs and Incas sooner or later resigned their rights to represent heaven or ended up under the guillotine.

In anthropological perspective, the emergence of bourgeois parliamentary democracies in seventeenth- and eighteenth-century Europe was a rare reversal of that descent from freedom to slavery which had been the main characteristic of the evolution of the state for 6,000 years. Wittfogel has opposed Marx and Engels' contention that all history is the history of class struggle with the observation that "class struggle is the luxury of multi-centered and open societies." Perhaps a better way to put this—for I would not deny that class struggle existed in hydraulic societies in at least latent forms—is to say that only in the recent history of Europe and America have the lower classes achieved the liberty to struggle openly for control of the state. No one who detests the practice of kowtowing and groveling, who values the pursuit of scientific knowledge of culture and society, who values the right to study, discuss, debate, and criticize, or who believes that society is greater than the state can afford to mistake the rise of European and American democracies as the normal product of a march toward freedom. It is equally dangerous to suppose that capitalism represents the end point of cultural evolution. And one cannot ignore the threat which the intensification of the capitalist mode of production now presents to the preservation of those precious rights and freedoms that have hitherto, if briefly, flourished under its auspices.

Capitalism's harshest critics—Karl Marx among them—have always conceded that the surge in the output of food and manufacturers associated with the rise of European business firms, banks, and other entrepreneurial organizations was without precedent. Never before had so many individuals tried harder to increase production more rapidly in so great a diversity of enterprises. I believe the secret of this "great leap forward" in productive effort was the release of ambitious individuals from political, social, and moral restraints on self-serving attempts to accumulate wealth. European entrepreneurs were the first people in the history of the world who could go about their business without worrying if some "internal bureau of plunder" was about to cut them down to size. Equally important, they could accumulate wealth without having to worry about sharing it with friends and relatives who helped them get rich. Like "big men," entrepreneurs accumulated wealth by making their followers—now called employees—work harder. But unlike Solomon Island *mumis*, entrepreneurs did not have to beg, cajole, and entice. Possessing capital, the entrepreneur could buy "help" and hire "hands" (plus backs, shoulders, feet, and brains). And the entrepreneur did not have to promise to give everything away at the next company picnic. Since his followers were not the "big man's" relatives or fellow villagers, it was easy for him to disregard their requests for a larger share in the product. Moreover, the helping hands-backs-shoulders-feet-brains had little choice in the matter. Deprived of access to lands and machines, the "help" could not work at all unless they accepted the legitimacy of the entrepreneur's claim to the "meat and the fat." The "help" assisted the entrepreneur not so they could all have a feast, but simply to keep from starving. In sum, the "big man" entrepreneur was free at last to regard the accumulation of capital as an obligation higher than the redistribution of wealth or the welfare of his followers.

Capitalism, then, is a system that is committed to an unbounded increase in production in the name of an unbounded increase in profits. Production, however, cannot be increased in an unbounded way. Freed from the restraints of despots and paupers, capitalist entrepreneurs still have to confront the restraints of nature. The profitability of production cannot expand indefinitely. Any increase in the quantity of soil, water, minerals, or plants put into a particular production process per unit of time constitutes intensification. It has been the burden of this book to show that intensification inevitably leads to declining efficiencies. That declining efficiencies have adverse effects upon the average standard of living cannot be doubted.

What must be made clear is that environmental depletions also lead to declining profits. This relationship is not easily understood because, according to the laws of supply and demand, scarcities lead to higher prices. Higher prices, however, tend to lower consumption per capita (the market symptom of declining living standards). Profits can be sustained temporarily if the drop in per capita consumption is compensated for by an expansion in total sales based on population growth or the conquest of international markets. But sooner or later the curve of rising prices caused by environmental depletions will begin to rise faster than the curve of rising consumption and the rate of profit must begin to fall.

The classic entrepreneurial response to a fall in the rate of profit is exactly the same as under any mode of production that has been overintensified. To compensate for environmental depletions and declining efficiencies (which manifest themselves as falling rates of profit), the entrepreneur seeks to lower the costs of production by introducing labor-saving machines. Although these machines require more capital and hence usually have higher start-up costs, they result in lowering the unit cost of the product.

Thus a system that is committed to perpetual intensification can survive only if it is equally committed to perpetual technological change. Its ability to maintain living standards depends on the outcome of a race between technological advance and the relentless deterioration of the conditions of production. Under the present circumstances, technology is about to lose that race.

[illegible]

[illegible] tall.

The [illegible] profit [illegible] machines. [illegible] though these machines consume more capital and [illegible]

[illegible]

15
The Industrial Bubble

All rapidly intensifying systems of production, whether they be socialist, capitalist, hydraulic, neolithic, or paleolithic, face a common dilemma. The increment in energy invested per unit time in production will inevitably overburden the self-renewing, self-cleansing, self-generating capacities of the ecosystem. Regardless of which mode of production is involved, there is only one means of avoiding the catastrophic consequences of declining efficiencies: to shift to more efficient technologies. For the past 500 years Western scientific technology has been competing against the most rapidly and relentlessly intensifying system of production in the history of our species.

Thanks to science and engineering, the average standard of living in the industrial nations is higher than at any time in the past. This fact, more than any other, bolsters our faith that progress is inevitable—a faith, incidentally, shared as much by the Comintern as by the U.S. Chamber of Commerce. What I want to emphasize here is that the rise in living standards began only 150 years ago, while the race between rapid technological change and intensification has been going on for 500 years. During most of the post-feudal epoch, living standards hovered close to pauperdom and frequently fell to unprecedented depths despite the introduction of an unbroken series of ingenious labor-saving machines.

As Richard Wilkinson has shown, all the important technological changes introduced into England between 1500 and 1830 were made under duress and in direct response either to resource shortages or to population growth and relentless reproductive pressures. Behind the whole process was an increasingly acute scarcity of agricultural land which forced people into manufacturing and town-based means of making their livelihood. The periods of greatest technological innovation were those of greatest population increase, highest cost of living, and greatest amount of suffering among the poor.

During the sixteenth century, when population soared upward again for the first time since the Black Death, mining and manufacturing grew as fast as during the industrial revolution of the eighteenth century. Brass-making and metal trades flourished. The iron industry entered the phase of mass production as it passed from small forges to large blast furnaces. Glass-making, salt-boiling, brewing, and brick-making all underwent rapid expansion and intensification. The English ceased to export raw wool and turned to the manufacture of finished cloth. But England's forests could not support the enormous increase in the consumption of wood and charcoal for construction and fuel. To relieve the great seventeeth-century "timber famine," coal mining was intensified. To get at the coal, miners dug deeper shafts, which put the mines below the water level. To get the water out, they dug drains into the hillsides. When the mines got too deep for such drains, they tried harnessing horses to lift pumps, then water wheels, and finally steam vacuum pumps.

Meanwhile, most mills continued to be run on water power. As land became scarcer, the price of wool rose. Soon it became cheaper to import cotton from India than to raise sheep in England. To run the cotton mills more water power was needed. But good water wheel sites soon became scarce. Then and then only did Watt and Boulton design the first steam engine intended to produce rotary motion for the spinning machines.

As manufacture expanded, the volume of trade increased. Pack animals could no longer bear the loads. Merchants increased their use of wagons and carts. But the wheels tore up the roads, dug pits in them, turned them into quagmires. So companies were formed to provide alternative forms of transport. They built networks of canals and experimented with horse-drawn railways. Large numbers of animals were needed to haul the canal boats and pull the wagons and carts, but the arable land available for growing hay kept shrinking. Soon the cost of feeding hay to horses exceeded the cost of feeding coal to locomotives. Then and only then—in 1830—did the age of the steam locomotive begin.

In Wilkinson's words, all of this was "essentially an attempt to keep abreast of the growing difficulties of production encountered by an expanding society." At no point prior to 1830 did the technology that was being shaped by the cunning force of some of the greatest minds in England ever really get ahead of the system's voracious appetite for natural resources. And 500 years after the Black Death the poverty and misery of English working classes remained essentially unchanged.

Conventional assessments of the standard of living in the eighteenth century paint a rosier picture by concentrating on the growth of an urban middle class. No doubt the middle-class grew steadily in absolute numbers from 1500 on, but it did not constitute a significant percentage of the European population before the third quarter of the nineteenth century. The distribution of wealth before then closely resembled the situation in many contemporary underdeveloped countries. One could easily have been deceived by the bustle and civic amenities of eighteenth-century London or Paris, just as one can easily be deceived today by the skyscrapers in Mexico City or Bombay. But beneath the glitter enjoyed by 10 percent of the population, there was only bare subsistence and misery for the remaining 90 percent.

The rise of the middle class in the United States tends to warp our perception of history, since it grew at a more rapid pace than in Europe. But the American colonial experience was an anomaly. The Americans took over a continent where no dense population had previously existed. Even a bronze age people would have been able to eke out a hundred years of rising living standards from a wilderness so richly endowed with soils, forests, and minerals. The only real test of the fruits of the first three centuries of rapid technological change took place in Europe, where the advance of science not only failed to relieve the plight of the peasants, but gave birth to novel forms of urban penury and degradation.

Certain facts seem incontrovertible. The larger machines became, the longer and harder the people who ran them had to work. By the 1800's factory hands and miners were putting in twelve hours a day under conditions that no self-respecting Bushman, Trobriander, Cherokee, or Iroquois would have tolerated. At the day's end, after contending with the continuous whine and chatter of wheels and shafts, dust, smoke, and foul odors, the operators of the new labor-saving devices retired to their dingy hovels full of lice and fleas. As before, only the wealthy could afford meat. Rickets, a new crippling disease of the bones caused by a lack of sunshine and dietary sources of vitamin D, became endemic in the cities and factory districts. The incidence of tuberculosis and other diseases typical of low-grade diets also increased.

Direct and indirect infanticide continued to be practiced on a scale that was probably as great as in medieval times. Most cases of what the law might have considered negligent or deliberate infanticide were passed off as accidents. While "overlaying" remained high on the list, unwanted children were also drugged to death with gin or opiates, or were deliberately starved. According to William Langer, "In the 18th century it was not an uncommon spectacle to see the corpses of infants lying in the streets or on the dunghills of London and other large cities." Abandonment at the door of a church would have been preferred, but the chance of discovery was too great. Eventually Parliament decided to intervene and set up foundling hospitals with various systems for collecting unwanted infants without risk to the donor. On the Continent, infants were passed through revolving boxes set in the walls of foundling hospitals.

But government was not capable of sustaining the cost of rearing children to adulthood, and foundling hospitals quickly became de facto slaughterhouses whose prime function was to authenticate the state's claim to a monopoly over the right to kill. Between 1756 and 1760 there were 15,000 admissions to London's first foundling hospital; of those admitted, only 4,400 survived to adolescence. Additional thousands of foundlings continued to be destroyed by wet nurses employed by parish workhouses. In order to economize, parish officers assigned the infants to women who were nicknamed "killing nurses" or "she-butchers" because "no child ever escaped their care alive." On the Continent admissions to foundling institutions increased steadily even during the early years of the nineteenth century. In

France admissions rose from 40,000 a year in 1784 to 138,000 in 1822. By 1830 there were 270 revolving boxes in use throughout France, with 336,297 infants legally abandoned during the decade 1824–1833. "Mothers who left their babies in the box knew that they were consigning them to death almost as surely as if they dropped them in the river." Between 80 and 90 percent of the children in these institutions died during their first year of life.

As late as the 1770's Europe had what demographers call a "pre-modern" population: high birth and death rates (about forty-five and forty per thousand, respectively), a .5 percent per annum rate of increase, and a life expectancy at birth of about thirty years. Less than half the people born survived to fifteen years of age. In Sweden, where the eighteenth-century censuses are more reliable than elsewhere, 21 percent of the infants whose births were registered died within the first year.

After 1770 some parts of Europe entered what demographers call an "early transitional" phase. There was a notable decline in the death rate, while the birth rate remained approximately unchanged. This does not necessarily mean that the standard of living was improving. The study of "early transitional" populations in modern underdeveloped countries indicates that declines in death rates and consequent increments in population growth are compatible with unchanging or even deteriorating standards of health and welfare. Benjamin White, for example, has found in a recent study of impoverished central Javanese peasants that parents will rear additional children if this brings only a slight balance of benefits over costs. This relationship between numbers of children and income helps to explain why many underdeveloped countries seem so unresponsive to population control by voluntary family planning methods. Where the net benefits of rearing children exceed the costs, a family that somehow succeeds in rearing more children will be slightly better off than its neighbors, even if in the meantime the standard of living of the population as a whole may be declining.

The late eighteenth century in Europe was a time when there was a great demand for child labor. Within the household, children participated in a variety of "cottage industries," helping to card wool, spin cotton, and manufacture clothing and other items under contract to entrepreneurs. As the locus of manufacture shifted to the factories, children often became the main source of labor since they could be paid less than adults and were more docile. It is safe to conclude, therefore, that the falling death rate during the early phases of the industrial revolution was due at least in part to the increased demand for child labor rather than wholly to a substantial overall improvement in diet, housing, or health. Children who previously would have been neglected, abandoned, or killed in infancy were now given the dubious privilege of living to the age at which they could begin to work in a factory for a few years before they succumbed to tuberculosis.

The failure of the first three centuries of post-feudal mechanization and scientific engineering was apparent to everyone. After all, widespread misery and suffering on the Continent provided the spark that ignited the French Revolution. In 1810 the workers in the factory districts of England were chanting "bread or blood." More and more, the impoverished masses had to steal in order to eat. Annual convictions for larceny in England rose 540 percent between 1805 and 1833; 26,500 people were hanged between 1806 and 1833, mostly for thefts of minor sums of money. In 1798 the fear of revolution and the appalling plight of the working class in the midst of technical progress and economic growth had led the English parson Thomas Malthus to propound his famous doctrine that poverty and distress were inevitable. The means of subsistence had been increasing even faster. Malthus did not claim that population would never get into balance with food supply; rather, he warned that unless population was restricted through abstinence, it would be checked by wars, infanticide, famines, plagues, abortions, and undesirable forms of contraception. As far as the past was concerned, Malthus was absolutely correct. Where he went wrong was in failing to foresee how industrial production in combination with new modes of contraception would soon create a rapid and unprecedented rise in the standard of living.

Malthus and other nineteenth-century economists whose forebodings came to be known as the "dismal science" were challenged by Karl Marx and other reformists and radicals on the grounds that the poverty and misery into which the peasants and workers of Europe had sunk was a result of laws peculiar to the political economy of capitalism and not of human existence in general. According to Marx, capitalists made their profits from exploiting labor; under capitalism, wages would always be driven down to subsistence levels regardless of whether population was rising or falling. Marx insisted that the internal laws of capitalism would inevitably lead to the concentration of wealth in the hands of a few plutocrats and the pauperization of everybody else. Like Malthus, he failed to predict the rapid and unprecedented rise in standard of living which was shortly to take place.

Neither Malthus nor Marx—the one obsessed with the law of reproduction, the other obsessed with the law of production—grasped the fact that the industrial revolution was creating an entirely new relationship between production and reproduction. Unlike all previous major shifts in modes of production, the industrial revolution of the nineteenth century resulted in an enormous spurt forward in labor efficiency accompanied not by an increase but by a decrease in the rate of population growth. From a peak of about 1.0 percent per year in the early 1800's, the rate of growth fell to 0.5 percent a century later, even though the amount of food and the number of other basic subsistence items available per capita were increasing far more rapidly. Although emigration to the Americas helped to slow the overall European rate of growth, a drop in the birth rate from 45 per thousand to less than 20 per thousand accounts for most of the decline.

This phenomenon is called the demographic transition. Around the world, economists and statesmen pin their hopes for economic development on the expectation that a fall in birth rates is a normal response to the introduction of more efficient technologies. But in anthropological perspective, nothing could be more abnormal. Every major shift in labor productivity has hitherto been accompanied or followed by a rapid increase in population density. This seems to have been true of the paleolithic to neolithic transition, of the Yanomamo shifting from stone to steel tools, of the Mesoamericans shifting from slash-and-burn to *chinampas,* of the Chinese shifting from rainfall to irrigation. And it appears to be specifically true of Europe from the bronze age on; certainly from early medieval times to the beginning of the nineteenth century, every period of rapid technological change was also a period of rapid population growth.

Let me try to explain why the demographic transition took place. It seems to me to have been caused by the conjunction of three extraordinary cultural events: the fuel revolution, the contraceptive revolution, and the job revolution. I'll take these up one at a time. By the fuel revolution, I mean the hundred-, thousand-, even millionfold increase in labor productivity brought about by the application of steam, diesel, gasoline, electric, and jet engines to agriculture, industry, mining, and transport. The utilization of these engines on a scale large enough to compensate even for the relatively slow rate of population growth of the past 100 years was entirely dependent on the sudden release of vast amounts of previously untapped energy stored up inside the earth in the form of coal and oil. I have difficulty in imagining how the harnessing of so much energy in such a short span of time would not have resulted in at least modest gains in living standards for substantial numbers of people. That coal and oil happen to be nonrenewable sources of energy (unlike trees, water, wind, and animal muscle power, to which previous generations had restricted themselves) is a significant fact which I shall return to in a moment.

By the contraception revolution, I mean the invention of safe and inexpensive means of reducing fertility through mechanical and chemical devices. The condom was widely advertised during the eighteenth century, but it was made out of sheep gut and used primarily as a protection against syphilis. With the invention of the vulcanization process in 1843, industrial technology could be used for the mass production of "rubbers." Along with these, the middle class began to use vaginal douches and vaginal plugs toward the end of the nineteenth century, and by the early twentieth century working-class families were doing the same. Infanticide dropped, as can be seen in the sharp decline in infant mortality. And so did the birth rate. Prior to 1830 the

English birth rate stood at close to 40 per thousand, approximately the rate found in such modern underdeveloped countries as India and Brazil. By 1900 it had dropped below 30 per thousand and by 1970 below 20 per thousand.

As Mahmood Mandami's study of the use of contraceptives in India has proven, mere availability of effective and relatively painless and cheap contraceptive devices would not by itself have brought about such dramatic declines in the birth rate. Modern contraception lowers the cost of interfering with the reproductive process. But families still have to be motivated to want to interfere with the course of nature; they have to want to rear fewer children. Here, then, enters the job revolution. As I've already suggested, the motivation to restrict fertility is essentially a question of the balance between the benefits and costs of parenthood. With industrialization, the cost of rearing children increases—especially after the introduction of child labor laws and compulsory education statutes—because the skills which a child must acquire in order to earn a living and be of benefit to its parents take longer to learn. At the same time, the whole context and manner in which people earn their livings becomes transformed. The family ceases to be the locus of any significant form of production activity (other than that of cooking meals and begetting children). Work is no longer something done by family members in or near the family farm or business. Rather, it is something done at an office, store, or factory in the company of other people's family members. Hence the return flow of benefits from rearing children hinges more and more on their economic success as wage earners and their willingness to help out in the medical and financial crises that parents can expect in their waning years.

The availability of painless contraception and the altered structure of economic tasks—the contraception revolution and the job revolution—provide the key to many puzzling aspects of contemporary social life. Longer life spans and spiraling medical costs make it increasingly unrealistic to expect children to give comfort and security to their aging parents. Thus we are in the process of substituting old-age and medical insurance programs for the preindustrial system in which children took care of their aged parents. When this process is completed, the last vestige of significant counterflow in the parent-child account will have disappeared.

The cost to parents of rearing a middle-class child to college age in the United States now stands at $80,000, only a minuscle portion of which is returned in money, goods, or services. (I do not deny that the intangibles, such as the joys of watching children grow up, also influence behavior. But who is to say that the joy of waching ten children grow up to be carhops is greater than the joy of watching one grow up to be a surgeon? Or that it is more rewarding for a woman to rear one surgeon than to be one herself and rear none?) That is why the U.S. birth rate continues to fall and divorces, unmarried consensual unions, childless marriages, homosexuality and homosexual marriages are all on the increase. And that is why experimental modes of family life, sexual "liberation," and "generation gaps" also suddenly make news.

To sum up: We can now see how technology got the upper hand in the race against intensification, depletion, and declining efficiency. The industrial world tapped an enormous fresh supply of cheap energy at the same time that it was able to apportion this bonanza among a population that was increasing far below its reproductive potential. But the race is far from over.

The advantage can only be temporary. We are slowly beginning to comprehend that a commitment to machines that run on fossil fuels is a commitment to depletions, declining efficiencies, and declining rates of profits in the strongest possible degree. Coal and oil cannot be recycled; they can only be used up at a faster or slower rate.

Experts, of course, disagree as to how long the usable supplies of coal and oil will last at present rates of consumption. Dr. M. King Hubert of the Shell Oil Company and the United States Geological Survey calculates that the peak in oil production will occur in 1995 and that coal production will peak in 2100. The real question is not when the last drop of oil will be gone nor is it when the last ton of coal will be mined. The effect of depletion on the standard of living becomes unbearable long before the last blade of grass or last horse or reindeer is gone. The farther and deeper we search for coal and oil, the more costly all industrial operations become. Under these circumstances the rate at which energy is applied to the production of food and other sources of energy merely acts to speed up the rate at which declining efficiencies become manifest in the rising costs of goods and services. As coal and oil become scarcer, their costs will go up. And since virtually every product and service in industrial society depends on large energetic inputs derived from these sources, inflation will steadily reduce the ability of the average person to pay for the goods and services now regarded as essential for health and well-being.

How fast and how low standards of living in the industrial nations will fall depends on how long conversion to alternative energy sources is delayed. The possibility of deep impoverishment should not be dismissed. In the face of inevitable and imminent shortages of fossil fuels, we are not yet cutting back on the rate at which we are squandering these resources. In fact, we are still rapidly expanding the scope of fossil fuel technologies and attempting to compensate for rising prices with more and more lavish injections of fossil fuels into "labor-saving" machines and production processes.

Food production, to take the most critical example, has now become totally dependent on our oil supply. Agricultural traction, lifting, hauling, and transport were captured first. Now we have reached the stage where the conditioning of the soil through chemical fertilizers and the defense of plants through herbicides, pesticides, insecticides, and fungicides have also become totally dependent on an ever-increasing supply of petrochemicals. The so-called "green revolution" is an oil revolution in which higher crop yields per acre have been made possible by continuous injections of vast amounts of fossil fuel energy into the production of plant varieties specially bred for their ability to respond to petrochemical inputs.

As David Pimentel of Cornell University has shown, in the United States 2,790 calories of energy are now being used to produce and deliver one can of corn containing 270 calories. The production of beef now requires even more prodigious energy deficits: 22,000 calories to produce 100 grams (containing the same 270 calories as in the can of corn). The bubble-like nature of this mode of production can be seen from the fact that if the rest of the world were suddenly to adopt the energy ratios characteristic of U.S. agriculture, all known reserves of petroleum would be exhausted in eleven years. Or, to put it in a slightly different form: the faster the underdeveloped world industrializes, the sooner the industrial world must develop a new mode of production.

Epilogue and Moral Soliloquy

Before the fuel revolution, plants and animals were the main source of energy for social life. Scattered about the earth on millions of farms and villages, plants and animals collected the energy of the sun and converted it into forms appropriate for human use and consumption. Other sources of energy, such as the wind and falling water, were no less dispersed. The only way for despots to cut people off from their energy supply was to deny them access to the land or the oceans. This was an extremely difficult task and very costly under most conditions of climate and terrain. Control over water, however, was more readily managed. And where water could be controlled, plants and animals could be controlled. Further, since plants and animals were the main sources of energy, control over water was control over energy. In this sense the despotisms of hydraulic society were energy despotisms—but only in a very indirect and primitive way.

The fuel revolution has opened up the possibility for a more direct form of energy despotism. Energy is now being collected and distributed under the supervision of a small number of bureaus and corporations. It comes from a relatively small number of mines and wells. Hundreds of millions of people can technically be shut off from these mines and wells, starved, frozen, plunged into darkness, rendered immobile by the turn of a few valves and the flick of a few switches. As if this were not already sufficient cause for alarm, the industrial nations have begun to compensate for the impending exhaustion of coal and oil by converting to nuclear power—a far more concentrated source of energy than the fossil fuels. There already exists the electronic capability for the tracking of individual behavior by centralized networks of surveillance and record-keeping computers. It is highly probable that the conversion to nuclear energy production will provide precisely those basic material conditions most appropriate for using the power of the computer to establish a new and enduring form of despotism. Only by decentralizing our basic mode of energy production—by breaking the cartels that monopolize the present system of energy production and by creating new decentralized forms of energy technology—can we restore the ecological and cultural configuration that led to the emergence of political democracy in Europe.

This raises the question of how we can consciously select improbable alternatives to probable evolutionary trends. Surveying the past in anthropological perspective, I think it is clear that the major transformations of human social life have hitherto never corresponded to the consciously held objectives of the historical participants. Consciousness had little to do with the processes by which infanticide and warfare became the means of regulating band and village populations: women became subordinate to men; those who worked hardest and kept the least became those who worked the least and kept the most; "great providers" became great believers; sacrificial meat became forbidden flesh; animal sacrificers became vegetarians; labor-saving devices became the instruments of drudgery; irrigation agriculture became the trap of hydraulic despotism.

Our ancestors, of course, were no less psychologically conscious than we are in the sense of being alert, of having thoughts and making decisions based on the calculation of the immediate cost/benefits of alternative types of action. To say that their consciousness did not play a role in directing the course of cultural evolution is not to say that they were zombies. I suggest that they were unaware of the influence of modes of production and reproduction on their attitudes and values and that they were wholly ignorant of the long-term cumulative effects of decisions made to maximize short-term cost/benefits. To change the world in a conscious way one must first have a conscious understanding of what the world is like. Lack of such an understanding is a dismal portent.

As a cultural determinist, I have sometimes been accused of reducing human values to a mechanical reflex and of portraying individuals as mere puppets. These are doctrines that are alien to my understanding of cultural processes. I insist simply that the thought and behavior of individuals are always channeled by cultural and ecological restraints and opportunities. Successive modes of production and reproduction largely determine the nature of these channels. Where the mode of production calls for "big man" redistributors, ambitious men will grow up to boast about their wealth and give it all away. Where the mode of production calls for "big man" redistributors, ambitious men will grow up to boast about their wealth and give it all away. Where the mode of production calls for "big men entrepreneurs," ambitious men will grow up to boast about their wealth and keep it all for themselves. I do not pretend to know why Soni became a great feast-giver or why John D. Rockefeller became a great hoarder of wealth. Nor do I know why one individual rather than another wrote *Hamlet*. I am perfectly willing to let such questions dissolve into perpetual mystery.

Cultural causality is another matter. Many humanists and artists recoil from the proposition that cultural evolution has hitherto been shaped by unconscious impersonal forces. The determined nature of the past fills them with apprehension as to the possibility of an equally determined future. But their fears are misplaced. It is only through an awareness of the determined nature of the past that we can hope to make the future less dependent on unconscious and impersonal forces. In the birth of a science of culture others profess to see the death of moral initiative. For my part, I cannot see how a lack of intelligence concerning the lawful processes that have operated so far can be the platform on which to rear a civilized future. And so in the birth of a science of culture I find the beginning not the end of moral initiative. Let the protectors of historical spontaneity beware: If the processes of cultural evolution are what I have discerned, they are morally negligent to urge others to think and act as if such processes did not exist.

I hold it perniciously false to teach that all cultural forms are equally probable and that by mere force of will an inspired individual can at any moment alter the trajectory of an entire cultural system in a direction convenient to any philosophy. Convergent and parallel trajectories far outnumber divergent trajectories in cultural evolution. Most people are conformists. History repeats itself in countless acts of individual obedience to cultural rule and pattern, and individual wills seldom prevail in matters requiring radical alteration of deeply conditioned beliefs and practices.

At the same time, nothing I have written in this book supports the view that the individual is helpless before the implacable march of history or that resignation and despair are appropriate responses to the concentration of industrial managerial power. The determinism that has governed cultural evolution has never been the equivalent of the determinism that governs a closed physical system. Rather, it resembles the causal sequences that account for the evolution of plant and animal species. Retrospectively, guided by Darwin's principle of natural selection, scientists can readily reconstruct the causal chain of adaptations that led from fish to reptiles to birds. But what biologist looking at a primitive shark could have foreseen a pigeon? What biologist looking at a tree shrew could have predicted *Homo sapiens?* The intensification of the industrial mode of production and the technological victory over Malthusian pressures undoubtedly portend an evolution of new cultural forms. I do not know for certain what these will be, nor does anyone else.

Since evolutionary changes are not completely predictable, it is obvious that there is room in the world for what we call free will. Each individual decision to accept, resist, or change the current order alters the probability that a particular evolutionary outcome will occur. While the course of cultural evolution is never free of systemic influence, some moments are probably more "open" than others. The most open moments, it appears to me, are those at which a mode of production reaches its limits of growth and a new mode of production must soon be adopted. We are rapidly moving toward such an opening. When we have passed through it, only then, looking backwards, shall we know why human beings chose one option rather than another. In the meantime, people with deep personal commitments to a particular vision of the future are perfectly justified in struggling toward their goal, even if the outcome now seems remote and improbable. In life, as in any game whose outcome depends on both luck and skill, the rational response to bad odds is to try harder.

Acknowledgments, References, and Notes

Culture and Nature

I am preparing a more technical volume (Harris, 1979)* to clarify my general philosophical and scientific premises in relationship to alternative paradigms. An earlier work (Harris, 1968) tells the story of the development of cultural materialism up to the 1960's. The specific theme of this book—the relating of cultural evolution to intensification and depletions—closely resembles the theoretical position of Michael Harner (1970). Other scholars who have preceded me in emphasizing the relationship between intensification and cultural evolution are Ester Boserup (1965), Robert Carneiro (1970), Brian Spooner (1972), Philip Smith (1972), Colin Renfrew (1974), Richard Wilkinson (1973), M.N. Cohen (1975), and Malcolm Webb (1975). Major differences of definition, emphasis, and scope separate my own approach from all of these predecessors. However, if any or all of them see in what I have written an exact duplicate of a theory which they can call their own, I shall be happy to acknowledge their priority in its formulation. For an overview of cultural differences and similarities see my textbook (Harris, 1974).

Murders in Eden

For a description of contemporary hunter-collectors see Lee and De Vore (1968) and Bicchieri (1972). See Steward

*For full citations see the entry in the bibliography under author and date.

(1955) and Service (1968) for surplus above subsistence theory. For the accomplishments of the upper paleolithic see Prideaux (1973) and Marshack (1972). Marshall Sahlins (1972) says hunter-collectors are the "original affluent society." See Butzer (1971) for the relationship between ice age ecology and culture. On work patterns see Lee (1968, 1969), Johnson (1975), and Edmondson (1976); for the Mehinacu see Gregor (1969). Hunter-collectors' preadaptation to agriculture is discussed by Cohen (1975, p. 82 ff). For hunter-collector density data see Kroeber (1939), Lee (1968), and David (1973). On stone age demography, disease, and health see Hassan (1973, 1975), Cockburn (1971), Wood (1975), Armelagos and McArdle (1975), Black (1975), Livingstone (1968), Dumond (1975), Boyd (1972), Howell (in press), Birdsell (1968, 1972), and Coale (1974). On abortion and mechanical and chemical contraceptives see Devereux (1955) and Nurge (1975). On geronticide see Hoebel (1954, pp. 76–79) and Warner (1937). For infanticide see Dickeman (1975a), Balikci (1967), Chagnon (1968), and Freeman (1971). On carrying infants see Lee (1972). For lactation method see Frisch and McArthur (1974), Frisch (1975), Kolata (1974), Van Ginneken (1974), and Divale and Harris (1976).

The Origin of Agriculture

Most archaeologists refer to the Levant, Egypt, Anatolia, and Mesopotamia as the Near East. I have used the term "Middle East" to designate this region in keeping with geopolitical usage. On scavenging see Shipman and Phillips-Conroy (1977) and Brain (in press). See Butzer (1971, 1975) and Flannery (1969) for postglacial changes. For the pleistocene megafauna problem in the New World see MacNeish (in press); the quote is from Mosimann and Martin (1975, p. 308). I am grateful to Richard MacNeish for permitting me to use his manuscript *Energy and Culture in Ancient Tehuacan*. See also MacNeish (1972) and the reports of the Tehuacán Valley Project of the Peabody Museum of Archaeology. For early Middle Eastern domestication I have relied on Flannery (1973), David Harris (in press), Harlan (in press), Zohary and Hopf (1973), Ducos (1969), and Chaplin (1969). Flannery (1973, p. 284) believes in the mysterious changes. For neolithic rates of population growth see Carneiro and Hilse (1966), Smith and Young (1972), and Butzer (1976). For Andean domestication of animals see Pires-Ferreira et al. (1976). I am aware of the possibility that agriculture involving rice, root crops, and tree crops may have originated independently in Southeast Asia. If so, the specific model I have been using would have to be modified—but not discarded. See Solheim (1970), Vishnu-Mittre (in press), Harlan (in press), David Harris (in press). An independent origin for agriculture seems likely for China, but this would strengthen the model if it is substantiated. See Ping-ti Ho (1975).

The Origin of War

For peaceful cultures see Lesser (1968); on the archaeology of violence see Roper (1969, 1975). For hunter-collector war see Divale (1972). For anthropology of war see Fried et al. (1968) and Nettleship et al. (1975). The Tiwi are described by Hart and Pilling (1960); the Murngin, by Warner (1930); the Dani, by Heider (1972). For the social solidarity function of war see Wright (1965) and Wedgwood (1930). For *war as play* see Lowie (1954). Robert Ardrey is a popular advocate of *war as human nature*. See Montagu (1976) for a thorough review and refutation of this position. For dispersion effects see Vayda (1961, 1971). The quote is from Birdsell (1972, pp. 357–58). See Livingstone (1968) for effects of modern war on population. See Divale and Harris (1976) for evidence on links between war and female infanticide. For the role of women in production see Morren (1974) and Lee (1969).

Proteins and the Fierce People

Quotes are from Chagnon (1974, pp. 127, 194–195). For settlement size see Lathrap (1973) and Meggers (1971). For sex ratios see Chagnon (1973, p. 135), Lizot (1971), and Smole (1976). The quote about fighting over women is from Chagnon (1968b, p. 151); about peripheral villages (1968b, p. 114). The next quote is from Lizot (1971, pp. 34–35). See Neel and Weiss (1975) and Chagnon (1975). See Smole (1976) for history of Yanomamo contacts with Europeans. The earlier quote is from Chagnon (1968, p. 33). For the discussion of animal protein in the tropical forest I am greatly indebted to Daniel Gross (1975), Eric Ross (1976), and Jane Ross (1971). My source for U.S. animal protein is Pimentel et al. (1975, p. 754). The quote is from Smole (1976, p. 175). Helena Valero's story is in Biocca (1970). See also Siskind (1973).

The Origin of Male Supremacy and of the Oedipus Complex

See Reed (1975) for an exhumation. For attempts to show that women's subordination has been overemphasized see Friedl (1967), Sweet (1967), Lamphere (1975), Hoffer (1975), and Reiter (1975). For attacks on male blinders see Kaberry (1970) and Linton (1973). The statistics from Murdock refer to the computer punch card version of the *Ethnographic Atlas*. See also Murdock (1967). The standard work on kinship and marriage is Murdock (1949). On the Nagovisi see Nash (1974). The term "dowry" is also sometimes applied to a woman's share of parental inheritance given to her at marriage. This should be called anticipatory inheritance rather than dowry. See Lévi-Strauss (1969). For more on asymmetric institutions see the Introduction to Rosaldo and Lamphere (1974) and Friedl (1975). For Iroquois warfare I have relied on Scheele (1950) and Morgan (1962). See Divale (1975) and Divale et al. (1976) for matrilocality and external warfare. The quote on Iroquois marriage is from Morgan (1962, p. 325). On Iroquois women see Brown (1975). On pastoralism see Salzman (1971). The errant feminist is quoted by Scheele (1950, p. 48). The next quote is from Morgan (1962, p. 324). The next quote is from Brown (1975, pp. 240–41). On the Oedipus complex see Hall and Lindzey (1967), Barnouw (1973), and Malinowski (1927). For a good example of the inverted causal priorities of Freudianism see Walsh and Scandalis (1975).

The Origin of Pristine States

I am grateful to Morton Fried (see especially Fried, 1967) and to Barbara Price (especially Price, 1977) for long-term assistance in thinking about the origin of the state. See Webb (1975) for a discussion of the regions in which pristine states may have developed. Redistribution as a form of exchange was originally defined by the economist Karl Polanyi and introduced into anthropology by Polanyi et al. (1957). The link between redistribution and social stratification was suggested first by Marshall Sahlins (1958). For quotes about *mumis*, see Oliver (1955, pp. 439, 411, 399, 421). See Hogbin (1964) for Kaoka "big men." On Trobrianders see Malinowski (1920, 1922, 1935) and Uberoi (1962). See Renfrew (1973) for comparisons between Cherokee and European "henge" cultures. The quotes on the Bunyoro are from Beattie (1960, pp. 34, 36). My scenario for the evolution of pristine states draws upon Carneiro (1970) but rejects "social" circumscription as an alternative to ecological circumscription. Webb's (1975) scenario is closest to mine. For population estimates see Butzer (1976) and Sanders (1972). See Briffault (1963) for matrilineal argument. See Renfrew (1973) for "fat ladies."

The Pre-Columbian States of Mesoamerica

For examples of the romantic approach see Morley and Brainerd (1956), Thompson (1954), Coe (1968), and Covarrubias (1957). I have relied on Willey (1966) and Weaver (1972) for my basic facts about Mesoamerican prehistory. My ecological interpretations would not have been possible without the synthesis proposed by William Sanders and Barbara Price (1968). See Grennes-Ravitz and Coleman (1966) and Hammond (1974). For Maya population estimates see Haviland (1969), Sanders (1972), and Cook (1972). For trade theory of Maya state see Rathje (1971) and for its refutation see Price (1977). Lundell's (1937) study of the Petén is still the best available. See Gifford (1972) and Grove et al. (1976) for earliest Maya settlements. For slash-and-burn see Cowgill (1962), Boserup (1965), Meggers et al. (1973), and Conklin (1963). For the people who eat forests see Condominas (1957). See Puleston (1974), Turner (1974), and Cook (1972). For breadnut trees see Puleston and Puleston (1971). See Mathenay (1976). For the Maya collapse, see Culbert (1973). For the rise of Teotihuacán see Sanders (1972) and Sanders and Price (1968). See Millon (1973) but ignore his hysterical attack against ecologists. For *chinampas* see Palerm (1967). For demographic patterns in the Valley of Mexico see Parsons and Blanton (1969).

The Cannibal Kingdom

Michael Harner alone deserves credit (or blame) for the discovery (or rediscovery) of Aztec cannibalism and for the explanation that I offer for Aztec cannibalism in this chapter. See Harner (1975, 1977a, b). However, I have independently gone over the primary sources, especially Díaz (1956, pp. 217–20), De Sahagún (1950, pp. 4, 589), Durán (1964, p. 121), and Tápia (1971). For Iroquois heart-eating see Scheele (1950, p. 101). For pre-Columbian cannibalism see Flinn et al. (1976). For a summary of Staden's account see Métraux (1945). The Jesuit missionary was Le Mercier in Thwaites (1959, Vol. 13, pp. 59–79). See Sagan (1974). For the strength in human flesh see Dornstreich and Morren (1974). See Cook (1946), Díaz (1965, p. 119), Tápia (1971, p. 583), Soustelle (1962, p. 101), Cook (1946, p. 283), De Sahagún (1950, pp. 24, 29), and Durán (1964, p. 122).

The Lamb of Mercy

For reviews of cannibalism in the Old World see Tannahill (1975) and Sagan (1974). I have relied on summaries of human sacrifice in Hastings' (1921) *Encyclopedia of Religion and Ethics.* See also Lévi (1966), Rosengarten (1966), and Yerkes (1952). For the "cult of the severed head" see Piggott (1965, p. 230); for Druids see Piggott (1975). See Gelb (1973). The quotes are from Hastings (1921). See W. Smith (1956), Schneider (1957), and Dyson-Hudson and Dyson-Hudson (1969). The quote is from Smith (1956). See my account of the events surrounding the last supper in Harris (1974). See Tannahill (1975, p. 84) for "contemptible" animals. Hammurabi's words are from Driver and Miles (1955, pp. 7–13). See Mencius (1970, pp. 483, 135–36). On Incas see Rowe (1947) and Mason (1957). See Pires-Ferreira (1976).

Forbidden Flesh

The data on productivity of plants versus animals are from the National Research Council (1975, p. III ff). For discussion of dietary role of protein see Taylor and Pye (1966) and FAO/WHO (1973). For efficiency and physiology of the pig see National Research Council (1975), Pond and Manes (1974), and Mount (1968). For archaeological evidence of the domesticated pig, see Epstein (1971, Vol. 2 pp. 349–50), Ducos (1969), and Zeuner (1963). See E. Ross (1976) for general theory of taboos on hunted animals. See Zeuner (1963, pp. 134–35), Whyte (1961, pp. 69–76), and Reifenberg (1955) for environmental impact of intensification on the Middle East. See Alland (1974, p. 67) for criticism of pig theory. See Epstein (1971, p. 342) for pig in Egypt: see Epstein (1971, p. 354) and Hawkes (1973, p. 101) for pig in Mesopotamia. See Whyte (1971) and Jacobsen and Adams (1958) on silting and salt problem. See Young (1972) for intensification in early Mesopotamia.

The Origin of the Sacred Cow

See Allchin (1968, p. 321), Allchin and Allchin (1968, pp. 114, 259), Hawkes (1973), Marshall (1931), and Thapar (1966). See Prakash (1961, pp. 15, 16) and Bose (1961, p. 109). *The Cambridge History of India* is a standard source. See Prakash (1961, pp. 175–76) and Maitz (1957, pp. 94–95) for Gupta period. See Davis (1951), Spengler (1971), and Nath (1929) for historical demography. See Bose (1961, p. 131 ff) for deforestation and Mahabharata drought. For the cultural ecology of cattle in India see M. Harris (1974, 1971, 1966), Raj (1971, 1969), Heston (1971), Dandekar (1969), Odend'hal (1972), and Embassy of India (1975). See Gandhi (1954). For discussion of lactase see Harrison (1975). See Gandhi (1954). For discussion of lactase see Harrison (1975). For comparisons of Indian and Chinese ecosystems see Buck (1964), Raj (1969), Singh (1971), Gavan and Dixon (1975), Shen (1951, p. 290), Phillips (1945), and Sprague (1975). The Mao quote is from Raj (1971, p. 717). See Varma (1967) for modern Ganges Valley.

The Hydraulic Trap

For world population trends see Spengler (1974). See David (1951), Butzer (1976), and Bielenstein (1947). For the remainder of this chapter I have relied heavily on Karl Wittfogel's *Oriental Despotism*. See also Wittfogel

(1931, 1960, 1970, 1972). The Marx quote is from the article "British Rule in India" (New York Daily Tribune, 1853). See Wittfogel (1972, p. 62). See Adams (1966, p. 68) and Butzer (1976). Perkins (1968) makes the same mistake for China. See Bielenstein (1947) for Yellow River floods. I am grateful for the advice and criticism of Sinologist-anthropologist-colleague-friend Myron Cohen. See Wittfogel (1972) and Ulmen (1975) for review of impact of hydraulic theory on research. Also M. Harris (1968) and Price (1971). See Mitchell (1973) for clarification of hydraulic theory. See Woodbury and Neely (1972) for irrigation in Tehuacán.

The Origin of Capitalism

See Piggott (1965, pp. 229, 235, 140). For Rome see Africa (1974). See Bloch (1961, 1966). See Wittfogel (1957, p. 44). See Wolf (1966, p. 30 ff) and Van Bath (1963) for European medieval demography and economy. For the history of the plow see Wailes (1972). See Wallerstein (1975, p. 20) and Lopez (1974). For "crisis of feudalism" see Wallerstein (1975, p. 21 ff) and Postan (1972). See Wilkinson (1973, pp. 76–77). On infanticide see Russel (1948), Kellum (1974), Langer (1974), Trexler (1973a, b), Shorter (1975, p. 168 ff), and Dickeman (1975). See M. Harris (1974) for witchcraft, messianism, and peasant revolts, 1300–1500. See Russell and Russell (1973) for relationship between Black Death and ecological crisis of feudalism. Also Nohl (1961). For Chinese technology see Needham (1970), Needham and Ling (1959), Elvin (1974), and Wittfogel (1957, pp. 78, 329).

The Industrial Bubble

Wilkinson (1973, p. 76 ff, p. 112 ff). For living conditions in Europe see Braudel (1972, 1973), Engels (1958), Eden (1928), Pinchbeck (1969), Polanyi (1944), and Langer (1972, pp. 96, 98). For mortality in Sweden and demographic transition see Llewellyn-Jones (1974). Also Ehrlich and Ehrlich (1970) and Ford and DeJong (1970). See Langer (1963) and Glass and Eversley (1965) for eighteenth-century decline in mortality. See White (1973, 1975). For cottage industries see Landes (1966). Crime statistics are from Rusche and Kirchheimer (1939). For social context of Malthusians see Polgar (1975) and Beales (1959). For Marx-Malthus controversy see Meek (1971). See Himes (1963) and Llewellyn-Jones (1974) for history of contraception. See Banks (1953) and Coale (1969) for decline of fertility. For the culminating effects and estimates of the rising costs of child-rearing see Minge-Kalman (1977). For depletion of coal and oil see National Petroleum Council (1973), Penner and Icerman (1974), Hubert (1976), and Commoner (1976). For the "oilification" of food see M. Harris (1973), Jennings (1976), Wade (1973), Pimentel et al. (1973, 1975), Pimentel (1976), Borgstrom (1973), Steinhart and Steinhart (1974), and Leach (1975).

Bibliography

Adams, Robert McC.
1966 *The Evolution of Urban Society: Early Mesopotamia and Prehispanic Mexico.* Chicago: Aldine.

Africa, Thomas W.
1974 *The Immense Majesty: A History of Rome and the Roman Empire.* New York: Thomas Y. Crowell.

Alland, Alexander
1974 "Adaptation." Annual Review of Anthropology 4:59–73.

Allchin, Bridget and Raymond Allchin
1968 *The Birth of Indian Civilization.* Baltimore: Penguin.

Allchin, F. R.
1968 "Early Domestic Animals in India and Pakistan." In Ucko and Dimbleby (eds.), pp. 317–21.

Angel, J. Lawrence
1975 "Paleoecology, Paleodemography and Health." In Polgar (ed.), pp. 167–90.

Armelagos, George and Allan McArdle
1975 "Population, Disease, and Evolution." American Antiquity 40,2:1–10.

Balikci, Asen
1967 "Female Infanticide on the Arctic Coast." Man 2:615–25.

Banks, J. A.
1953 *Prosperity and Parenthood.* London: Routledge.

Barnouw, Victor
1973 *Culture and Personality*. Homewood, Ill.: Dorsey Press.

Beales, H. L.
1959 "The Historical Context of the Essay on Population." In D. V. Glass, ed., *Introduction to Malthus*, pp. 1–24. London: Frank Case.

Beattie, John
1960 *Bunyoro: An African Kingdom*. New York: Holt, Rinehart & Winston.

Bicchieri, M. G. (ed.)
1972 *Hunters and Gatherers Today*. New York. Holt, Rinehart & Winston.

Bielenstein, Hans
1947 "The Census of China During the Period 2–742 A.D." Bulletin of the Museum of Far Eastern Antiquities 19:125–65.

Biocca, Ettore
1970 *Yanomama: The Narrative of a White Girl Kidnaped by Amazonian Indians*. New York: Dutton.

Birdsell, Joseph
1968 "Some Predictions for the Pleistocene Based on Equilibrium Systems Among Recent Hunter-Gatherers." In Lee and De Vore (eds.), pp. 229–49.
1972 *Human Evolution: An Introduction to the New Physical Anthropology*. Chicago: Rand McNally.

Black, Francis
1975 "Infectious Diseases in Primitive Societies." Science 187:515–18.

Bloch, Marc
1961 *Feudal Society*. Chicago: University of Chicago Press.
1966 "The Rise of Dependent Cultivation and Seignorial Institutions." In M. M. Postan, ed., *The Agrarian Life of the Middle Ages*, pp. 235–90. London: Cambridge University Press.

Borgstrom, Georg
1973 *The Food and People Dilemma*. North Scituate, Mass.: Duxbury Press.

Bose, A. N.
1961 *Social and Rural Economy of Northern India, 600 B.C.–200 A.D.* Calcutta: Firma K. L. Mukhopadhyay.

Boserup, E.
1965 *The Conditions of Agricultural Growth*. Chicago: Aldine.

Boyd, R.
1972 "Urbanization, Morbidity, and Natality." In Ucko, Dimbleby, and Tringham (eds.), pp. 345–52.

Brain, C. K.
(in press) "Some Aspects of the South African Australopithecine Sites and Their Bone Accumulations." In C. Jolly, ed., *Early Man in Africa*. London: Duckworth.

Braudel, Fernand
1973 *Capitalism and Material Life 1400–1800*. New York: Harper & Row.
1972 *The Mediterranean and the Mediterranean World in the Age of Phillip II*. New York: Harper & Row.

Briffault, Robert
1963 *The Mothers*. New York: Grosset & Dunlap.

Brown, Judith
1975 "Iroquois Women: An Ethnohistoric Note." In Reiter (ed.), pp. 235–51.

Buck, John
1964 (1937) *Land Utilization in China*. New York: Praeger (Vol. 1), Vol. 2 (Statistics), and Vol. 3 (Atlas). Chicago: University of Chicago Press.

Butzer, Karl
1971 *Environment and Archaeology: An Ecological Approach to Prehistory*. Chicago: Aldine.

1975 "Patterns of Environmental Change in the Near East During Late Pleistocene and Early Holocene Times." In Fred Wendorf and A. Marks, eds., *Problems in Prehistory: North Africa and the Levant*, pp. 389–411. Dallas: Southern Methodist University.

1976 *Early Hydraulic Civilization in Egypt: A Study in Cultural Ecology*. Chicago: University of Chicago Press.

Cambridge History of India

1923–1927 *Cambridge History of India*. Cambridge: Cambridge University Press.

Carneiro, Robert

1970 "A Theory of the Origin of the State." Science 169:733–38.

Carneiro, Robert and D. Hilse

1966 "On Determining the Probable Rate of Population Growth During the Neolithic." American Anthropologist 68:177:81.

Chagnon, Napoleon

1968a *Yanomamö: The Fierce People*. New York: Holt, Rinehart & Winston.

1968b "Yanomamö Social Organization and Warfare." In Fried, Harris, and Murphy (eds.), pp. 109–59.

1974 *Studying the Yanomamö*. New York: Holt, Rinehart & Winston.

1975 "Genealogy, Solidarity, and Relatedness: Limits to Local Group Size and Patterns of Fissioning in an Expanding Population." Yearbook of Physical Anthropology 19:95–110.

Chaplin, Raymond

1969 "The Use of Non-morphological Criteria in the Study of Animal Domestication from Bones Found on Archaeological Sites." In Ucko and Dimbleby (eds.), pp. 231–46.

Coale, Ansley

1970 "The Decline of Fertility in Europe from the

French Revolution to World War II." In S. J. Behrman, L. Corsa, and R. Freedman, eds., *Fertility and Family Planning: A World View*. Ann Arbor: University of Michigan Press.

1974 "The History of Human Population." Scientific American 231:41–51 (September).

Cockburn, T. A.

1971 "Infectious Diseases in Ancient Populations." Current Anthropology 12:45–62.

Coe, Michael

1968 *America's First Civilization: Discovering the Olmec*. New York: American Heritage.

Cohen, Mark N.

1975 "Population Pressure and the Origins of Agriculture." In Polgar (ed.), pp. 79–121.

Commoner, Barry

1976 *The Poverty of Power: Energy and the Economic Crisis*. New York: Alfred A. Knopf.

Condominas, George

1957 *Nous avons mangé la forêt de la Pérre-Genie Goo*. Paris: Plon.

Conklin, Harold

1963 *The Study of Shifting Cultivation*. Washington: Pan American Union.

Cook, Sherburne

1946 "Human Sacrifice and Warfare as Factors in the Demography of Pre-Colonial Mexico." Human Biology 18:81–102.

1972 *Prehistoric Demography*. Reading (Mass): Addison-Wesley.

Covarrubias, Miguel

1957 *Indian Art of Mexico and Central America*. New York: Alfred A. Knopf.

Cowgill, Ursula

1962 "An Agricultural Study of the Southern Maya Lowlands." American Anthropologist 64:273–86.

Culbert, T. P. (ed.)
1973 *The Classic Maya Collapse.* Albuquerque: University of New Mexico Press.

Dandekar, V. M.
1969 "Cow Dung Models." Economic and Political Weekly (Bombay) 2:1267–71 (August).

David, Nicholas
1973 "On Upper Paleolithic Society, Ecology and Technological Change." In Renfrew (ed.), pp. 275–303.

Davis, Kingsley
1951 *The Population of India and Pakistan.* Princeton: Princeton University Press.

De Sahagún, Bernadino
1950–63 *General History of the Things of New Spain.* Santa Fe, N.M.: School of American Research.

Devereux, George
1955 *A Study of Abortion in Primitive Societies.* New York: Julian Press.

Díaz, Bernal
1956 *The Discovery and Conquest of Mexico 1517–1521.* New York: Farrar, Straus & Giroux.

Dickeman, Mildred
1975a "Demographic Consequences of Infanticide in Man." Annual Review of Ecology and Systematics 6:100–37.
1975b "Female Infanticide and Hypergyny: A Neglected Relationship." Paper presented at the meeting of the American Anthropological Association, San Francisco.

Divale, William
1972 "Systematic Population Control in the Middle and Upper Paleolithic." World Archaeology 42, 2:222–41.
1975 "An Explanation for Matrilocal Residence." In Raphael (ed.), pp. 99–108.

Divale, W. T., F. Chamberis, and D. Gangloff
1976 "War, Peace and Marital Residence in Pre-Industrial Societies." Journal of Conflict Resolution 20:57–78.

Divale, William and M. Harris
1976 "Population, Warfare, and the Male Supremacist Complex." American Anthropologist 78:521–38.

Dornstreich, Mark and G. Morren
1974 "Does New Guinea Cannibalism Have Nutritional Value?" Human Ecology 2:1–12.

Driver, G. R. and J. C. Miles (eds.)
1955 *The Babylonian Laws*, Vol. 2. Oxford: Clarendon Press.

Ducos, P.
1969 "Methodology and Results of the Study of the Earliest Domesticated Animals in the Near East (Palestine)." In Ucko and Dimbleby (eds.), pp. 265–76.

Dumond, Don E.
1975 "The Limitation of Human Population: A Natural History." Science 187:713–20.

Durán, Diego
1964 *The Aztecs: The History of the Indies of New Spain*. New York: Orion.

Dyson-Hudson, Rada and N. Dyson-Hudson
1969 "Subsistence Herding in Uganda." Scientific American 220(2):76–89.

Eden, Frederick
1928 *The State of the Poor*. London: G. Routledge & Sons.

Edmondson, W. C.
1976 *Land, Food and Work in East Java*. New England Monographs in Geography, 4. Armidale, N.S.W. Australia.

Ehrlich, Paul and A. Ehrlich
1970 *Population, Resources, Environment*. San Francisco: W. H. Freeman.

Elvin, Mark
1974 *The Pattern of the Chinese Past.* Stanford: Stanford University Press.

Embassy of India
1975 "Indian Economy and Cattle Use." India News, November 7.

Engels, Friedrich
1958 *The Condition of the Working Class in England.* London: Oxford University Press.

Epstein, H.
1971 *The Origin of the Domestic Animals of Africa.* 2 Vols. New York: Africana Publishing Corporation.

FAO/WHO
1973 *Energy and Protein Requirements.* FAO Nutrition Meetings Report Series, No. 52. Rome: Food and Agricultural Organization of the United Nations.

Flannery, Kent
1969 "Origins and Ecological Effects of Early Domestication in Iran and the Near East." In Ucko and Dimbleby (eds.), pp. 73–100.
1973 "The Origins of Agriculture." Annual Review of Anthropology 2:270–310.

Flinn, Lynn, C. Turner, and A. Brew
1976 "Additional Evidence for Cannibalism in the Southwest: The Case of LA 4528." American Antiquity 41:308–18.

Ford, T. R. and G. F. DeJong (eds.)
1970 *Social Demography.* Englewood Cliffs: Prentice-Hall.

Freeman, M.
1971 "A Social and Economic Analysis of Systematic Female Infanticide." American Anthropologist 73:1011–18.

Fried, Morton H.
1967 *The Evolution of Political Society: An Essay in*

Political Anthropology. New York: Random House.

Fried, Morton, M. Harris, and R. Murphy (eds.)
1968 *War: The Anthropology of Armed Conflict and Aggression*. Garden City, N.Y.: Natural History Press.

Friedl, Ernestine
1967 "The Position of Women: Appearance and Reality." Anthropological Quarterly 40:97–108.
1975 *Women and Men: An Anthropologist's View*. New York: Holt, Rinehart & Winston.

Frisch, Rose
1975 "Critical Weights, A Critical Body Composition, Menarche and the Maintenance of Menstrual Cycles." In Elizabeth Watts, F. Johnston, and G. Lasker, eds., *Biosocial Interrelations in Population Adaptation*, pp. 319–52. The Hague: Mouton.

Frisch, Rose and J. McArthur
1974 "Menstrual Cycles: Fatness as a Determinant of Minimum Weight for Height Necessary for Their Maintenance or Onset." Science 185:949–51.

Gandhi, M. K.
1954 *How to Serve the Cow*. Ahmedabad: Navajivan Publishing House.

Gavan, J. D. and J. Dixon
1975 "India: A Perspective on the Food Situation." Science 188:541–49.

Gelb, Ignace
1972 "From Freedom to Slavery." In D. O. Edzard (ed.), 18th Recontre Assyriologique Internationale. Munich: Bayerischen Akademic Der Wissenschaften.
1973 "Prisoners of War in Early Mesopotamia." Journal of Near Eastern Studies 32:70–98.

Gifford, James
1974 "Recent Thoughts Concerning the Interpretation

of Maya Prehistory." In Hammond (ed.), pp. 77–98.

Glass, D. V. and D. Eversley (eds.)
1965 *Population in History*. Chicago: Aldine.

Gregor, Thomas A.
1969 "Social Relations in a Small Society: A Study of the Mehinacu Indians of Central Brazil." Ph.D. dissertation, Columbia University.

Grennes-Ravitz, Ronald and G. Coleman
1976 "The Quintessential Role of Olmec in the Central Highlands of Mexico." American Antiquity 41: 196–205.

Gross, Daniel
1975 "Protein Capture and Cultural Development in the Amazon Basin." American Anthropologist 77:526–49.

Grove, David C. et al.
1976 "Settlement and Cultural Development at Chalcatzingo." Science 192:1203–10.

Hall, Calvin and G. Lindzey
1967 "Freud's Psychoanalytic Theory of Personality." In Robert Hunt, ed., *Personalities and Cultures: Readings in Psychological Anthropology*, pp. 3–29. Garden City: Natural History Press.

Hammond, Norman
1974 "The Distribution of Late Classic Maya Major Ceremonial Centers." In Hammond (ed.), pp. 313–34.

Hammond, Norman (ed.)
1974 *Mesoamerican Archaeology: New Approaches*. Austin: University of Texas Press.

Harlan, Jack
(in press) "Origins of Cereal Agriculture in the Old World." In C. Reed, ed., *Origins of Agriculture*. The Hague: Mouton.

Harner, Michael
1970 "Population Pressure and the Social Evolution

of Agriculturists." Southwestern Journal of Anthropology 26:67–86.

1975 "The Material Basis for Aztec Sacrifice." Paper read at the Annual Meeting of the American Anthropological Association, San Francisco.

1977 "The Ecological Basis for Aztec Sacrifice." American Ethnologist 4:117–35.

Harris, David

(in press) "The Origins of Agriculture: Alternate Pathways Toward Agriculture." In C. Reed, ed., *Origins of Agriculture*. The Hague: Mouton.

Harris, Marvin

1966 "The Cultural Ecology of India's Sacred Cattle." Current Anthropology 7:51–59.

1968 *The Rise of Anthropological Theory: A History of Theories of Culture*. New York: Thomas Y. Crowell.

1971 "Comments on Alan Heston's 'An Approach to the Sacred Cow of India.'" Current Anthropology 12:199–201.

1973 "The Withering Green Revolution." Natural History 82, 2:20–22.

1974 *Cows, Pigs, Wars and Witches: The Riddles of Culture*. New York: Random House.

1975 *Culture, People, Nature: An Introduction to General Anthropology*. New York: Thomas Y. Crowell.

1979 *Cultural Materialism: The Struggle for a Science of Culture*. New York: Random House (in preparation).

Harrison, Gail

1975 "Primary Adult Lactase Deficiency: A Problem in Anthropological Genetics." American Anthropologist 77:812–35.

Hart, C. W. M. and A. R. Pilling

1960 *The Tiwi of North Australia*. New York: Holt, Rinehart & Winston.

Hassan, Ferki
1973 "On Mechanisms of Population Growth During the Neolithic." Current Anthropology 14, 5:535–42.
1975 "Size, Density and Growth Rate of Hunting-Gathering Populations." In Polgar (ed.), pp. 27–52.

Hastings, James (ed.)
1921 *Encyclopedia of Religion and Ethics*. New York: Charles Scribner & Sons.

Haviland, William
1967 "Stature at Tikal, Guatemala: Implications for Ancient Maya Demography and Social Organization." American Antiquity 32:316–25.
1969 "A New Population Estimate for Tikal, Guatemala." American Antiquity 34:429–33.

Hawkes, Jaquetta
1973 *The First Great Civilizations*. New York: Alfred A. Knopf.

Heider, Karl
1972 *The Dani of West Irian*. Reading, Mass.: Addison-Wesley.

Herskovits, Melville
1952 *Economic Anthropology*. New York: Alfred A. Knopf.

Heston, Allan et al.
1971 "An Approach to the Sacred Cow of India." Current Anthropology 12:191–209.

Himes, N. E.
1963 *Medical History of Contraception*. New York: Gamut Press.

Hoebel, E. Adamson
1954 *The Law of Primitive Man*. Cambridge: Harvard University Press.

Hoffer, Carol
1975 "Bundu: Political Implications of Female Solidarity in a Secret Society." In Raphael (ed.), pp. 155–64.

Hogbin, H. Ian
1964 *A Guadalcanal Society: The Kaoka Speakers.* New York: Holt, Rinehart & Winston.

Howell, Nancy
1976 "The Population of the Dobe Area !Kung." In Richard Lee and I. De Vore, eds., *Kalahari Hunter-Gatherers: Studies of the !Kung San and Their Neighbors.* Cambridge: Harvard University Press, pp. 137–51.

Hubert, M.
1976 "Scientist Is Hopeful on World Resources." New York Times, December 2.

Jacobsen, Thorkild and R. Adams
1958 "Salt and Silt in Ancient Mesopotamian Agriculture." Science 128:1251–58.

Jennings, Peter
1976 "The Amplification of Agricultural Production." Scientific American 235(3):180–95.

Johnson, Allen
1975 "The Allocation of Time in a Machiguenga Community." Ethnology 14:301–10.

Kaberry, Phyllis
1970 *Aboriginal Woman, Sacred and Profane.* London: Routledge. (Initially published 1939.)

Kellum, Barbara
1974 "Infanticide in England in the Later Middle Ages." History of Childhood Quarterly 1:367–88.

Kolata, Gina
1974 "!Kung Hunter-Gatherers: Feminism, Diet and Birth Control." Science 185:932–34.

Kroeber, Alfred L.
1939 *Cultural and Natural Areas of Native North America.* Berkeley: University of California Press.

Lamphere, Louise
1975 "Women and Domestic Power: Political and Economic Strategies in Domestic Groups." In Raphael (ed.), pp. 117–30.

Landes, David (ed.)
1966 *The Rise of Capitalism*. New York: Macmillan.
Langer, William
1963 "Europe's Initial Population Explosion." American Historical Review 69:1–17.
1972 "Checks on Population Growth, 1750–1850." Scientific American: 92–99.
1974 "Infanticide: A Historical Survey." History of Childhood Quarterly 1:353–65.
Lathrap, Donald
1973 "The 'Hunting' Economies of the Tropical Forest Zone of South America: An Attempt at Historical Perspective." In Daniel Gross, ed., *Peoples and Cultures of Native South America*, pp. 83–95. New York: Natural History Press.
Leach, Gerald
1975 *Energy and Food Production*. Washington: Institute for Environment and Development.
Lee, Richard
1968 "Problems in the Study of Hunters and Gatherers." In Lee and De Vore (eds.), pp. 3–12.
1969 "!Kung Bushmen Subsistence: An Input-Output Analysis." In A. Vayda, ed., *Environment and Cultural Behavior*, pp. 47–49. Garden City: Natural History Press.
1972 "Population Growth and the Beginnings of Sedentary Life Among the !Kung Bushmen." In Spooner (ed.), pp. 329–42.
Lee, Richard and I. De Vore (eds.)
1968 *Man the Hunter*. Chicago: Aldine.
Lesser, Alexander
1968 "War and the State." In Fried, Harris, and Murphy (eds.), pp. 92–96.
Lévi, Sylvain
1966 *La doutrine du sacrifice dans les Brâhmanas*. Paris: Presses Universitaires de France.
Lévi-Strauss, Claude
1969 *The Elementary Structures of Kinship*. Rev. ed.

Trans. by J. H. Bell, J. R. von Sturmer, and Rodney Needham, eds. Boston: Beacon.

Linton, Sally
1973 "Women the Gatherer: Male Bias in Anthropology." In Sue Ellen Jacobs, ed., *Women in Perspective: A Guide for Cross Cultural Studies.* Urbana: University of Illinois Press.

Livingstone, Frank
1968 "The Effect of War on the Biology of the Human Species." In Fried, Harris, and Murphy (eds.), pp. 3–15.

Lizot, Jacques
1971 "Aspects économiques et sociaux du changement cultural chez les Yanomamis." L'Homme 11:2–51.

Llewellyn-Jones, Derek
1974 *Human Reproduction and Society.* London: Faber & Faber.

Lopez, Robert S.
1974 *The Commercial Revolution of the Middle Ages: 950–1350.* Englewood Cliffs, N.J.: Prentice-Hall.

Lowie, Robert
1954 *Indians of the Plains.* New York: McGraw-Hill.

Lundell, Cyrus
1937 *The Vegetation of Petén.* Washington, D.C.: Carnegie Institution.

MacNeish, Richard
1972a "The Evolution of Community Patterns in the Tehuacán Valley of Mexico, and Speculation about the Cultural Processes." In P. J. Ucko, R. Tringham, and G.W. Dimbleby, eds., *Man, Settlement, and Urbanism*, pp. 67–93. Cambridge, Mass.: Schenkman.

1972b *The Prehistory of Tehuacán Valley*, Vol. IV. Austin: University of Texas Press.

(in press) "Speculations About the Discovery of the New World by Paleoindians." American Scientist.

n.d. *Energy and Culture in Ancient Tehuacan.* Manuscript.

Maitz, S. K.

1957 *Economic Life of Northern India in the Gupta Period. Cir.* A.D. *300–500.* Calcutta: World Press Private.

Malinowski, Bronislaw

1920 "War and Weapons Among the Natives of the Trobriand Islands." Man 20:10–12.

1922 *Argonauts of the Western Pacific.* New York: Dutton.

1927 *Sex and Repression in Savage Society.* London: Routledge and Kegan Paul.

1935 *Coral Gardens and Their Magic,* 2 Vols. London: Allen & Unwin.

Marshack, Alexander

1972 *The Roots of Civilization.* New York: McGraw-Hill.

Marshall, John

1931 *Mohenjo-daro and the Indus Civilization,* 3 Vols. London.

Mason, J. Alden

1957 *The Ancient Civilizations of Peru.* Harmondsworth (England): Penguin.

Mathenay, Ray

1976 "Maya Lowland Hydraulic Systems." Science 193:639–46.

Meek, Ronald

1971 *Marx and Engels on the Population Bomb.* Berkeley: Ramparts Press.

Meggers, B.

1971 *Amazonia: Man and Culture in a Counterfeit Paradise.* Chicago: Aldine.

Meggers, Betty, E. Ayensu, and W. Duckworth

1973 *Tropical Forest Ecosystems in Africa and South America: A Comparative Review.* Washington, D.C.: Smithsonian Institution Press.

Mencius
1970 *The Works of Mencius*, trans. by James Legge. New York: Dover.

Métraux, Alfred
1945 "Tribes of the Middle and Upper Amazon River." In J. H. Steward, ed., *Handbook of South American Indians*, pp. 687–712. Washington, D.C.: Bureau of American Ethnology Bulletin 143(3).

Millon, René
1973 "The Study of Urbanism at Teotihuacan, Mexico." In Hammond (ed.), pp. 335–62.

Minge-Kalman, Wanda
1977 *The Evolution of Domestic Production: Changes During the Peasant to Worker Transition in Europe*. Ph.D. dissertation, Columbia University.

Mitchell, William
1973 "The Hydraulic Hypothesis: A Reappraisal." Current Anthropology 4: 532–34.

Montagu, Ashley
1976 *The Nature of Human Aggression*. New York: Oxford University Press.

Morgan, Lewis H.
1962 *League of the Iroquois*. New York: Corinth Press.

Morley, S. G. and G. Brainerd
1956 *The Ancient Maya*. Palo Alto: Stanford University Press.

Morren, George
1974 "Settlement Strategies and Hunting in a New Guinea Society." Ph.D. dissertation, Columbia University.

Mosimann, James G. and Paul S. Martin
1975 "Simulating Overkill by Paleoindians." American Scientist 63, 3.

Mount, Lawrence
1968 *The Climatic Physiology of the Pig*. London: Edward Arnold.

Murdock, George P.
1949 *Social Structure.* New York: Macmillan.
1967 *Ethnographic Atlas.* Pittsburgh: University of Pittsburgh Press.

Nag, Moni (ed.)
1975 *Population and Social Organization.* The Hague: Mouton.

Nash, Jill
1974 *Matriliny and Modernization: The Nagovisi of South Bougainville.* New Guinea Research Bulletin.

Nath, Pran
1929 *A Study in the Economic Condition of Ancient India.* London.

National Petroleum Council
1973 *U.S. Energy Outlook: Oil and Gas Availability.* Washington, D.C.: National Petroleum Council.

National Research Council
1974 *Agricultural Production Efficiency.* Washington, D.C.: National Academy of Sciences.

Needham, Joseph
1970 *Clerks and Craftsmen in China and the West.* Cambridge (England): Cambridge University Press.

Needham, Joseph and W. Ling
1959 *Science and Civilization in China,* Vol. III. Cambridge (England): Cambridge University Press.

Neel, James and K. Weiss
1975 "The Genetic Structure of a Tribal Population, the Yanomamo Indians." American Journal of Physical Anthropology 42:25–52.

Nettleship, Martin, R. Givens and A. Nettleship (eds.)
1975 *War, Its Causes and Correlates.* The Hague: Mouton.

Nohl, Johannes (ed.)
1961 *Black Death: A Chronicle of the Plague Compiled from Contemporary Sources.* New York: Humanities Press.

Nurge, Ethel

1975 "Spontaneous and Induced Abortion in Human and Non-Human Primates." In Raphael (ed.), pp. 25–36.

Odend'hal, Stewart

1972 "Energetics of Indian Cattle in Their Environment." Human Ecology: 1, 1:3–32.

Oliver, Douglas

1955 *A Solomon Island Society: Kinship and Leadership Among the Siuai of Bougainville.* Cambridge: Harvard University Press.

Palerm, Angel

1967 "Agricultural Systems and Food Patterns." *Handbook of Middle American Indians* 6:26–52.

Parsons, Jeffrey and R. Blanton

1969 *Prehispanic Demography in the Eastern Valley of Mexico: The Texcoco, Ixtapalapa, and Chalco Areas.* Unpublished manuscript.

Penner, S. S. and L. Icerman

1974 *Energy: Demands, Resources, Impact, Technology and Policy.* Reading, Mass.: Addison-Wesley.

Perkins, Dwight

1968 *Agricultural Development in China 1368–1968.* Chicago: Aldine.

Phillips, Ralph et al.

1945 *Livestock of China.* U.S. Department of State Publication 2249. Far Eastern Series: 9. Washington, D.C.

Piggott, Stuart

1965 *Ancient Europe.* Edinburgh: The University Press.

1975 *The Druids.* New York: Praeger.

Pimentel, David, L. E. Hurd, A. C. Bellotti, et al.

1973 "Food Production and the Energy Crisis." Science 182:443–49.

Pimentel, David, W. Dritschilo, J. Krummel, and J. Krutzman

1975 "Energy and Land Constraints in Food Protein Production." Science 190:754–61.

Pimentel, David
1976 "Expert Says Only Hope to Feed World Is with Food Production Unlike That in U.S." New York Times, December 8.

Pinchbeck, Ivy
1969 *Women Workers and the Industrial Revolution 1750–1850*. New York: Kelley Reprints.

Ping-ti Ho
1975 "The Indigenous Origins of Chinese Agriculture." In C. Reed, ed., *Origins of Agriculture*. The Hague: Mouton.

Pires-Ferreira, J., E. Pires-Ferreira, and P. Kaulicke
1976 "Preceramic Animal Utilization in the Central Peruvian Andes." Science 194:483–90.

Polanyi, Karl
1944 *The Great Transformation*. New York: Rinehart.

Polanyi, Karl, C. Arensberg, and H. Pearson (eds.)
1957 *Trade and Market in the Early Empires*. Glencoe, Ill.: The Free Press.

Polgar, Steven
1975 "Birth Planning: Between Neglect and Coercion." In Nag (ed.) pp. 177–202.

Polgar, Steven (ed.)
1975 *Population, Ecology and Social Evolution*. The Hague: Mouton.

Pond, W. G. and J. H. Manes
1974 *Swine Production in Temperate and Tropical Environments*. San Francisco: Freeman.

Postan, Michael
1972 *The Medieval Economy and Society: An Economic History of Britain in the Middle Ages*. London: Weidenfeld & Nicolson.

Prakash, Om
1961 *Food and Drinks in Ancient India: From Earliest Times to C. 1200* A.D. Delhi: Munshi Ram Manohar Lal.

Price, Barbara
1971 "Prehispanic Irrigation Agriculture in Nuclear America." Latin American Research Review 6:3–60.
1977 "Turning State's Evidence: Problems in the Theory of State Formation." Unpublished paper.

Prideaux, Tom (ed.)
1973 *Cro-Magnon Man*. New York: Time-Life.

Puleston, D. E.
1968 *Brosimum Alicastrum as a Subsistence Alternative for the Classic Maya of the Central Southern Lowlands*. Ann Arbor, Mich.: University Microfilms.
1974 "Intersite Areas in the Vicinity of Tikal and Uaxactun." In Hammond (ed.), pp. 301–11.

Puleston, D. E. and O. S. Puleston
1971 "An Ecological Approach to the Origin of Maya Civilization." Archaeology 24:330–37.

Raj, K. N.
1969 "Investment in Livestock in Agrarian Economies: An Analysis of Some Issues Concerning 'Sacred Cows' and 'Surplus Cattle.' Indian Economic Review 4:1–33.
1971 "India's Sacred Cattle: Theories and Empirical Findings." Economic and Political Weekly 6:717–722. (March 27).

Raphael, Dana (ed.)
1975 *Being Female: Reproduction, Power, Change*. The Hague: Mouton.

Rathje, William
1970 "Socio-political Implications of Lowland Maya Burials: Methodology and Tentative Hypotheses." World Archaeology 1:359–74.
1971 "The Origin and Development of Lowland Classic Maya Civilization." American Antiquity 36:275–85.

Reed, Evelyn
1975 *Woman's Evolution*. New York: Pathfinder Press.

Reifenberg, A.

1953 "The Struggle between the Desert and the Sown." Desert Research. Proceedings, International Symposium held in Jerusalem, May 1952, pp. 378–91. Jerusalem: Research Council of Israel Special Publication.

Reiter, Rayna (ed.)

1975 *Toward an Anthropology of Women*. New York: Monthly Review Press.

Renfew, Colin

1973 *Before Civilization*. New York: Alfred A. Knopf.

Renfrew, Colin (ed.)

1974 *The Explanation of Culture Change: Models in Prehistory*. Pittsburgh: University of Pittsburgh Press.

Roper, Marilyn

1969 "A Survey of the Evidence for Intrahuman Killing in the Pleistocene." *Current Anthropology* 10:427–59.

1975 "Evidence of Warfare in the Near East from 10,000 to 4,000 B.C." In Nettleship, Givens, and Nettleship (eds.), pp. 299–344.

Rosaldo, M. Z. and L. Lamphere (eds.)

1974 *Women, Culture, and Society*. Stanford: Stanford University Press.

Rosengarten, Yvonne

1966 *Le régime des offrandes dans la société sumérienne d'après les textes presargoniques de Lagas*. Paris: E. de Boccard.

Ross, Eric

(in press) "Food Taboos, Diet and Hunting Strategy: The Adaptation to Animals in Amazon Cultural Ecology." Current Anthropology.

Ross, Jane

1971 "Aggression as Adaptation: The Yanomamo Case." Mimeographed. Columbia University.

Rowe, John
1947 "Inca Culture at the Time of the Spanish Conquest. In Julian Steward, ed., *Handbook of South American Indians*. Bureau of American Ethnology Bulletin 143:183–330.

Rusche, Georg and O. Kirchheimer
1939 *Punishment and Social Structure*. New York: Columbia University Press.

Russel, Josiah
1948 *British Medieval Population*. Albuquerque: University of New Mexico Press.

Russell, Claire and W. Russel
1973 "The Natural History of Violence." In Charlotte Otten, ed., *Aggression and Evolution*, pp. 240–273. Lexington, Mass.: Xerox College Publishing.

Sagan, Eli
1974 *Human Aggression, Cannibalism, and Cultural Form*. New York: Harper & Row.

Sahlins, Marshall
1958 *Social Stratification in Polynesia*. American Ethnological Society Monographs. Seattle: University of Washington Press.
1972 *Stone Age Economics*. Chicago: Aldine.

Salzman, Philip (ed.)
1971 "Comparative Studies of Nomadism and Pastoralism." Anthropological Quarterly 44, 3:104–210.

Sanders, William T.
1972 "Population, Agricultural History, and Societal Evolution in Mesoamerica." In Spooner (ed.), pp. 101–53.

Sanders, W. T. and B. Price
1968 *Mesoamerica: The Evolution of a Civilization*. New York: Random House.

Scheele, Raymond
1950 *Warfare of the Iroquois and Their Northern Neighbors*. Ph.D. dissertation, Columbia University.

Schneider, Harold
1957 "The Subsistence Cattle Among the Pakot and in East Africa." American Anthropologist 59: 278–300.

Service, Elman
1969 "The Prime-Mover of Cultural Evolution." Southwestern Journal of Anthropology 24:396–409.

Shen, T. H.
1951 *Agricultural Resources of China.* Ithaca: Cornell University Press.

Shipman, Pat and J. Phillips-Conroy
1977 "Hominid Tool-making Versus Carnivore Scavenging." American Journal of Physical Anthropology 46:77–86.

Shorter, Edward
1975 *The Making of the Modern Family.* New York: Basic Books.

Singh, R. L. (ed.)
1971 *India: A Regional Geography.* Varanasi, National Geographic Society of India.

Siskind, Janet
1973 *To Hunt in the Morning.* New York: Oxford University Press.

Smith, Philip E.
1972 "Land-use, Settlement Patterns and Subsistence Agriculture: A Demographic Perspective." In Ucko, Tringham, and Dimbleby (eds.), pp. 409–25.

Smith, Philip and C. Young, Jr
1972 "The Evolution of Early Agriculture and Culture in Greater Mesopotamia: A Trial Model." In Spooner (ed.), pp. 5–19

Smith, William
1956 *The Religion of the Semites.* New York: Meridan Books.

Smole, William J.
1976 *The Yanomamo Indians: A Cultural Geography.* Austin: University of Texas Press.

Solheim, William
1970 "Relics from Two Diggings Indicate the Thais Were the First Agrarians." New York Times January 12.

Soustelle, Jacques
1962 *Daily Life of the Aztecs on the Eve of the Spanish Conquest*. Stanford: Stanford University Press.

Spengler, Joseph
1971 *Indian Economic Thought: A Preface to Its History*. Durham, N.C.: Duke University Press.
1974 *Population Change, Modernization, and Welfare*. Englewood Cliffs, N.J.: Prentice-Hall.

Spooner, Brian (ed.)
1972 *Population Growth: Anthropological Implications*. Cambridge: M.I.T. Press

Sprague, G. F.
1975 "Agriculture in China." Science 188:549–55.

Steinhart, J. and C. Steinhart
1974 "Energy Use in the U.S. Food System." Science 184:307–15.

Stevenson, Robert
1968 *Population and Political Systems in Tropical Africa*. New York: Columbia University Press.

Steward, Julian
1955 *Theory of Culture Change*. Urbana: University of Illinois.

Sweet, Louise
1967 "The Women of 'Ain and Dayr.'" Anthropological Quarterly 40.

Tannahill, Reay
1975 *Flesh and Blood: A History of the Cannibal Complex*. New York: Stein & Day.

Taylor, C. M. and O. F. Pye
1966 *Foundations of Nutrition*, 6th ed. New York: Macmillan.

de Tápia, Andrés
1971 "Relación Hecha por el Señor Andrés de Tápia sobre la Conquista de México." In J. G. Icazbal-

ceta, ed., *Colección de Documentos para la Historia de México:* Nendeln/Liechtenstein: Kraus reprint, Vol. 2, pp. 554–94.

Thapar, Romila
1966 *A History of India.* Baltimore: Penguin.

Thompson, J. E.
1954 *The Rise and Fall of Maya Civilization.* Norman: University of Oklahoma Press.

Thwaites, Reuben
1959 (1637) *The Jesuit Relations and Allied Documents,* Vol. 13. New York: Pageant Book Co.

Trexler, Richard
1973a "Infanticide in Florence: New Sources and First Results." History of Childhood Quarterly 1:98–116.
1973b "The Foundlings of Florence, 1395–1455." History of Childhood Quarterly 1:259–84.

Turner, B. L., II
1974 "Prehistoric Intensive Agriculture in the Maya Lowlands." Science 185:118–24.

Uberoi, J. P. Singh
1962 *Politics of the Kula Ring: An Analysis of the Findings of Bronislaw Malinowski.* Manchester: Manchester University Press.

Ucko, Peter and G. W. Dimbleby (eds.)
1969 *The Domestication and Exploitation of Plants and Animals.* Chicago: Aldine.

Ucko, Peter, G. W. Dimbleby, and R. Tringham (eds.)
1972 *Man, Settlement and Urbanism.* London: Duckworth.

Ulmen, G. L.
1975 "Wittfogel's Science of Society." Telos 24:81–114.

Van Bath, B. H.
1963 *The Agrarian History of Western Europe:* A.D. *500–1850.* London: Edward Arnold.

Van Ginneken, J. K.
1974 "Prolonged Breastfeeding as a Birth-Spacing Method." Studies in Family Planning 5:201–08.

Varma, K. N.
1967 *Population Problem in the Ganges Valley.* Agra: Shiva Lal Agarwala.

Vayda, Andrew P.
1961 "Expansion and Warfare among Swidden Agriculturalists." American Anthropologist 63:346–58.
1971 "Phases of the Process of War and Peace Among the Marings of New Guinea." Oceania 42:1–24.

Vishnu-Mittre
(in press) "The Archaeobotanical and Palynological Evidences for the Early Origin of Agriculture in South and Southeast Asia." In M. Arnott, ed., *Gastronomy: The Anthropology of Food and Food Habits.* The Hague: Mouton.

Wade, Nicholas
1973 "The World Food Situation: Pessimism Comes Back Into Vogue." Science 181:634–38.

Wailes, Bernard
1972 "Plow and Population in Temperate Europe." In Spooner (ed.), pp. 154–79.

Wallerstein, Immanuel
1974 *The Modern World-System.* New York: Academic Press.

Walsh, Maurice and B. Scandalis
1975 "Institutionalized Forms of Intergenerational Male Aggression." In Nettleship, Givens, and Nettleship (eds.), pp. 135–56.

Warner, W. Lloyd
1930 "Murngin Warfare." Oceania 1:457–94.
1937 *A Black Civilization.* New York: Harper & Bros.

Watt, Kenneth
1968 *Ecology and Resource Management: A Quantitative Approach.* New York: McGraw-Hill.

Weaver, Muriel
1972 *The Aztecs, Maya, and Their Predecessors.* New York: Seminar Press.

Webb, Malcolm
1975 "The Flag Follows Trade: An Essay on the Necessary Integration of Military and Commercial Factors in State Formation." In Jeremy Sabloff and C. C. Lamberg Karlovsky, eds., *Ancient Civilization and Trade.* Albuquerque: University of New Mexico Press.

Webster, David
1975 "Warfare and the Evolution of the State." American Antiquity 40:464–70.

Wedgwood, Camilla
1930 "Some Aspects of Warfare in Melanesia." Oceania 1:15–33.

White, Benjamin
1973 "Demand for Labor and Population Growth in Java." Human Ecology 1, 3:217–36.
1975 "The Economic Importance of Children in a Javanese Village." In Nag (ed.), pp. 127–46.

Whyte, R. D.
1961 "Evolution of Land Use in Southwestern Asia." In L. D. Stamp, ed., *A History of Land Use in Arid Regions.* UNESCO Arid Zone Research 17:14.

Wilkinson, Richard
1973 *Poverty and Progress: An Ecological Perspective on Economic Development.* New York: Praeger.

Willey, Gordon
1966 *An Introduction to American Archaeology,* Vol. 1. Englewood Cliffs, N.J.: Prentice-Hall.

Wittfogel, Karl A.
1931 *Wirtschaft und Gesellschaft Chinas.* Leipzig: C. L. Hirschfeld.
1957 *Oriental Despotism: A Comparative Study of Total Power.* New Haven: Yale University Press.
1970 *Agriculture: A Key to the Understanding of Chi-*

nese Society Past and Present. Canberra: Australian National University Press.

1972 "The Hydraulic Approach to Pre-Spanish Mesoamerica." In R. MacNeish (ed.), pp. 59–80.

Wolf, Eric

1966 *Peasants.* Englewood Cliffs, N.J.: Prentice-Hall.

Wood, Corinne

1975 "New Evidence for the Late Introduction of Malaria into the New World." Current Anthropology 16:93–104.

Woodbury, Richard and J. Neely

1972 "Water Control Systems of the Tehuacan Valley." In R. MacNeish (ed.), pp. 81–153.

Wright, Quincy

1965 *A Study of War.* Chicago: University of Chicago Press.

Wyon, John and J. Gordon

1971 *The Khanna Study: Population Problems in the Rural Punjab.* Cambridge: Harvard University Press.

Yerkes, Royden

1952 *Sacrifice in Greek and Roman Religions and Early Judaism.* New York: Scribners.

Young, Cuyler

1972 "Population Densities and Early Mesopotamian Origins." In Ucko, Dimbleby, and Tringham (eds.).

Zeuner, Frederic

1963 *A History of Domesticated Animals.* New York: Harper & Row.

Zohary, Daniel and M. Hopf

1973 "Domestication of Pulses in the Old World." Science 182:887–94.

Index

About the Author

MARVIN HARRIS has taught at Columbia University since 1953 and from 1963 to 1966 was Chairman of the Department of Anthropology. He has lectured by invitation at most of the major colleges and universities in the United States. In addition to field work in Brazil, Mozambique, and Ecuador on the subjects of cross-cultural aspects of race and ethnic relations, the effects of colonialism, and problems of underdevelopment seen in ecological perspective, Harris has pioneered in the use of videotape techniques in the study of family life in this country.

Author of several books, among them the influential *Rise of Anthropological Theory: A History of Theories of Culture* and the popular undergraduate text *Culture, Man and Nature: An Introduction to General Anthropology*, Harris writes regularly for *National History* magazine and is a frequent contributor to the professional journals, *American Anthropologist* and *Current Anthropology*. His other books include *Cows, Pigs, Wars, and Witches* and *Cultural Materialism*.